The Political Rights of Migrant Workers in Western Europe

The Political Rights of Migrant Workers in Western Europe

edited by

Zig Layton-Henry

SAGE Modern Politics Series Volume 25
Sponsored by the European Consortium for
Political Research/ECPR

SAGE Publications
London · Newbury Park · New Delhi

Preface and Chapters 1, 5 and 9 © Zig Layton-Henry 1990
Chapter 2 © Catherine Wihtol de Wenden 1990
Chapter 3 © Jan Vranken 1990
Chapter 4 © Tomas Hammar 1990
Chapter 6 © Uwe Andersen 1990
Chapter 7 © Jan Rath 1990
Chapter 8 © Gérard de Rham 1990

First published 1990

SAGE Publications Ltd
28 Banner Street
London EC1Y 8QE

SAGE Publications Inc
2111 West Hillcrest Drive
Newbury Park, California 91320

SAGE Publications India Pvt Ltd
32, M-Block Market
Greater Kailash – I
New Delhi 110 048

British Library Cataloguing in Publication data

The political rights of migrant workers in Western Europe.
   (Sage modern politics series; V. 25)
   1. Western Europe.   Migrant personnel.   Civil rights
   I. Layton-Henry, Zig
   323.1′4

   ISBN 0-8039-8271-2

Library of Congress catalog card number 89-062960

Typeset by AKM Associates (UK) Ltd, Southall, London
Printed in Great Britain by Billing and Sons Ltd, Worcester

Contents

Preface and Acknowledgements   vi

1   The Challenge of Political Rights
    Zig Layton-Henry   1

2   The Absence of Rights: the Position of Illegal Immigrants
    Catherine Wihtol de Wenden   27

3   Industrial Rights
    Jan Vranken   47

4   The Civil Rights of Aliens
    Tomas Hammar   74

5   Immigrant Associations
    Zig Layton-Henry   94

6   Consultative Institutions for Migrant Workers
    Uwe Andersen   113

7   Voting Rights
    Jan Rath   127

8   Naturalisation: The Politics of Citizenship Acquisition
    Gérard de Rham   158

9   Citizenship or Denizenship for Migrant Workers?
    Zig Layton-Henry   186

Index   196

Notes on the Contributors   200

Preface and Acknowledgements

This book is concerned with the position of post-war immigrants to Western Europe and in particular with their access to social, civil and political rights. The migration to Western Europe, particularly in the 1960s and 1970s, of millions of migrant workers and political refugees and their families in search of work, security and a better future for themselves constitutes a major challenge to the concept of citizenship in modern industrial democracies. In the pre-war period most members of European states, with the notable exceptions of France and Switzerland, were citizens with full legal, civil and political rights. However, post-war immigration has created large communities of long-settled foreign citizens in most Western European countries.

These foreign migrants and their families are members of their new countries of work and residence even though psychologically they may feel, and in practice define themselves, as members of their countries of origin. They are members of their countries of residence because of their physical presence and length of stay in these countries. They participate in the labour markets of the receiving countries, pay taxes to their governments, contribute to social security and receive benefits in return, they rear and educate their children in its schools, worship in its churches and mosques and participate in a wide variety of other community activities. However, in spite of their increasingly long residence which appears close to a situation of permanent settlement, a large proportion remain non-citizens either because they do not wish to change their national identity and give up the citizenship of their country of origin or because the process of naturalisation is difficult or expensive, or both. Some countries do not allow dual nationality, and the decision to give up the citizenship of one's country of birth may feel close to treachery, a violation of one's national identity and personal honour.

The growth of a second and even a third generation born and educated in Western Europe raises even more acutely the questions of membership in and citizenship of a modern democratic state. Can people be considered members of a state that they have never been to and whose language and customs they may only imperfectly understand? Infrequent holiday visits hardly constitute a tie or membership of a state. One can, of course, be a citizen of a far-away state and there may be strong historical, cultural and practical reasons for retaining the citizenship of the country of one's parents or grandparents, such as ownership of property or the desire to return. However, should the right to participate in local and national decision-making depend on a legal definition of citizenship or on the actual membership of a community? Should immigrant workers, who may be permanent residents in their new country, be excluded from political participation because they do not wish to become naturalised citizens and give up the citizenship of the state they or their parents were born in? Should they have no say in how their taxes are spent? Has the democratic slogan of the Americans in the eighteenth century of *No taxation without representation* been replaced in the twentieth century, for non-citizen residents at least, of *No representation without naturalisation*? These are some of the issues that will be considered and analysed in this book.

In the first chapter the political issues raised by post-war immigration will be outlined and analysed, in particular the question of political rights. The organisation of the book follows the trend in Western Europe to extend gradually economic, industrial, social and political rights to these new members of West European states. Thus Chapter 2 examines those immigrants who have practically no rights at all; namely, illegal entrants and undocumented workers. Chapter 3 considers the first rights that most immigrants acquire; namely, industrial rights. Chapter 4, 'The Civil Rights of Aliens', examines the civil rights of immigrants in Western democracies, and Chapter 5 considers the growth of immigrant associations which can play an important role in the political system in promoting and defending the rights of immigrants. Chapter 6 examines the special arrangements that have been made in some European countries for foreign immigrants to participate in elections to advisory or consultative bodies and thus have an indirect influence on issues that concern them, and Chapter 7 analyses voting rights. Finally, Chapter 8 looks at the politics of citizenship acquisition and the thorny problem of naturalisation. Finally, the conclusion sums up with the recommendations of the authors.

The countries examined in this book – Belgium, France, the Federal Republic of Germany, Great Britain, the Netherlands, Sweden and Switzerland – are those West European states which have experienced the largest immigration. The authors are all specialists in the area of immigration policy and ethnic minority research in these seven countries. However, the book has been written thematically and not on a country-by-country basis. Certain themes are more important in some of the countries than in others, and this is reflected in the organisation and content of the chapters. Each of the authors was responsible for collecting the data on his country and for preparing the chapter on the theme assigned to him. However, all members of the project collaborated in the preparation of the book as a whole. Zig Layton-Henry was chairman of the research group and has been responsible for editing the book and preparing it for publication. We wish to thank Barbara Layton-Henry and Dorothy Foster for their considerable help in typing and word processing the manuscript.

The writing of this book has been a collaborative enterprise encouraged and sponsored by the European Consortium for Political Research which has as one of its main aims the promotion of comparative research. The project has also been supported and financed by the Nuffield Foundation. We acknowledge with gratitude the support of both these institutions, without whose help the project would not have been possible.

Zig Layton-Henry
Kenilworth

1

The Challenge of Political Rights

Zig Layton-Henry

This book is concerned with one of the greatest unforeseen challenges confronting the advanced industrial countries of Western Europe. This challenge involves the struggle to extend full economic, political and civic rights to the millions of post-Second World War migrant workers and their families who have moved from the European periphery and the Third World, often former colonies of the European states, to settle in Western Europe.

From the perspective of the European societies accepting these immigrants, this challenge involves a perception of these migrant workers as permanent settlers requiring integration into their economic, social and political systems. From the perspective of the migrants, the challenge is how to achieve social justice, respect and fair treatment for themselves and their families without having to pay an unacceptable price in terms of compromising their national indentities, cultural heritage and aspirations for their children. This challenge is particularly significant because it contradicts many of the assumptions and expectations of the political elites and publics, both in the countries of emigration and those of immigration.

There are no recent European parallels to post-war immigration. European migration in the nineteenth and early twentieth centuries was largely a massive exodus to North America and to colonial territories around the world. Migration to Europe generally involved Europeans returning from other continents. Internal migration within Europe tended to be on a modest scale. Intra-European migrations in the nineteenth century involved Irish immigration to Britain, Polish immigration to Germany and, at the end of the century, Jewish migration from Russia to Western Europe. These migrants did face resentment and hostility from people in the countries they settled in, but with one major and horrendous exception they were eventually accepted and assimilated. The exception is, of course, the Holocaust. Jewish communities all over Nazi-occupied Europe were exterminated during the Second World War. The example of the Holocaust shows how distinctive minority groups, even those which appear well integrated, may be vulnerable to scapegoating and terror by majorities under such conditions as economic recession, invasion and war.

Where assimilation did take place this process can be described as 'one-sided', in the sense that immigrants had to take on the language, customs and loyalties of their new country before they were accepted on equal terms. As the migrants were few in number and were also European, this process of assimilation was relatively straightforward and was usually accomplished by the second generation.

Previous experience of migration had thus not prepared European political elites or publics for either the scale or the cultural, religious, linguistic and ethnic diversity of post-Second World War immigration. In the early post-war period, there was considerable intra-European migration as people displaced by the war found new homes and as West European countries, engaged in post-war reconstruction, recruited labour from prisoners of war, refugees, displaced persons and then from areas of labour surplus such as Ireland, Italy, Spain and Portugal. Traditional European emigration to North America, Australia and Africa, which had been disrupted by the war, resumed immediately after the war ended.

In the 1950s, and more especially in the 1960s, the character of immigration into the major industrial states of Western Europe changed. The migration of workers from the less industrialised parts of Europe was supplemented and overtaken by a movement of workers and political refugees from the Third World, often from the colonial territories of the receiving states. At first this migration of non-Europeans was considered to be a temporary phenomenon caused by the post-war boom in the West European economy and the struggle for independence in many European colonies. It was widely assumed that most of the Turks, Moroccans, Algerians, Pakistanis, Bangladeshis, Caribbeans, West Africans and other Third World migrants would eventually return to their native countries. The few who would decide to settle would integrate, as had happened with previous migrants, on the receiving society's terms. There might have to be a period of accommodation and adaptation, but integration and assimilation into the native population would take place in the long term (Patterson, 1963).

The size and diversity of post-war migration to Western Europe has been unprecedented. Most analysts of this migration estimate that at least 15 million people have been added to the populations of West European states (Castles and Kosack, 1973; Castles et al., 1984; Hammar, 1985a; Krane, 1979; Power, 1979), and also that millions more have been involved in the migration process as seasonal workers, illegal workers or guest-workers who have become naturalised citizens of such countries as France, Sweden and Britain. However, most migrant workers have not naturalised, and the foreign populations of Western European states have risen dramatically, especially in the 1960s and 1970s. Table 1.1 gives an indication of the present size of the foreign populations in the seven major receiving countries of Western Europe.

Table 1.1   *The foreign populations of the seven major receiving countries of Western Europe, 1984*

	000s	%		000s	%
Belgium	897.6	9.0	Netherlands	558.7	3.9
France	4,485.7	8.1	Sweden	390.6	4.7
Germany (FRG)	4,378.9	7.2	Switzerland	839.6	13.0
Great Britain	1,736	3.2			

Sources: M. Frey and V. Lubinski, *Probleme infolge hoher Auslanderkonzentration in ausgewahlten europäischen Staaten*, Federal Institute for Population Research, Wiesbaden, 1987. British Labour Force Surveys, 1984–6

Table 1.1 does not fully reflect the scale of migration to all of these countries, because of the high rate of naturalisation that has occurred in France and Sweden, for example, and also because a large number of migrant workers from the Third World had the citizenship of the receiving European country through colonial ties. This was particularly true for much of the immigration to Great Britain[1] and also for many immigrants to the Netherlands and France.

Nor do figures of the size of the foreign population in Western Europe indicate the diversity of post-war labour migration. In Switzerland most migrant workers have been, and are, predominantly European, especially Italians and Spaniards, although in recent years Switzerland has accepted small numbers of non-Europeans as refugees. In the Federal Republic of Germany (henceforward Germany), the first foreign migrant workers were Southern Europeans, predominantly Italians, Yugoslavs, Spaniards and Greeks, but these were soon overtaken by Turks, who now form by far the largest group. In 1984 there were 1,426,000 Turks, 600,000 Yugoslavs, 545,000 Italians and 287,000 Greeks resident in Germany (Système d'Observation Permanente des Migrations (SOPEMI, 1986). In Sweden the largest proportion of migrant workers came from neighbouring Finland, also a partner in the Nordic Union, but there are also significant numbers of Yugoslavs and Turks. There are in addition many Estonians and Poles who can more accurately be described as political refugees. The Estonians fled to Sweden at the end of the Second World War, while Poles have sought asylum during the whole period since 1945.

In the Netherlands, the largest groups of foreign migrant workers are the Turks, Moroccans and Spaniards, but there are in addition important communities of migrants from the Dutch Antilles and from former colonies of Indonesia and Surinam. The best-known of these are probably the South Moluccans. The Netherlands also has a very large number of foreign residents from other European Community countries and the United States, but these people occupy skilled and professional jobs, often on a temporary basis, and are often working for multi-national companies. They are in a more privileged position than the less skilled migrant workers who form the major focus of this study.

The situation in Belgium is rather similar to that in the Netherlands; there are large numbers of migrant workers from the Mediterranean, such as Turks and Moroccans, and also large numbers of professional foreign residents working for the European Commission, multi-national companies and other international organisations. These European professionals are highly paid, have a privileged status, and usually return to their home country. This makes it inappropriate to classify them as migrant workers in the same sense as the mass of unskilled workers from less developed countries.

As in the Netherlands, post-war migration to France has consisted of a mixture of colonial or post-colonial migrant workers (some with French citizenship), and foreign workers – usually from neighbouring countries. Between 1963 and 1965, Algeria was considered part of France, so migrant workers from Algeria during this period had French citizenship. Some migrant workers from the former French colonies in North and West Africa had special status owing to bilateral treaties under which they were recruited (Verbunt, 1985). However, most of these special arrangements were ended between 1975 and 1977. Italy, Portugal and Spain provided the major source of foreign workers to France during the post-war period, though there are also significant numbers of Turks, Vietnamese and Pakistanis.

Migration to Britain has been significantly different from that to other European countries to the extent that foreign workers have formed a very small proportion of its migrant workers. Most migrant workers have come either from Ireland or from British colonies or former colonies in the Caribbean and Indian sub-continent. The Irish have always been treated as British if resident in the United Kingdom. This is because even after the Republic of Ireland left the Commonwealth in 1948, no British government has wished to remove the economic, social and political rights that the Irish have traditionally enjoyed in Britain. In fact, the Ireland Act was specifically passed by the British parliament in 1949 in order to confirm the rights of Irish residents in Britain. Similar legislation was not passed in 1973 when Pakistan left the Commonwealth. New Pakistani immigrants to Britain became aliens and in theory lost the political rights that earlier

Pakistani migrants as Commonwealth citizens had enjoyed. In practice no distinctions have been made between Pakistanis who settled in Britain before or after 1 January 1973, and all have been allowed to exercise full political rights. Caribbean and Asian migrants to Britain were British subjects either directly as members of British colonies or as citizens of British Commonwealth countries, but they are distant geographically and, to varying degrees, culturally. The Irish are a native people of the British Isles, even though many are now foreign citizens. However, popular attention regarding migration has ignored the Irish and focused on non-white immigration from the New Commonwealth.

It is already clear that there are a large number of terms that can be and are used to describe the people involved in the mass migration to Western Europe in the post-war period. They are described by such terms as 'immigrants', 'migrant workers', 'guest-workers', 'foreign workers', 'colonial workers', 'post-colonial migrants', 'economic refugees' and 'refugees'. The diversity of the people involved in post-war migration makes it impossible to agree on a single term to describe these migrants and their family members. A variety of terms is thus used in this book and it is necessary to define some of these terms. The word 'immigrant' has acquired the popular meaning of a person who moves to a country with the intention of taking up permanent residence. However, in most European countries the official definition of an immigrant, used in the collection of statistics, for example, is of a person who moves to a country and resides there for longer than a specified period which is often quite short, usually from three to six months. This official definition is used in this book. Immigration refers to the physical entrance of immigrants either singly or as a group into a country (Hammar, 1985a).

A migrant can be defined as a person who moves from one country to another. A migrant worker is a person who moves from one country to another specifically to find work. The term 'migrant workers' will be used in this book to describe first-generation migrant workers with few skills who came to Western Europe to take the low-paid manual jobs that native Europeans could not be recruited to do. In Germany these workers are commonly called 'guest-workers', implying that they were specifically invited to come but that their stay was assumed to be temporary.

Foreign workers are workers who have a diffferent nationality from that of their country of work and residence. They can be distinguished from colonial or post-colonial migrant workers, many of whom do have the citizenship of the 'mother country' to which they have migrated. Many colonial or post-colonial migrants were migrant workers looking for work and a higher standard of living for themselves and their children. Many others, however, were political refugees fleeing from violence and civil war. This was particularly the case with migrants to the Netherlands and France. 'Economic refugee' is a term which is often used to describe people claiming the status of refugee, and who ask for political asylum on the grounds that they are unable or unwilling to return to their country of origin because of a well-founded fear of persecution on account of race, religion, nationality, membership in a particular social group or because of their political views, but who are suspected of seeking residence in a West European country *primarily* to find work. In West Germany after the halt in labour recruitment in 1973–4 there was a large rise in the numbers of people seeking political asylum. Many of these were suspected of being 'economic refugees' rather than political refugees. A problem for the receiving countries is that many of the Third World countries from which migrant workers come do have repressive regimes or substantial internal violence; for example, Turkey, Yugoslavia, Morocco, Sri Lanka and the Philippines. It may thus be hard to distinguish genuine political refugees from migrant workers.

Many of the people with whom this book is concerned are not migrants or immigrants themselves. They are the children or even the grandchildren of migrants. However, they often retain the citizenship of their parents' country of origin and often suffer many of the disadvantages and discrimination suffered by their parents or grand-parents. These people are often referred to as 'the second generation'. The term 'ethnic minority', although its meaning does vary in the seven countries, may be used when the established communities founded by post-war immigrants are being considered.

The first generation of post-war migrants to Western Europe were predominantly concerned with finding work and earning money for the benefit of themselves and their families. They were not too concerned about rights to participate in the institutions and processes of their country of (temporary) residence. The growth of a second generation born and brought up in Germany, France or Switzerland, but which does not have German, French or Swiss citizenship or identity, raises the question of political rights, identity and citizenship in a much more acute form.

The major focus of this book is thus those post-war migrants and their families who have established themselves in these seven European countries. Foreign migrant workers who lack citizenship rights are the major concern, but we also wish to examine the position of those immigrants who have acquired the citizenship of their new country of residence either through naturalisation or through registration or automatic entitlement as members of colonies or former colonies of the country to which they migrated for work. Although many immigrants have the citizenship of countries such as Britain, France and the Netherlands, they are often treated in a discriminatory way because of chauvinism or racism.

Migrant workers with high status, professional skills and large salaries – for example, doctors, academics and executives of multinational corporations – are generally excluded from consideration, as the focus of the book is on the large majority of migrant workers, mostly from the Third World, who have relatively few skills and have moved to Western Europe in search of whatever work they could find.

In the various countries of Western Europe, different terms are used to describe migrant workers and their descendants. These terms are often political statements and indicate that the user holds particular views about immigration and the status of migrant workers as members of his society. In Switzerland, migrant workers are described as 'foreigners' (Ausländer), 'foreign labour' (ausländischer Arbeitskräfte) or 'foreign workers' (Fremdarbeiter). Many Swiss feel there is a serious problem of 'over-foreignisation' (Uberfremdung). There have been several determined campaigns to limit the size of the foreign population: for example, the various Schwarzenbach initiatives in the 1970s. In 1981 an initiative to improve the position of foreigners in Switzerland was defeated by 84 percent to 16 percent in the subsequent referendum (Hoffmann-Nowotny, 1985).

The hostility of the Swiss to immigration is partly because of the fact that it is a small, rich country with a high proportion of foreign workers, but it is also due to the delicate political balance between the different linguistic and religious groups which make up the Swiss population. Substantial permanent immigration has been accepted in Switzerland, but continuing immigration could upset this carefully constructed political equilibrium. Cultural pluralism thus militates against immigration in the Swiss case. Article 16 of the Swiss Federal Law of Abode and Settlement of Foreigners, enacted in 1931, requires that, 'When deciding about immigration and immigrants, the authorities should take into account the nation's cultural and economic interest, the situation in the labour market, and the degree of over-foreignisation (Hoffman-Nowotny, 1985). This remains the dominant Swiss approach to immigration matters, and underlines their preference for the temporary recruitment of migrant workers on a rotation basis.

In the Federal Republic of Germany, migrant workers are often referred to as 'guest-workers' (Gastarbeiter), and again the term emphasises the temporary nature of labour recruitment and the fact that migrant workers are not full members of German society. They are 'guests', but even welcome guests do not stay permanently. The expectation that migrant workers will eventually return to their native countries is a myth that is reinforced by prominent politicians, including Chancellor Kohl, who reiterate that Germany is not a country of immigration – despite the large size of the foreign population and the fact that the average length of stay is now over fifteen years. The problems associated with the creation of a German state, the history of recent wars, and boundary changes, and the present division of Germany into two states, may contribute to the reluctance of German politicians to accept foreign workers, Turks in particular, as permanent settlers and so ease their integration into German society. At the same time people coming from the German Democratic Republic are *always* welcomed. However, the very large numbers of foreign workers in Germany, the large increase in family settlement, and the very long period of stay of most workers has forced many Germans to realise that permanent settlement has now taken place, despite the statements of some of their politicians.

Recently an attempt has been made, with considerable success, to popularise a new term, 'ausländische Mitbürger' or foreign fellow citizens. Nevertheless, the term continues to stress the foreign character of the migrants and is often used in this way. Thus in 1982, speaking before a crowd in Dortmund, Helmut Kohl argued that 'the number of foreign fellow citizens in Germany should be reduced' (Thränhardt, 1988).

In France, the term 'immigrant' refers to migrant workers and their families who have settled, even if they have French nationality. The French state has a tradition of encouraging immigration to compensate for France's historically low birth-rate and the losses of two world wars. Immigrants are encouraged to settle and naturalise and become assimilated as Frenchmen and women. The extent and diverse nature of post-war immigration has meant that this process has been less easy than in the past and many migrant groups, particularly Maghrebians, have resisted assimilation. This has increased the hostility of the French public towards immigrants, which in turn strengthens the solidarity and resistance of immigrants to assimilation. But it also encourages some immigrant groups to campaign for a change in the popular view of an assimilated Frenchman, so that being French is no longer restricted to European Christians but can include people of Arab, Asian and African descent who are Muslim, black African Christians or Vietnamese Buddhists.

In Sweden, Belgium and the Netherlands, most, if not all, migrant workers are generally described as 'minorities' – foreign or ethnic. The use of the term 'minority' reflects the expectation in these countries that most migrant workers will settle permanently in their new countries of work and residence, even though they may not have intended to do so when they first migrated. The extension of local voting rights to foreigners who have been resident three years or more in Sweden and five years or more in the Netherlands is part of a recognition by policy-makers in these countries that labour migration has resulted in permanent settlement and that all permanent members of a society should participate in the decision-making process. Sweden had little experience of foreign immigration before the 1960s and considered itself to be a small homogeneous country. Most migrant workers coming to Sweden were fellow Nordics from Finland, a country previously united with Sweden until the nineteenth century. However, unlike the Irish migrating to Britain, the Finns do not have a common language with their Swedish neighbours, and experience some difficulties because of this – for example, in the education of their children (although 20 percent of Finnish migrants to Sweden belong to Finland's Swedish-speaking minority). It was not difficult for Swedish policy-makers to convince the public of the benefits of some positive measures to encourage the integration of foreign immigrants.

In Holland the early post-war immigrants were people from the Dutch East Indies (Indonesia), mostly with Dutch citizenship, to whom the Dutch had moral obligations. This was also true for later migrants from Surinam and the Antilles. It was not too difficult for Dutch traditions of pluralism to be extended to include these new groups, although the traditional 'pillars' of Dutch society – Protestantism, Catholicism and liberal-secularism – were far removed from the Islamic culture of the later Turkish and Moroccan immigrants. However, Dutch traditions of liberalism have been maintained in their treatment of post-colonial and foreign migrants. The situation in Belgium is similar to that in the Netherlands, although local voting rights have not yet been granted. There has been some concern in Belgium that immigration will upset the fragile but politically important language compromise between the Dutch-speaking Flemings and French-speaking Walloons, as most immigrants find jobs in Brussels or Wallonia and become French-speaking rather than Dutch-speaking.

In Britain, policy-makers recognised from the earliest phase of migration that settlement would inevitably take place. This was partly based on the knowledge of economic conditions in the colonies, the tradition of migration among Jamaicans and Indians, and also on the fact that the migrants, being British subjects, had the right to settle if they wished to do so. It was assumed that economic factors would be the major stimulus encouraging permanent settlement. The term 'ethnic minorities' is now widely used in Britain to refer to West Indian, Asian and African immigrants and their descendants. The terms 'black' or 'black British' are also widely used in the academic literature, and these terms have strong political connotations. This is because they are often used to include both Afro-Caribbeans and members of the various South Asian communities – namely, Indians. Pakistanis and Bangladeshis. The use of 'black' or 'black British' in this way is intended to indicate that all non-whites face common experiences of racism, racial discrimination and racial disadvantage. The groups included in the terms 'black' or 'ethnic minorities' are, of course, extremely diverse in terms of their countries of origin, religions, languages and cultural traditions, and in many ways it is very unsatisfactory to put them together in one category. Furthermore, it is ambiguous and confusing to use the term 'ethnic minorities' to include only non-white groups, or non-whites plus other people of non-British origin – for example, Cypriots, Poles, Jews and Hungarians. This is because Britain is a multi-national state with its own native ethnic minorities, namely the Scots, Welsh and Irish. The Irish are both a native ethnic minority – in the sense that they are native to the British Isles and part of Ireland remains in the United Kingdom – and a foreign ethnic minority in that most Irish are citizens of the Irish Republic and prize their Irish national identity. Many Irish are unskilled migrant workers who travel to Britain to find manual jobs, especially in the construction industry. Some come to Britain on a seasonal basis. They are therefore comparable with Finnish workers migrating to Sweden or Portuguese workers travelling to France.

As can be seen from the above discussion, there are considerable problems involved in attempting to adopt a common set of terms to describe the people and their descendants who are the major concern of this book. The terms vary in different countries and the groups involved in the migration process were themselves extremely diverse. A variety of terms will thus be used depending on whether the analysis is focusing on migrant workers, foreign migrant workers or the second generation. We have tried to be as consistent as possible in our use of these terms.

The Project Countries

The seven major West European democracies chosen for this study – namely Belgium, France, Great Britain, the Federal Republic of Germany, the Netherlands, Sweden and Switzerland – were selected because they have attracted the large majority of migrant workers who have moved to Western Europe in search of work and a higher standard of living for themselves and their families. The Federal Republic of Germany, France, Britain and Switzerland all have very large numbers of migrant workers. Switzerland has the highest proportion of any European state. Sweden has a relatively small proportion of migrant workers but has led the way in developing a positive policy to encourage the integration, equal treatment and permanent settlement of its foreign immigrants. It has notably extended voting rights to foreign migrant workers in local and regional elections. Belgium has a large proportion of migrant workers, but its own language and regional divisions make it politically difficult to follow the lead of its Dutch neighbour in extending local voting rights.

The study includes pluralist federal states (Switzerland and Germany), unitary states (France, Sweden and the Netherlands), and those in between (Britain and Belgium). The variety of political arrangements among them, and their differing political cultures and traditions, will enable us to test whether the willingness to extend participatory rights to migrant workers is associated with particular political arrangements, internal conflicts or consensus, or with the strength of particular political traditions.

The size, degree of industrialisation, homogeneity and confidence in national security and identity may all also influence the willingness of a country to accept immigrants as participants in the political system. The seven countries are all advanced industrial states whose political systems can be described as multi-party democracies, but they vary in size, homogeneity, degree of federalism, the nature of their electoral systems and their historical traditions. An examination of the ways in which they have granted rights to migrant workers may enable us to specify the conditions under which civil, industrial, political and social rights are granted, and whether the long-term trend is for migrant workers and their families to be accepted as full members, even citizens, of their new countries of residence, or whether there are serious obstacles to their treatment as full and equal members.

Citizenship rights

Marshall divides citizenship rights into three major categories: civil, political and social (Marshall 1963). By civil rights he means those rights necessary for individual freedom: liberty of the person, freedom of speech, thought and faith, the right to own property and to conclude valid contracts, and the right to justice. He emphasises that the right to justice is crucial because it is the right to defend and assert one's rights on terms of equality with others by due process of law. Thus the institutions most directly associated with civil rights are the courts of justice.

The crucial element of political rights is the right to participate in the exercise of political power and the decision-making process. The most obvious means by which this is achieved is by voting in local and national elections. The institutions most closely associated with these rights are local and regional councils and the national government. Social rights have developed later than civil and political rights and include the right to a minimum standard of living and to a share in economic welfare and social security benefits. They also include the right to benefit from general educational and health provision and to live the life of a civilised human being according to the standards prevailing in society. The institutions most closely associated with social rights are the educational system and the social services.

In this book we shall also be examining industrial rights, which can be defined as a special sub-category of civil rights. Industrial rights include the right to belong to a trade union, to participate in elections for trade-union offices, to participate in elections to companies' councils and the right to strike. The ability to exercise industrial rights effectively is vitally important for migrant workers whose major priority in migrating was to find and maintain themselves in work. Furthermore, if they are foreign workers without the right to vote in local and national elections, participation in a company's councils and trade unions might be the most effective means to defend their interests.

Access to rights

All sovereign states regulate the movement of people to and from their territory and control their access to the benefits of the modern welfare state. The very principles of the welfare state, according to Freeman (1986) encourage a distinction between members and non-members. He argues that the international state system is marked by considerable economic inequalities, so that some states can afford much higher welfare benefits and socially determined living standards than the rest of the world. The very existence of such unequal benefits is a stimulus to migration, but unlimited migration would undermine the high level of these benefits. Therefore migration has to be controlled if these socially determined privileges are to be maintained. As the welfare state establishes principles of distributive justice that depart from free market principles, it has to be legitimised on the basis of solidarity that comes from common membership of a human community. This concept implies the existence of people who are not members and who are therefore excluded. The benefits of the welfare state are thus normally restricted to citizens (though in practice permanent residents may qualify for many of these benefits), and non-citizens may be wholly or partially excluded (Freeman, 1986).

However, another means of legitimising welfare benefits is through taxation – in Britain, for example, through National Insurance contributions. Those who contribute towards financing the welfare state should be entitled to its benefits. This would include foreign migrant workers who pay taxes and who therefore should be recognised as members of the welfare state. However, in all European states there is some resentment that foreigners, and especially recent immigrants (who are often considered to be foreign, even though they may be entitled to citizenship as members of a colony or former colony), should benefit from the health and social security provision that the modern welfare state bestows on its citizens.

Thus a number of barriers, or gates, control the access of potential immigrants to West European states. Associated with each of these gates is access to a larger number of rights and fewer restrictions. The first gate is that of *admission*. Some who seek entry as refugees or immigrants are refused, and are unable to proceed beyond this first stage. However, it is usually not difficult to gain temporary admission as a tourist, visitor, student, businessman or seasonal worker. Initially migrant workers were recruited for a temporary period under specific conditions restricting them to particular occupations and areas. They often had to report to the police and were not allowed to bring their wives and children with them. Everybody with a temporary permit has an insecure status, even when they comply with the regulations. Breaking the conditions of entry by, for example, doing forbidden work, committing a criminal act or overstaying the period of residence, can result in deportation.

The second gate is that of *permanent residence*. Once a person has lived in a country for a certain period, he can apply for permanent residence and an employment permit free of restrictions. Once this is achieved, the migrant worker has a much more secure and free status. He can bring his wife and children to live with him and he becomes much more a full member of his new society. In fact, he becomes a potential settler. He gains most of the rights – civil, social and industrial – that are enjoyed by citizens. Usually the major restriction that permanent foreign residents have, when compared with citizens, is the lack of political rights, especially voting rights in local and national elections. They are also banned from being candidates in local and national elections and are often forbidden from belonging to political parties.

This group of foreign citizens with substantial rights and security has become so numerous and important that some commentators have argued that their status should be recognised by a new term, namely 'denizens'.[2] This new term is meant to emphasise that the traditional sharp distinction between foreigner and citizen has been eroded and that large numbers of foreign citizens have established close, intensive, secure and long-standing relations with their country of residence. They are members of these countries even though they are legally foreigners and have not wished, and may not wish, to become natural-ised citizens. If the status of denizenship became widely recognised it would provide an additional alternative to the sharp choice between being a citizen or non-citizen of a state (Hammar, 1990).

In order to obtain full political rights, the non-citizen migrant worker must pass through the final gate to *citizenship* through the process of naturalisation. One can thus develop a typology linking rights to the status of different types of migrant worker, as outlined in Table 1.2.

Table 1.2   *The status and rights of migrant workers*

Very few rights	Illegal entrants Illegal workers
Few rights	Seasonal workers Temporary workers
Some security	Workers recruited under bilateral agreements
Considerable rights and security	Foreign workers with permanent residence status (denizens)
Full rights including political rights	Post-colonial workers with citizenship; naturalised citizens; native-born second- generation with citizenship

As migrant workers were recruited and allowed access to Western Europe as workers, it tended to be in the industrial and economic sphere that initially they were granted the fullest rights. Even economic rights, however, were conditional upon legal recruitment and the possession of the necessary employment and residence permits. Those migrant workers who entered European countries illegally had very few rights and were vulnerable to arbitrary deportation.

Some countries – for example, France – have allowed extensive illegal immigration, and the position of illegal migrant workers represents the most extreme case of absence of rights in the typology. Illegal workers have some minimal rights – for example, the right to appeal against deportation and the right to be treated humanely – but they have no rights to residence, work, social security benefits and, in practice, the protection of the law. If they seek redress of wrongs committed against them by, for example, seeking the help of the police, their illegal status may be discovered and they may be deported. They are thus open to severe exploitation by employers and landlords.

The extension of social and humanitarian rights to migrant workers has depended partly on the policy adopted by the receiving country towards recruitment. If a tough rotation policy was adopted, as was the case in Switzerland, then the social rights of migrants were, at least at first, severely restricted. They could not bring their families with them, they had to leave after a certain period, and they could not qualify for permanent residence. In Germany, in spite of official adherence to a guest-worker policy, family reunification has been allowed and migrant workers have stayed for so long that permanent settlement has clearly taken place. In France, where illegal immigration was allowed by the authorities for most of the 1960s and part of the 1970s, there has arisen the expectation that there will be periodic amnesties to regularise the status of these workers.

Once family reunification takes place and migrant communities become established, then access to social and political rights becomes much more important. The presence of wives and children makes access to decent accommodation and housing a high priority. Also health care, social security and other welfare benefits are more important. The community may desire more permanent and substantial places of worship and access to educational institutions to ensure that their children can be taught the customs and traditions of their home society in addition to the normal school curriculum. They may also want the services they use, such as maternity provision and health care, to be sensitive to the cultural traditions of their community. In order to achieve these goals, political influence will be necessary.

The final stage in the acquisition of rights by a new member of a society is the acquisition of full political rights, especially voting rights, which is often seen as conferring full membership. The willingness of West European democracies to grant citizenship to migrant workers varies considerably. In Switzerland, naturalisation is both difficult and expensive. In Germany, it is also very difficult. In Britain, citizenship has traditionally been easy to acquire or reclaim, but recent trends are to make the acquisition of citizenship more difficult and to tie access to social and welfare rights more closely to citizenship. Citizens of Commonwealth countries had an automatic right to British citizenship but, since the Nationality Act of 1981, the trend has been to treat Commonwealth and non-Commonwealth citizens on the same basis as far as immigration and social rights are concerned, although 'patrials' – that is, people with a close connection with the United Kingdom through descent from a British grandparent – continue to have privileged access to the UK. Commonwealth citizens continue to enjoy full political rights. Since 1979, naturalisation in Britain has become more expensive. In France, naturalisation has traditionally been encouraged as part of the policy of assimilation and to increase the French population. It is thus relatively easy for foreign migrant workers, especially the second generation, to acquire French citizenship. Belgium and the Netherlands have recently changed their nationality laws to make it easier for foreign residents to become naturalised citizens. In Sweden too, naturalisation is very cheap and much encouraged. Both Sweden and the Netherlands have extended local voting rights to foreign migrant workers to encourage their integration and involvement in their new societies. Norway, Denmark and Ireland have passed similar legislation, though in the case of Ireland the main reason was to grant reciprocal voting rights to British residents in the Irish Republic, thus protecting the voting rights of Irish residents in Britain.

Figure 1.1   *Ease of access to various rights of foreign migrant workers*

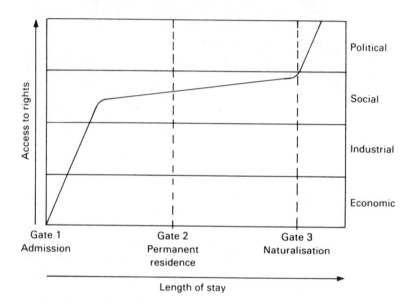

However, even in those countries which have led the way in extending voting rights to foreign migrant workers, reformers have found a deep-seated resistance to the granting of national voting rights to foreign residents (Hammar, 1986; Tung, 1986). Participating in parliamentary elections seems to be of great symbolic importance as a national political act, and citizens are not prepared to extend this right easily to people unwilling to take the positive step of becoming a member of the national community through the process of naturalisation. Nevertheless, as temporary labour recruitment has been transformed into permanent settlement, the general trend among all Western European states has been gradually to extend the rights of foreign migrant workers.

This trend has gone hand-in-hand with tougher restrictions on the right to be admitted. Since the end of the post-war European boom in 1973, labour recruitment has been severely controlled in all the advanced industrial countries of Western Europe, and in some cases it has been reversed. As labour recruitment has declined, there has been considerable increase in concern about the numbers of people seeking asylum in Western Europe, particularly from the Third World. This has resulted in the introduction of greater restrictions on the rights of people claiming the status of refugees. This is partly because some European governments claim that many asylum seekers are not political refugees at all, but economic refugees – that is, they are really migrant workers unable to obtain entry and employment permits. In 1986 Sweden and Denmark passed legislation to refuse access to the asylum procedure for those who arrived from a safe third country.

The government of Germany has been most concerned with the problem of asylum seekers because, under its constitution, there is great difficulty in refusing admission to asylum seekers and considerable scope for appeals and therefore delay in resolving such cases. Recently the British government has taken additional powers to control the entry of refugees, because of the number of Tamils seeking asylum from Sri Lanka. The Immigration (Carriers' Liability) Bill passed in 1987 makes carriers (notably airlines) liable to financial penalties in respect of passengers brought by them to the UK without valid documents.

In Switzerland, the problem of asylum seekers was dramatically emphasised by a referendum on 5 April 1987, when civil rights groups and the churches challenged the government's legislation taking additional powers to restrict the entry of refugees. The opponents of the government claimed that these new powers undermined Switzerland's long tradition of giving sanctuary to refugees. However, the amendments to the asylum laws giving the extra powers to the government were supported by 67.4 percent of the Swiss electorate.

Table 1.3 shows the increase in the number of asylum seekers in selected European countries between 1984 and 1986.

The political challenge
The settlement of foreign migrant workers in Western Europe has caused a reassessment of the concept of membership of a modern state. In the pre-war period, almost all members of European states were citizens with full legal, civil and political rights, but now many members of Western democracies are not citizens. They are certainly members of these states participating in the labour and housing markets, paying taxes, bringing up families and sending their children to school. They contribute to and receive welfare benefits, and are involved in the social and cultural life of their local communities. In some neighbourhoods, foreign workers are a high proportion, even a

Table 1.3   *The numbers of persons seeking asylum in selected European countries, 1984–6*

Country	1984	1985	1986
Austria	7,400	6,700	8,700
Belgium	4,000	6,300	7,500
Britain	3,900	5,500	3,900
Denmark	4,300	8,700	9,300
France	16,100	28,900	26,300
Germany	34,400	73,900	99,700
Netherlands	2,600	5,700	5,900
Norway	400	800	2,700
Sweden	11,300	15,000	15,000
Switzerland	7,400	9,700	8,500
Total	91,000	161,200	187,500

Source: Asylum Seekers in the United Kingdom, Essential Statistics, British Refugee Council, Sept. 1987

majority, of the population, but they are generally excluded from political decision-making at both local and national levels.

The presence of large numbers of migrant workers challenges the sharp distinction between citizen and non-citizen in Western democracies. All those resident in a state are, at least temporarily, members of that state, and may, for example, be subject to military service in time of war. All residents normally have some legal and civil rights. It might thus be more sensible to suggest that there is a continuum of rights attached to the membership of a state rather than a sharp distinction between member and non-member, citizen and non-citizen. Those members with the fewest rights or none at all might be groups such as illegal immigrants, asylum-seekers or refugees. The only rights of these groups may be to seek entry and to appeal against expulsion. They may have few allies in their intended country of residence, and few resources. In comparison, legally resident aliens or denizens may be considered to have a high degree of security and legal protection, and lack only such political rights as the right to vote and to stand for public office.

Citizens can, of course, be assumed to have full legal, civil and political rights, though certain groups may be discriminated against legally or in practice. In some countries naturalised citizens may not hold certain political or security-sensitive offices.[3] Other citizens may continue to be regarded as 'foreign' even though they have acquired citizenship. Racial discrimination, for example, may lead to certain groups being treated as second-class citizens.

Post-war migrant workers fall into all these categories of membership of West European states. Those who have full citizenship are most often migrants from the former British, Dutch or French colonies; but in some countries – for example, Sweden and France – many migrant workers have become naturalised citizens of their new country. This is, however, exceptional. In most of Europe, migrant workers have retained their old citizenships. In some, but not all, West European states, the European-born children of migrant workers are entitled to claim the citizenship of their country of birth and residence, but many are reluctant to renounce their parents' country and cultural heritage.

The importance of political rights
Castles and Kosack emphasise that migrant workers have not come to homogeneous, friendly, peaceful societies, but to class societies where the means of production are owned by a small minority and where class oppression is the norm. Migrants are assigned a low place in these inegalitarian societies, which are characterised by conflict and coercion (Castles and Kosack, 1973). This is a fairly accurate description of the economic structure of most West European states, but it is not the whole picture. West European countries are also highly developed welfare states and, on the whole, they have long traditions of liberal democracy. The European notion of citizenship implies equality for all citizens giving them equal access to the benefits of the Welfare state and equal political, civil and social rights (Turner, 1986).

These characteristics of European states may work in contrary directions as far as migrant workers are concerned. The traditions of liberal democracy, equal treatment for citizens and regard for individual human rights is a resource for foreign immigrants, asylum-seekers or politically embarrassing aliens, but they all have some protection in constitutional bills of rights, the law of the land, or under such treaties as the European Convention of Human Rights or the United Nations Charter. Even illegal immigrants and refugees may be able to appeal to civil liberties groups, the churches, trade unions or political groups which have an interest in upholding democratic values and individual liberties, and in defending poor or oppressed groups. Legally resident aliens have substantially more rights than illegal immigrants or refugees, and their rights cannot easily be restricted or violated without eroding the rights of citizens too. There is thus likely to be considerable resistance to attacks on their rights as legally resident aliens.

One should not overemphasise the protection given to foreign citizens by bills of rights or liberal democratic values. On occasion, states may ride roughshod over the rights of legally resident aliens. It has been argued by writers such as Castells (1975) that the political and legal isolation of migrant workers, owing to their predominantly foreign status, makes them particularly vulnerable to exploitation.

Some writers have even argued that foreign workers live under a kind of arbitrary police state: 'If the police state is that in which administrative authority may arbitrarily, and with more or less complete freedom of decision, apply all the measures for which it wishes to take the initiative . . . then foreigners in France are living under such a regime' (Pauly and Diederich, 1983).

Many authors draw attention to the difference between the *de jure* and *de facto* treatment of foreign migrant workers. Paul Lagarde points out that, with reference to France

> Nowhere do the tests formally forbid aliens from engaging in political activities, but the Minister of the Interior, each time he has to justify an expulsion, replies that the alien expelled has failed to fulfil the obligation of political neutrality imposed on all aliens resident in France, which amounts to depriving the alien of all possibility of action and expression at [the] political level. In other countries, the political liberty of the alien is constrained by the notion of public order. In any case, for the alien there is a severer punishment than for the national, namely expulsion. (Pauly and Diederich, 1983)

In Britain, as well as in France, aliens can be deported arbitrarily for violating public order or the security of the state. The British Home Secretary can decide that an alien's presence is not 'conducive to the public good' and he can then be deported virtually without appeal. Aliens who commit serious crimes in Britain can be recommended for deportation by the courts after they have been sentenced and have served their sentences.

Operations by the police – for example, to apprehend illegal immigrants – may result in the harassment of particular groups of aliens or citizens. People of foreign appearance may also be asked to prove their immigrant status when they come into contact with officials and may be reluctant to claim benefits that are due to them, or to take action to redress grievances.

This lack of political rights has led, according to Miller, to a thesis of political quiescence. Migrant workers are portrayed as an apolitical mass whose apathy and inferior political status weakens the working class politically and industrially. Those migrant workers who are interested in politics may also be more concerned with the politics of their homeland than that of their new country of residence. The political elites of Western European states have thus divided the proletariat and buttressed their own ascendancy by importing workers who cannot participate fully in the class struggle (Miller, 1981).

Not everybody agrees either that migrant workers are a passive political force or that they are completely denuded of political rights. Some groups on the extreme left see migrant workers as a potentially revolutionary vanguard precisely because they are not integrated into the political system. The native working class are often compromised, from a revolutionary point of view, by allegiances to established social democratic and labour parties either through membership of unions affiliated to these parties or directly as party members and supporters.

On the political right, migrant workers are often seen as a threat to national unity, an alien wedge potentially disruptive and disloyal. This may even be the case when they are citizens. In Britain, Enoch Powell warned that immigration could bring a threat of division, violence and bloodshed of American dimensions (Schoen, 1975). Casey argues that 'there is no way of understanding British and English history that does not take seriously the sentiments of patriotism that go with a continuity of institutions, shared experience, language, customs and kinship'; and that 'the moral life finds its fulfilment in an actual, historic human community and, above all, in a nation state' (1982). He argues that immigrant groups do not have these shared experiences and loyalties and are therefore most unlikely to identify themselves with the traditions and loyalties of the host nation (Casey, 1982). The clearest exponent of this view is Powell who, in one of his speeches, concluded that 'the West Indian or Indian does not, by being born in England, become an Englishman. In law he became a United Kingdom citizen by birth; in fact he is a West Indian or Asian still' (Powell, 1969).

Martin Heisler has a similarly pessimistic view concerning the presence of large semi-settled foreign minorities in Western societies, which he sees as an added complication in the government of these states (1986). His view is that the governing power of Western democracies has been eroded by immigration. Moreover, domestic and international constraints prevent the reversal of most of the unforeseen and undesirable social and economic problems that have followed the policies which created these large foreign minorities. He concludes by arguing that it was a political mistake to have permitted this migration. Heisler neglects the considerable economic and social benefits that migration has contributed to Western European societies, but he is right in drawing attention to the political challenge that large foreign minorities present to European states (Heisler, 1986).

The political role attributed to migrant workers by the extreme left and right have received less attention than the thesis of political quiescence. But, as Miller (1981) argues, there is much evidence to suggest that the thesis of political quiescence has been accepted too easily. On the contrary, foreign migrant workers possess a considerable range of rights in Western democracies. Most have a legal right to residence and employment, and they have the right to free speech, to practise their religion, to form their own associations, to publish newspapers, to join unions and to participate in public demonstrations. They can engage in extra-parliamentary activities, seek allies among sympathetic groups such as churches, trade unions and political parties, and may receive assistance and support from their home government. The size and concentration of their communities is a source of security and resources and, even though they lack the vote, gives them local political influence. In the case of Muslim migrant workers, they may be able to seek and acquire support from co-religionists abroad, such as the governments of Saudi Arabia and Libya.

Increasingly, West European governments have recognised the potential danger of large disenfranchised, unassimilated minorities in their societies. There is clearly a contradiction between the economic exploitation of immigrants and the precepts of the liberal democratic state, and a limit to the length of time that residence and membership in a state can be sustained without representation. Those who pay taxes should be consulted about how the taxes are spent unless the duration of their work and residence is very short. Even Conservative politicians are aware of this contradiction: for example, when he was President, Giscard d'Estaing said, 'immigrant workers, being part of our national productive community, should have a place in French society which is dignified, humane and equitable' (Verbunt, 1985).

The campaign for political rights
Since the nineteenth century, nationality and citizenship have in Europe been considered closely related concepts. Nationality suggests membership of a nation – that is, a body of people distinguished by common descent, language, culture or historical tradition. It may also mean the people of a state, though this meaning is closer to the concept of citizenship which has come to mean the members of a state or, more strictly, those people being, or having, the rights and duties of a citizen. Citizenship is thus the legal definition of those people with citizenship rights. The problem in Europe has been that many states have considered themselves to be nation states in which nationality and citizenship are the same. Moreover nationalism, whereby a communal group claims distinctive political institutions and sovereignty, has been used to justify separation from multi-national states such as the Austro-Hungarian, Ottoman or Russian empires. Even at the present time, communal groups in Spain, France and the United Kingdom are demanding by force the right to self-determination based on claims of belonging to distinct national groups.

Most European states contain ethnic, religious, linguistic and national minorities which may claim the right to independence. In some states it is hard to decide which is the dominant nationality. In the case of the United Kingdom and Yugoslavia, for example, people may identify themselves with a variety of nationalities such as English,

Scots or Welsh on the one hand, and Croat, Serbian or Albanian on the other. These local national identities compete with the overall British or Yugoslav national identity. The English, Scots and Welsh are conscious of shared history, economy, customs and values which give them a double identity as British as well as English, Scots or Welsh, but these local nationalisms may form the basis of demands for separatism and independence. Historical problems of creating a national identity or of upsetting the ethnic composition of the state may make some European regimes cautious about granting citizenship to large numbers of people who do not share the traditions, customs and loyalties of their existing citizens. They may also be concerned about upsetting existing political arrangements which the acquisition of large numbers of new citizens may involve.

One major exception to this general rule about restricting citizenship concerns those European powers with colonial territories overseas. In these cases, citizenship was often granted intentionally or unintentionally to some or all colonial subjects.

Citizenship has generally been granted either to all those born within a given state's territory – for example, Britain and the USA – or to those descended from a citizen father – the dominant European tradition. In addition, citizenship can be obtained by applying for and being accepted for naturalisation. The process of naturalisation has generally been seen by state authorities as involving a positive commitment to the state as demonstrated by a significant period of residence, a knowledge of its language and constitution, and an oath of allegiance.

The migration and settlement of millions of foreign migrant workers has challenged these traditional notions of citizenship, nationality and membership of a nation state. The realisation that migrant workers are becoming permanent settlers without applying for citizenship through naturalisation has created a novel situation – a situation that is a challenge to theories of representative democracy.

Citizenship in the advanced industrialised countries is a prized possession. It gives access to security, employment, high wages, a good standard of living, educational opportunities, health care, and freedom from hunger, even if the individual is unemployed. Every state controls access to its territory and citizenship. States discriminate in favour of their own citizens and against citizens of other states. They control the composition of their populations to preserve their national identity, and for cultural and security reasons. In addition, immigration control is seen as a means of maintaining high living standards and social welfare benefits. Post-war migration has challenged some of these national imperatives and created a new social and political reality. Even without the granting of citizenship, the presence of migrant workers and their families has transformed previously ethnically homogeneous states such as Sweden and Germany into multi-cultural societies.

The presence of large numbers of residents who are excluded from political decision-making means that representative government is no longer truly representative. This is especially true at the local level where, in some municipalities, a large proportion of residents are foreign and this proportion is expanding because of continued immigration (now largely because of family reunions), the youthfulness of the immigrant population and high birth-rates. Even in Rotterdam, a major European city, some 16 percent of the population is foreign, and, with the movement of Dutch people out of the city and the expansion of the foreign population, this proportion is rising steadily. It is not surprising, therefore, that the municipal authorities in Rotterdam have wished to involve foreign residents in decision-making, given that so many of their services are directed at these groups. The Rotterdam council thus strongly supported the extension of voting rights at the local level to foreign citizens. In contrast, the local authorities of German towns with large foreign minorities are often opposed to the extension of voting rights to migrant workers because this would change the political complexion of the municipal councils and would also provoke extreme popular hostility. In Germany, therefore, migrants have been encouraged to elect local advisory boards which local authorities can then consult.

The general trend, however, in the post-war period has been for the gradual extension of social, civil and political rights to migrant workers and their dependents. Even in Germany *länder* like Schleswig-Holstein and Hamburg have granted local voting rights to foreign residents. Restrictions on the employment and activities of foreigners have gradually been lifted, and in some countries naturalisation laws have been relaxed. The trend is not uniform, and sometimes tougher policies have been introduced but generally an expansion of rights has taken place. The next chapter examines the position of the most vulnerable, most exploited and least protected group: namely, illegal immigrants and undocumented workers.

Notes

1   It is impossible to obtain comparable figures for all seven countries. However, it is Great Britain which is most difficult to make comparable, because of the 'non-foreign' status of Commonwealth immigrants. The foreign-born population of Great Britain was 3,023,000 (5.6%) according to the Labour Force Survey, 1985. The total population of Great Britain in 1981 was 53,556,911 and of the United Kingdom 55,063,976. There are very few immigrants in Northern Ireland, so the focus of analysis in this chapter is Great Britain rather than the United Kingdom.

2 In origin the term 'denizen' referred to an alien admitted to citizenship by royal letters patent by the English Crown in the sixteenth century (Cohen, 1988). However, the term has fallen into disuse and it seems appropriate to give it this new meaning.

3 In the USA, the President must be a native-born citizen, as must the Prime Minister in Sweden. In Britain, naturalised citizens may be excluded from some positions in the armed forces. In France until recently a range of offices were excluded from naturalised citizens.

References

British Labour Force Surveys (1984–6) Office of Population, Censuses and Surveys. London: HMSO.

Casey, J. (1982) 'One Nation: The Politics of Race', *Salisbury Review*, 1 (Autumn).

Castells, M. (1975) 'Immigrant Workers and Class Struggles in Advanced Capitalism: The Western European Experience', *Politics and Society*, 5 (1).

Castles, S., H. Booth and T. Wallace (1984) *Here for Good*. London: Pluto Press.

Castles, S. and G. Kosack (1973) *Immigrant Workers and Class Structure in Western Europe*. Oxford: Oxford University Press.

Cohen, R. (1988) 'Citizens, Denizens and Helots: The Politics of International Migration Flows in the Post-war World', Centre for Research in Ethnic Relations, University of Warwick.

Freeman, G. (1979) *Immigrant Labor and Racial Conflict in Industrial Societies : The French and British Experience, 1945–1975*. Princeton, NJ: Princeton University Press.

Freeman, G. (1986) 'Migration and the Political Economy of the Welfare State', *Annals of the American Academy of Political and Social Science*, 485 (May).

Frey, M. and V. Lubinski (1987) *Probleme infolge hoher Auslander-konzentration in ausgewahlten europäischen staaten*, Federal Institute for Population Research, Wiesbaden.

Hammar, T. (1985a) *European Immigration Policy: A Comparative Study*. Cambridge: Cambridge University Press.

Hammar, T. (1985b) 'Citizenship, Aliens' Political Rights and Politicians' Concern for Migrants : The Case of Sweden', in R. Rogers (ed.), *Guests Come to Stay*. Boulder, Colo.: Westview Press.

Hammar, T. (1986) 'Citizenship : Membership of a Nation and of a State', *International Migration*, 4.

Hammar, T. (1990) *International Migration, Citizenship and Democracy*. Aldershot: Gower Publishing.

Heisler, M. O. (1986) 'Transnational Migration as a Small Window on the Diminished Autonomy of the Modern Democratic State', *Annals of the American Academy of Political and Social Science*, 485 (May).

Hoffmann-Nowotny, H. (1985) 'Switzerland', in T. Hammar (ed.), *European Immigration Policy : A Comparative Study*. Cambridge: Cambridge University Press.

Krane, R. E. (1979) *International Labour Migration in Europe*. New York: Praeger Press.

Marshall, T. H. (1963) 'Citizenship and Social Class', in *Sociology at the Crossroads*. London: Heinemann.

Miller, M. J. (1981) *Foreign Workers in Western Europe: An Emerging Political Force*. New York: Praeger Press.

Patterson, S. (1963) *Dark Strangers: A Study of West Indians in London*. London: Tavistock Publications.

Pauly, A. and R. Diederich (1983) 'Migrant Workers and Civil Liberties', European University Institute, Working Paper No. 45.

Powell, E. (1969) Text of a speech delivered to the annual conference of the Rotary Club of London, Eastbourne, 16 Nov. 1968, in B. Smithies and P. Fiddick (eds), *Enoch Powell on Immigration*. London: Sphere Books: 63–77.

Power, J. (1979) *Migrant Workers in Western Europe and the United States*. London: Pergamon Press.

Rogers, R. (1985) *Guests Come to Stay*. Boulder, Colo.: Westview Press.

Schoen, D. (1975) *Enoch Powell and the Powellites*. London: Macmillan.

SOPEMI (1986) *Continuous Reporting System on Migration*. Paris: OECD.

Thränhardt, D. (1988) 'West Germany – An Undeclared Immigration Country' (unpublished manuscript).

Tung, K. R. (1986) 'Voting Rights for Alien Residents – Who Wants it?' *International Migration Review*, 19 (3).

Turner, B. (1986) *Citizenship and Capitalism*. London: Allen & Unwin.

Verbunt, G. (1985) 'France', in T. Hammar (ed.), *European Immigration Policy: A Comparative Study*. Cambridge: Cambridge University Press.

2

The Absence of Rights:
the Position of Illegal Immigrants

Catherine Wihtol de Wenden

The first hurdle that intending migrants have to overcome is that of admission to their intended country of work and residence. In the post-war period, particularly after 1954, the West European economies were very short of labour and immigration was allowed and was even encouraged. In this situation millions of migrants found it relatively easy to gain admission and pass through the 'front door' into the European country of their choice. In this period immigration controls were very relaxed and often those migrants who did not comply with the immigration rules and gained unauthorised admission by the 'back door' found that it was easy to evade apprehension, find work and accommodation and, after a period of residence, have their position regularised either by an official amnesty or by qualifying in another way – for example, by length of stay or marriage to a person with permanent residence. In Britain after 1962 Commonwealth immigrants had to have employment vouchers, but those who entered without documents could not be deported if they evaded capture for only 24 hours. This rule contributed to illegal immigration between 1962 and 1968, when it was finally abolished.

In France between 1950 and 1972 the official view was that illegal immigration was a major benefit to the French economy, contributing to rapid levels of economic growth and higher living standards. It was not a problem that needed remedial action. The French policy in this period was to allow relatively open borders but to restrict access to welfare rights to those legally in residence. France has always operated strict internal controls of those within its borders, and foreign immigrants who broke the law or offended against the 'ordre public' could be arbitrarily expelled.

In the last fifteen years this relaxed attitude to immigration ceased with the ending of the great post-war European boom in 1973. All West European countries ended large-scale labour recruitment in the early 1970s and since then have taken strict action to protect their labour markets. Immigration has become a political issue of some importance in many European countries and this has also encouraged governments to impose stricter controls and to enforce them more vigorously. Intending migrants have to obtain work and residence permits before their arrival in the receiving country and, increasingly, these permits are only available to workers offering a high degree of professional expertise and experience. The expansion of the European Community (EC) in the 1980s is also likely to result in stricter controls on non-EC citizens. This is because the incorporation of Greece, Spain and Portugal has brought into the community major labour-exporting countries and will reduce the need for EC countries to recruit labour from outside. Transitional arrangements mean that in 1988 Greeks and in 1993 Spaniards and Portuguese will benefit from the free EC labour market and will be able to move anywhere within the EC to find work. All EC countries are expected to discriminate against non-EC nationals and in favour of EC citizens in their labour markets.

Definitions of Illegality

There are different types and approaches to the problem of illegal immigration in the different project countries. This is despite the efforts of the European Commission to implement a common policy. In Germany there are three main types of illegality: violations of (1) the law on work permits, (2) the law on the employment of temporary workers, and (3) the law on illegal residence. In 1980 it was officially estimated that there were about 200,000 illegal immigrants in Germany. However, the whole question surrounding illegality is complicated by the relations between Germany and Turkey, and by the German laws regarding politicial asylum. Most migrant workers in Germany are Turkish and so probably are most illegal migrants. As Turkey has a repressive political regime illegal migrants, when discovered, often claim the status of political refugees. The process of claiming political asylum is long and complicated and usually takes two years to resolve. It is only when asylum status has been refused that the claimant becomes an illegal immigrant and liable for deportation. Even so, only a quarter of those ordered to leave the country do so.

In Switzerland many types of illegality are linked to restrictions on permanent residence; for example, seasonal workers or annual workers may exceed their period of temporary residence or stay on after their permits have not been renewed. They may also bring their wives and children with them without authorisation. In addition, foreigners may enter the country without any authorisation or visa, they may make false statements about the purpose of their visit, pretending to be tourists or students. Some enter without passing through a frontier crossing point, or with forged papers or enter while ostensibly being in transit to another destination. Some workers break the conditions under which they entered and some people refused the status of political refugees try to stay.

In Belgium, as in all countries, illegal immigrants are persons of foreign nationality who enter without the required permits. These permits vary, depending on nationality, purpose and length of stay. Those who intend to stay longer than three months have to ask, before their arrival, for a residence permit. This has to be renewed each year. Non-citizens who have resided in Belgium for five years are entitled to settle. Illegal workers are those who lack the required employment and residence permits. If discovered they can be deported.

In Sweden, if a foreigner wishes to stay for more than three months he must apply for a residence permit before his arrival. Some foreign nationals need a visa even to come as visitors or tourists. An illegal worker is a foreigner who is gainfully employed without a work permit. Very few work permits have been issued since 1972 with the exception of a few hundred for people with specialist skills. There are thought to be very few illegal immigrants in Sweden. This is partly due to efficient and effective controls but also due to the existence of the Nordic labour market agreement which was established in 1954 and renewed in 1983. Most of Sweden's foreign migrant workers are Finns, and as fellow Nordics they are free from regulation and controls. Over half of the foreign population in Sweden comes from other Nordic countries. In recent years, asylum-seekers who have been refused asylum have been evading deportation and remaining in the country, often hidden by Swedish friends. The numbers are relatively small but are increasing.

In Britain before 1962, the major immigration flows came from Ireland or the Commonwealth, neither of which was subject to controls. Since then Commonwealth immigration has gradually become as strictly controlled as foreign immigration and now both come under the Immigration Act (1971). The trend has been for successive governments to control immigration more strictly and this has been especially so since 1979. The Conservative government has tightened controls and taken more vigorous action against illegal immigrants. The courts have widened the definition of illegality to include those who give false information to the immigration authorities, and to overstayers as well as those who avoid immigration control. Sometimes innocent people may find themselves in violation of the law. Recruitment agencies, for example, often recruit people for work in another country and offer to process the application forms for visas and other permits. Sometimes they deliberately omit or falsify information on these applications. The innocent migrant workers may then find themselves liable to deportation when these irregularities are discovered.

A wide variety of different forms of illegal immigration, work and residence thus exist. An immigrant may enter a country illegally, take up employment when this is forbidden, enter legally but stay longer than his visa allows. Some countries attempt to calculate the numbers of illegal immigrants within their borders but rarely are official estimates published. In Germany estimates are based on the prosecutions of employers; in Switzerland, according to the numbers discovered and expelled from the country; and in France, according to the numbers who present themselves for regularisation after the periodic announcement of amnesties. It is, of course, impossible to estimate the numbers of illegal entrants and workers, but one can speculate that it is substantially higher in countries like France which encouraged substantial 'spontaneous' immigration in the 1950s and 1960s than in Switzerland and Sweden where controls have been more effectively enforced.

The nature of illegality varies between the different European countries, depending on the control policy favoured by the state. In Britain, which has always operated strict border controls, illegal entry is rare. Instead, illegal workers in Britain tend to enter legally as visitors, tourists or students and then to break their entry conditions by overstaying and taking up forbidden employment.

The major categories of illegal immigrants and workers are:

1   Individuals who enter the country without passing through immigration controls. These are illegal immigrants or undocumented aliens.
2   Individuals who enter a country legally for a temporary period as visitors, tourists, students or seasonal workers but who extend their period of residence without permission. These are overstayers.
3   Individuals who have permission to stay but not to work. If they take up employment they become illegal workers or unauthorised workers.
4   Individuals who are legally employed under a restrictive contract who either decide to work beyond its expiration or who are employed in a manner not authorised by the contract. For example, they may change their employment without permission. These are also illegal or unauthorised workers.

The strictness with which these categories are defined and enforced varies according to the demands of the labour market and the salience of immigration as a political issue. During the period of rapid economic growth in France, especially after 1958, so-called 'spontaneous' immigration was not only allowed but even encouraged. As a consequence, large numbers of undocumented immigrants entered France and illegal status was not uncommon. At the end of the great European boom in 1973 all West European countries either stopped recruiting foreign workers altogether or imposed much stricter controls. In some countries, as unemployment rose efforts were made to encourage foreign workers to leave. Germany, for example, repatriated large numbers of migrant workers whose status was irregular. In contrast, Belgium granted an amnesty to many migrants with irregular status and legalised most of its illegal immigrants. In the case of France, both solutions were tried. However these radical steps did not have the results policy-makers have hoped for.[1] Attempts to repatriate illegals have not reduced the foreign migrant worker population significantly, and amnesties have also not reduced illegal immigration. In fact, regular amnesties or the hope of future amnesties may be a major factor encouraging more illegal immigration as aspiring migrants see the opportunity of being regularised after a period of illegal residence and work. In France, where illegal immigration was more or less official policy for twenty years, expectations of periodic amnesties came to be regarded as a right. When such amnesties became less common after 1973, campaigns were organised by illegal workers and their allies to demand regularisation of their status.

The Numbers of Illegal Immigrants

There is no accurate means of determining the number of illegal immigrants or unauthorised workers in Western Europe. In France, after a long period of tolerance, immigration, including illegal immigration, has now become a matter of political debate. Some politicians argue that the number of illegals is about 300,000 but refuse to reveal the basis for this estimate. In 1981 a special amnesty was announced by the government, and as a result more than 140,000 illegal immigrants, who had entered France before 1981, had their status legalised. Since then no amnesties have been allowed, except for family reunification or a successful application for political asylum. A survey undertaken by the Ministry of Labour during the amnesty programme of 1981–2 among 9,500 of those who successfully applied for legal status indicated that most illegals belong to the nationalities which contributed most of the migrant workers recruited before the imposition of controls in 1973. They formed part of the major migration flows. The reasons for this are clear, as the survey also revealed that women and young people were heavily over-represented among the illegal population. This suggests that many legally recruited foreign migrant workers often have difficulty obtaining permission for their wives and children to join them but send for them nevertheless (Cealis, Marie and Jansolin, 1983).

In Switzerland the government has always refused to estimate the number of illegals, but the organisations working with migrants estimate the numbers as varying between 30,000 and 150,000 or between 3 and 15 percent of the resident foreign population. This huge range indicates the difficulty of estimating illegal immigration. In 1982 the number of people deported from Switzerland as illegals was 2,326. The largest groups involved were Turks (558), Yugoslavs (510) and Portuguese (359). The numbers of deportations is rising as the police are under pressure to enforce the regulations more strictly.

Due to the strict border controls it has always been assumed that the numbers of illegal immigrants in Britain has been relatively small. Between 1962 and 1965 there was thought to be widespread evasion of the employment voucher scheme introduced by the Commonwealth Immigrants Act (1962). In the late 1960s the popular press gave considerable publicity to small parties of Asians landing on quiet beaches at night, but the numbers involved were probably only a few hundred.

In April 1974 the Home Secretary announced an amnesty for illegal immigrants who were citizens of Commonwealth countries or Pakistan and who had been adversely affected by the retrospective operation of the 1971 Immigration Act. Fewer than 2,500 applied for legalisation of their situation under the amnesty, and one-fifth of these were found to be ineligible as they were overstayers rather than illegal entrants (*Hansard*, 29th November 1977).

In recent years the Home Office has developed a more sophisticated system of internal immigration control. Computer technology now links the Home Office Immigration Service and the police force. But at present computer capacity is not adequate to track the millions of foreigners who visit the country every year, so selective checks are made. The number of deportations has been rising in recent years, from 544 in 1979 to 1,520 in 1986. Between 1981 and 1985 the annual average was about 1,400 (Ardill and Cross, 1987).

In Sweden the well-developed system of population registration makes internal control of aliens relatively efficient. All residents have a personal identification number which is necessary, for example, when visiting hospital or a doctor. Trade unions have a considerable influence on immigration policy and a major vested interest in protecting the labour market. Immigrant workers are thus more likely to be employed in areas, such as catering and domestic employment, where union influence is rather weak. A major issue related to illegal immigration for Sweden is that of asylum-seekers. The numbers of people claiming refugee status has been rising rapidly in recent years. Many of these destroy their papers on entering Sweden in order to avoid repatriation to the country of their last residence.

In Belgium, before deciding to halt immigration in 1974, the government decided to allow an amnesty for illegals already in the country and then to impose tougher sanctions afterwards. Some 12,000 illegal workers were regularised. In the Netherlands, 18,000 illegal immigrants applied to the government in 1975 for regularisation of their status under the terms of an amnesty. Some 15,000 of these applications were successful and the individuals were granted permanent residence.

Government Policy towards Illegals

In Europe in the 1980s immigration has become a major political issue. Rising unemployment and the exploitation of the immigration issue by politicians of the far right has caused governments to attempt to placate public opinion by controlling immigration more strictly and by taking tough action against illegals. Immigration policy is an area fraught with ambiguities and contradictions. This is because, although governments wish to stabilise the in-flow of foreign labour or reduce it to a minimum, some employers find illegal immigrants an adaptable, hard-working and uncomplaining workforce which is flexible, insecure and easily dispensable. Thus, from these employers' point of view, illegal migrant workers are the ideally exploitable source of labour: low paid, unorganised and uncomplaining.

In a period of recession governments have to be seen to be protecting their citizens' interests, particularly in the labour market. They may also accede to popular pressure to impose stricter immigration controls and encourage foreign workers to leave. However, the ability of governments to control immigration is limited by the sheer volume of late-twentieth-century travel and the need to maintain relatively open borders for businessmen, tourists, visitors and students. West European governments are thus often more concerned to give their populations the impression that tough action to control migration is being taken than actually to stop illegal immigration. Public opinion, it has been argued, is more sensitive to the aura of control than to the actual exercise of control (Costa-Lascoux and de Wenden, 1984).

National Policies towards Illegals

France
France was unique among West European states importing labour after the war, in so far as uncontrolled or illegal immigration was tolerated as the most efficient way of promoting economic growth at the lowest cost. Illegal migrants came from all the major areas sending migrant workers to France, in particular black Africa, Iberia and North Africa. The government of Portugal forbade its citizens to

emigrate and so Portuguese workers were illegal migrants by necessity. This did not prevent a massive Portuguese emigration, particularly to France. In 1948 the Portuguese represented 26 percent of illegal immigrants to France and by 1964 this had risen to 80 percent. On 29 July 1968 a government decree established a procedure for regularising the position of illegal immigrants.

The events of May 1968 and the economic crises of the early 1970s changed the whole climate of toleration towards foreign immigrants and to uncontrolled immigration. Employers and unions pressed for governmental control and politicians were concerned about the need to maintain law and order. The 'Fontanet decree' of 27 February 1972 attempted to establish a stricter implementation of the law. On 31 October 1973, following ministerial decisions, amnesty measures were suspended. At this time the changing climate of opinion was reflected in the dropping of the term 'uncontrolled immigration' and its substitution by 'illegal immigration'. In 1974 the number of illegal immigrants was estimated at some 385,000 (probably an underestimate), mainly concentrated in agriculture, forestry and construction.

Since the early 1970s the French government has attempted to bring immigration firmly under its control. This was the intention of the immigration legislation of 10 July 1976 and the decrees of 3 January and 11 July 1977.

Further restrictive legislation was introduced on 10 January 1980 (the Bonnet law), which applied to new applications for entry and residence in France. In May the same year the Secretary of State, Lionel Stoleru, announced he would consider, on an individual basis, applications for amnesty for those illegal workers resident in France since 1 March 1980 who had family responsibilities.

Since 1981 the government has directed its efforts to ending illegal immigration and improving the position of immigrants in the country. It has found it difficult to control immigration and enforcing the law is often arbitrary and repressive. At the same time money has been made available to encourage return migration and resettlement in the country of origin. This is one of the main planks of current government policy and was made law in July 1984.

The major recent initiatives were made soon after the Secretary of State in charge of migrant workers was appointed in June 1981. He wished to offer a six-month period of amnesty, until 31 December 1981, to illegals who could prove they had regular employment and were resident in France before 1 January 1981. Thus liberal initiatives were combined with regulations tightening border controls and penalising employers of illegal workers.

This offer of amnesty was a considerable success. Almost 150,000 immigrants applied for legalisation, and 140,000 of these were granted.

This was not the first such amnesty but was by far the most successful. The Ministry of Labour used this opportunity to survey the undocumented workforce and obtained information on 130,000 of those who were legalised. This information was supplemented by further surveys in the textile industry, catering and domestic service (Cealis, Marie and Jansolin, 1983). Seasonal workers, itinerant pedlars and Algerians (who are covered by a special agreement between France and its former colony) were treated and counted separately under the provisions of the amnesty.

The survey discovered that the participants were very young (80 percent under 32 years), predominantly unmarried (62.1 percent) and had only recently migrated to France (40 percent after 31 December 1979). They had entered France as tourists (68.4 percent) and had subsequently overstayed the three-month period allowed. Almost 60 percent were from countries which were recent sources of immigrants, such as Morocco, Tunisia, black Africa and Turkey. Only 20 percent were from traditional European sending countries and the remainder were from Third World countries which had not previously sent significant numbers to France, such as India, Pakistan, Sri Lanka and Haiti. The main distribution by nationality was as shown in Table 2.1.

Table 2.1 *Number and distribution by nationality of permanent foreign workers legalised during the 1981–2 exceptional regularisation*

	Numbers	%
Tunisians	21,405	17.3
Moroccans	20,677	16.7
Black Africans (Sub-Sahara)	18,399	14.9
Portuguese	15,711	12.7
Algerians	14,567	11.8
Turks	10,721	8.7
Mauritanians	2,811	2.3
Yugoslavs	2,736	2.2
Pakistanis	2,654	2.1
Spaniards	1,230	1.0
Other nationalities	12,668	10.3
Total permanent workers	123,579	100.0

Source: Claude Marie et al., Immigration clandestine. La Régularisation des Travailleurs 'sans papiers' (1981–2), supplément no. 106 (1083) of the *Bulletin Mensuel des Statistiques du Travail*, p.17

The survey revealed little short-term movement by these legalised workers away from their current employment. However, after legalisation, their position is greatly improved because they are entitled to the full range of social and economic welfare programmes available for workers in France. These include: pensions, sick leave, holidays with pay, medical insurance, family allowances and access to low-cost housing.

The main groups of workers who constitute illegals in France include those who failed to apply or applied and failed to be regularised, illegal immigrants who have arrived since 1 January 1981 and those people who have applied for refugee status and have been refused.

Great Britain

While immigration to Britain has been a major political issue in the post-war period, illegal immigration has only been of sporadic concern. This is because it has formed a relatively unimportant part of migration to Britain. The major sources of immigration to Britain – namely, Ireland and the Commonwealth – have not been subject to control until immigrants from the Commonwealth had to apply for employment vouchers under the 1962 Commonwealth Immigrants Act. This Act gave immigration officials the power to question Commonwealth citizens and refuse them admission. People refused admission could be removed. However, such action had to take place within 24 hours of arrival and, if a Commonwealth immigrant without an employment voucher, which was required under the 1962 Act, avoided contact with officials for 24 hours, he was safe and guilty of no offence. This loophole in the legislation resulted in significant evasion of the controls which was reported in the 1965 government white paper *Immigration from the Commonwealth*.

In 1968 the second Commonwealth Immigrants Act was passed. This placed a duty on all Commonwealth citizens (like aliens) to pass through immigration control. If they did not and were caught within 28 days they could be refused admission and be removed by executive order. They could be prosecuted but only within a period of six months of entry. In 1969 the Immigration Appeals Act and the Aliens (Appeals) Order 1970 gave alleged illegal entrants the right to appeal. However, the deportation powers were extended to overstayers and other people who broke the conditions of their leave to enter the UK. They could be deported without being prosecuted.

The Immigration Act (1971) further tightened the regulations regarding immigration controls and ended the distinction between Commonwealth citizens and aliens. The five-year immunity against deportation orders was restricted to Commonwealth citizens ordinarily resident in the UK on or before 1 January 1973. New arrivals could only gain immunity by becoming UK citizens.

In April 1974 the new Labour government granted an amnesty to Commonwealth immigrants adversely affected by the 1971 Immigration Act (*Hansard*, 11 April 1974). The number of people who came forward to take advantage of the amnesty was relatively small, which suggests that fears about large-scale evasion of the immigration controls were misplaced. The amnesty was extended in November 1977 to cover a wider range of illegal entrant and a closing date of 31 December 1978 was announced (*Hansard*, 29 November 1977). However, the numbers presenting themselves for regularisation of their status remained small as is shown in Table 2.2.

Table 2.2   *Applications for regularisation of entry to UK, 1974–9*

Year	Applications	Processed	Granted	Found ineligible
1974	1,380	587	407	180
1975	475	972	810	162
1976	302	459	334	125
1977	189	246	128	118
1978	50	86	73	13
1979	36	80	57	23
Total	2,432	2,430	1,809	621

Source: Hansard (House of Commons Official Report), cols 125–8, 29 Nov. 1977

The Home Office has always regarded overstaying and taking unauthorised employment as the main areas of concern. Employers are not liable to prosecution for employing illegal workers, but they have a duty to ensure that their workers pay National Insurance contributions and income tax and have the correct documents. Enforcement of these regulations is more difficult in industries with seasonal workers and a high turnover of staff. The main areas of employment of illegal workers are thus in hotels and restaurants, the textile industry, construction and domestic employment.

Illegal immigrants and overstayers, if they are Commonwealth citizens, are in an anomalous position in that they enjoy political rights, but, if discovered to be illegal entrants, can be deported. Illegal aliens – for example, Poles or Filipinos – have no political rights.

Since 1979 successive Conservative governments have imposed stricter controls on immigration and enforced these rules more strenuously. The courts have also expanded the concept of an illegal entrant from a person landing on a beach at night to gain entry under cover of darkness to a person who tells lies to an immigration officer, and even to overstayers like Safdar Hussain, who had established immunity from deportation through residence, went abroad for a holiday, and was then faced by deportation as an illegal entrant. The courts have been ready to extend the powers of the executive to include individuals who obtained entry by fraud as illegal entrants, powers which the Home Office ministers at the time did not think they had. The burden of proof is on the illegal entrant, who is extremely vulnerable as he can be deported without the higher level of proof which is needed in a court prosecution. In a recent case (*Zamir*) the House of Lords argued that 'an immigrant owes a positive duty of candour as to all material facts which denote a change of circumstance since the issue of an entry clearance. Zamir should have disclosed any change in circumstances which he knew or *ought to have known* was material.'[2] This case received considerable criticism from immigrant advisory organisations and lawyers who argued that it was not fair or humane to expect an immigrant, whose command of English might be fragmentary or non-existent, who had wound up his affairs in his home country, who has planned a new life in the UK and who has paid his fare, to tell an immigration officer every conceivable fact which might lead to refusal of entry. The courts have subsequently reversed some of the harsh judgments made in the *Zamir* case.

An indication of the trend towards a more restrictive policy can be obtained from Table 2.3.

Table 2.3   *Illegal entrants detected and removed, 1976–83*

	Commonwealth citizens		Aliens		Total	
	detected	removed	detected	removed	detected	removed
1976	210	140	180	130	390	270
1977	510	310	300	180	810	490
1978	440	260	500	250	940	510
1979	390	260	600	330	990	590
1980	580	320	1040	590	1620	910
1981	430	280	560	360	990	640
1982	610	280	650	330	1260	610
1983	426	492	404	323	830	815

Source: Control of Immigration Statistics; *Home Office Statistical Bulletin*

The Netherlands

Dutch policy towards illegal immigration has been influenced by four major factors: (1) the hostility of public opinion to illegal immigration; (2) the need to act responsibly and humanely towards people working in the country despite their illegal status; (3) the need to penalise employers; and (4) the need to maintain law and order.

In 1974 the government decided to end the uncontrolled immigration of migrant workers. As its proposals to promote voluntary return were rejected, restrictive immigration controls were introduced. However, for economic and humanitarian reasons it was decided not to expel illegal migrant workers. As an observer noted, 'In parliament the opinion prevailed that the government had a moral obligation to act sympathetically to these people.' In order to avoid raising hopes of an amnesty and encouraging further immigration from neighbouring countries, secret discussions were held between the government and parliament which led to an amnesty the following year.

On 30 May 1975 the government announced a legalisation programme for illegal migrant workers, providing they could comply with certain conditions. The most important condition was proof that they had entered the country before 1 November 1974. In addition, the migrants needed to have a valid passport, to pass a tuberculosis test, and to have been of the required age at the time of their entry – namely, 18–35 years for unskilled workers and 18–45 for skilled.

The government estimated that between 10,000 and 20,000 people would qualify for amnesty. In fact 18,000 illegal migrants applied, of whom 15,000 were granted legal residence. The process involved illegal migrants reporting to their local aliens police offices where the first decision was taken regarding their application. If it was rejected they could appeal to the Ministry of Justice to review their case (1,400 did so) and finally they could appeal to the courts (1,050 cases).

This amnesty and its administration was subject to considerable criticism (Groenendael, 1983). The procedures adopted varied, for example, between a stricter, legalistic approach in the large cities to more informal procedures in the smaller municipalities. Differences in execution were noted between Amsterdam, Rotterdam and Nijmegen. Different interpretations of the rules appeared to exist between the various aliens police offices.

Action groups assisting illegal migrant workers campaigned for a general amnesty instead of the conditional regularisation. Many demonstrations and actions were held to support this demand; for example, 182 Moroccans occupied a church and went on hunger strike to support their claim that they had been resident before 1 November 1974 in spite of being unable to provide adequate proof.

Since this major amnesty there has been no procedure to regularise illegal workers except a modest procedure adopted in 1980 after the new immigration law came into force. Some 850 illegals were regularised. The major instruments the government uses to control illegal immigration are internal controls such as checking identification papers and tightening border controls by the introduction of compulsory visas for a wider range of sending countries, such as Turkey, Morocco, Tunisia and Senegal. There is also a move to reduce the rights of illegals to social security benefits. Under the Economic Offence Act, Dutch employers commit an offence if they employ an illegal foreign worker. However, the law is only weakly enforced and the penalties are small.

The major groups of illegal workers in the Netherlands are thought to be the wives and children of foreign workers (both legal and illegal), return migrant workers entering illegally, overstaying tourists, Surinamese citizens, gypsies and Turkish Christians.

Germany
Illegal immigration has become a political issue in Germany since strict immigration controls were imposed in 1971. Both political and public opinion is strongly opposed to further foreign immigration and there is no prospect of an amnesty for illegal immigrants. The official view is that an amnesty would merely encourage further illegal immigration. 'We don't want to open the door to a new integration of foreigners,' said the German officials at the OECD Conference in 1986 (Walraff, 1986). In 1976 a central office for combating illegal labour traffic was created. Also federal and regional authorities co-operate in administering border controls. Foreigners who enter illegally can be returned to their previous country of residence. Employers can be prosecuted for employing illegal workers.

In 1985 the Federal Institute of Employment found more than 191,000 cases of illegal employment of foreign workers compared with 160,000 in 1984. In 1985 there were 106,000 prosecutions compared with 83,000 in 1984.

The free circulation of labour in the European Community (EC) that is now open to Greeks and will be open to the Spanish and Portuguese in 1993 will result in even stricter restrictions on non-EC citizens.

Sweden
Government policy on immigration, in Sweden, is greatly influenced by the trade unions. Both government and the unions are strongly opposed to illegal immigration, which has never been condoned. Nevertheless, some exists, especially in domestic service and restaurant work.

Public opinion in Sweden is also strongly opposed to illegal immigration but is more aware of the aura of control than its actual exercise. There is thus scope for the government to take a tough stand in public but to be more generous in practice.

In 1976, two decisions were taken by the Swedish government about Christian Turks who had come from eastern Turkey and claimed that they were threatened by Turks and by non-Christian neighbours of other nationalities. They requested asylum, but were refused as they were not persecuted by the Turkish state, only lacked the protection of that state. The number of people in this group, known as 'Assyrians', grew, and the government decided, in these two decisions, that those who had arrived illegally in Sweden before certain dates should be granted residence permits, as people in a refugee-like situation. At the same time, it was decided that similar cases in future would not be accepted and the individuals involved would be deported.

Switzerland

The Swiss government attempts to control immigration through strict border controls, but their effectiveness is limited by geographical factors, the importance of tourism and the large numbers of legal foreign immigrants. The local cantonal police investigate illegal employment in companies, as employers are responsible for paying social taxes on their foreign workers. Penalties for non-payment of social taxes or for accommodating illegal workers can be six months' imprisonment. However, the penalties for employing illegal workers are low, usually a small fine. Periodically illegal immigration becomes an issue in Switzerland and demands are made for stricter enforcement of the law and heavier penalties. These were proposed in both 1983 and 1986, and in September 1986 the Federal Council approved the proposal to increase penalties against employers using illegal workers. This was confirmed by a referendum in April 1987, and now employers face heavier financial penalties and the possibility of imprisonment. However, there is little knowledge of the extent of illegal immigration though some speculation at the local level – for example, by the local press. In December 1987 it was suggested that there were 10,000 illegal immigrants in Geneva (*Tribune de Genève*, 26 November 1987).

Government policy is much tougher in theory than in practice. This is in contrast to Swiss policy on political refugees, which is liberal in theory but restrictive in practice. However, the Swiss government has never been so liberal as to allow an amnesty for illegal immigrants. An amnesty was proposed in 1983 by left-wing groups but without success.

Political Asylum

The position of asylum-seekers and illegal immigrants is often confused, even though political refugees have a right of entry to West European countries if their claims of persecution are upheld. The confusion is partly due to the fact that illegal immigrants, when discovered, may claim the status of political refugees. This is because the countries from which they migrate tend not only to be poor but also to be governed by repressive regimes. Widespread violence and insurrection in many Third World countries means that migrants are often leaving to gain more personal security as well as searching for employment. It is thus often difficult to distinguish between migrant workers and political refugees. In Germany there has recently been a dramatic rise in asylum applications, from 19,737 in 1983 to 73,832 in 1985. In Switzerland there were 7,435 applications in 1984 and 9,703 in 1985. In Belgium there was also a rise from 3,693 in 1984 to 5,357 in 1985. In Sweden, which has a reputation for welcoming political refugees, applications have risen sharply, from 3,000 in 1983 to 14,000 in 1985. Swedish officials are thus considering and implementing measures to process applications more speedily and also to reduce the pressure from asylum-seekers.

Generally, within Western Europe governments have linked their policy on political refugees to their general immigration policy. In some cases the rise in applications for asylum has been interpreted as a strategy by migrant workers to bypass the tough immigration controls introduced in the 1970s. Regulations on the right to political asylum have thus been more strictly interpreted both as applications rise and as states act to protect their labour markets and appease anti-immigrant feelings among their electorates.

Access to Rights

It may seem strange to discuss the rights of illegal immigrants and unauthorised workers, because they have no right to be present in the country or at least should not be working. Moreover, they have committed criminal offences by avoiding immigration controls and/or by taking up work without permission. However, states often have an ambiguous and even contradictory attitude towards illegal workers. On the one hand, illegals are a positive resource taking unpleasant, low-paid work that native workers refuse to do. They work hard, often taking two or three jobs to make ends meet, they avoid contact with the police and government officials because, if discovered, they might be liable to instant removal or deportation after appeal. They are thus generally law-abiding and independent, not daring to ask for benefits to which they might be entitled and may well have contributed through taxation. They assume they are not entitled to unemployment, housing, health and welfare benefits, though usually they do send their children to school.

In some states like Britain, while it is a criminal offence to be an illegal worker, it is not an offence to employ illegal workers. However, even in states where it is illegal to employ unauthorised workers, the sanctions against employers are very weakly enforced. In some sectors of West European economies competition is so fierce, wages are so low and working conditions are so bad that it is hard to envisage employers surviving without the cheap and flexible labour that illegal workers offer (Moulier-Boutang, Garson and Silberman, 1986). Such sectors are hotel and restaurant work, contract cleaning, employment as domestic workers, and work in the garment trade, especially as a home worker. In Britain, privatisation, the weakening of minimum wage legislation, contract tendering of work in the public sector and similar initiatives have created more such jobs. In France, seasonal work in agriculture is often done by illegal workers.

Illegal entrants or illegal workers are vulnerable to exploitation by employers and landlords. They are forced to accept low pay, long hours, poor promotion, down-skilling and no holiday or sick pay. They are often charged high rents. They cannot complain because they can only keep their job with the connivance of their employer, and their accommodation with the assistance of their landlord. They are not protected by industrial legislation, trade unions or welfare state benefits. They are also vulnerable to people who know about their illegal status and who may inform on them to the authorities. If robbed or abused they dare not complain because of the justified fear that their immigration status will be checked by the police.

They may, as residents and taxpayers, be entitled to certain welfare benefits depending on the type of their illegality, but they are likely to fear that any contact with officials may result in the discovery of their status and the danger of expulsion. Illegal workers thus usually see themselves as outside the ambit of the welfare state and on the margins of society. They have to provide for themselves as best they can, although they may be able to get help from compatriots, immigrant associations, churches or mosques and sympathetic unions and politicians. A major exception to their lack of rights is access to education for their children. Education is compulsory for all children in West European countries, including non-nationals, and immigration status is not investigated.

Illegal immigrants, if discovered, are entitled to a fair hearing and to an appeal procedure where good conduct and length of work and residence may be taken into account on their behalf but not automatically. In Britain, it would be unusual to deport somebody who had been resident in the country for ten years though this is not automatic. In December 1986 Viraj Mendis, a Communist and a Sinhalese, sought sanctuary in the Church of the Ascension, Hulme, in Manchester, when he was threatened with deportation as an illegal immigrant. He claimed political asylum on the grounds that, as a known supporter of Tamil demands, his life would be in danger if he was returned to Sri Lanka. His claim for political asylum and his appeals were rejected and he was deported in January 1989. This was despite the fact that he had resided in Britain for 15 years (Ardill and Cross, 1987). Illegal immigrants are not entitled to apply for citizenship either for themselves or for their children, although, before the 1981 British Nationality Act, birth in Britain gave an automatic entitlement to citizenship no matter what was the status of the parents.

In November 1976 the EC Commission produced its first draft of a directive aimed at achieving measures in the Community against unauthorised employment. In 1978 a second draft was produced, aimed at penalising employers and recruiting agencies which violated the law. These proposals were highly controversial and were strongly opposed by some governments, including Britain, which objected to community interference in British criminal law, to employer penalties and improved appeal rights for illegals (Ardill and Cross, 1987).

The Case for Regularisation

The general trend in Western Europe has been towards tighter controls on immigration, on greater unwillingness to allow family reunification and an increase in deportations of those alleged to be illegal entrants or workers, as the police come under pressure to enforce the immigration laws more vigorously. These policies have a number of unfortunate consequences. They result in a substantial increase in police resources being devoted to the surveillance and prosecution of foreign minorities. Members of immigrant and foreign communities legally settled may be subject to constant police checks and raids on their businesses. Innocent people may be detained or unable to get permission to bring in their families. People may be deported for technical or unintentional breaches of the complicated immigration laws. People who are industrious, law-abiding (notwithstanding their immigration status) and valuable members of the community, and who may have lived in their community for many years, live in fear of discovery and deportation. This may affect their wives and children too.

While public opinion in all European countries is generally hostile to illegal immigration and wishes the law to be enforced, considerable support has been mobilised in Britain, France, the Netherlands and Sweden for individuals or groups threatened with deportation. In May 1980 more than 100 British members of parliament signed a motion in the House of Commons appealing to the Home Secretary not to deport Verghese and Meena Varki. Similarly, there was a local campaign, based in their village of residence, which saved the De Peiera family from deportation. In August 1984 Manchester City Council advertised in the *Guardian* against the deportation of three people whose marriages to British citizens had broken down. In 1983–4 NALGO (the National Association of Local and Government Officers) led a major national campaign against the deportation of one of its members, a social worker, Mohammed Idrish. He came to Britain from Bangladesh in 1976 to study at university, where he met and married a British girl. Unfortunately, the marriage broke down before he obtained permanent residence. Mr Idrish worked as a social worker at Dr Barnado's Homes after completing his university course. His campaign to stay has been supported by trade unions, ethnic minority organisations, the Council of Churches, local authorities and members of parliament. In October 1985 the Immigration Appeal Tribunal ruled that Mohammed Idrish's value to the community outweighed any public interest in his deportation. He was therefore allowed to stay in Britain.

The campaign by the Migrants Action Group in support of 400 Filipino workers in 1982–3 was successful in getting decisions to remain for three-quarters of those threatened with deportation. Many of these migrants were innocent victims of mistakes or fraud by the agencies which recruited them for work in Britain.

Similar campaigns in support of illegal workers and political refugees have become common in most West European countries in the 1980s. In the Netherlands it has been argued that illegals have become a semi-permanent pressure group in their efforts to influence Dutch government policy. Religious and social organisations have been active in their support. In 1975 these organisations supported the claim of a group of Moroccan illegal workers who fled into churches to escape deportation after their requests for legalisation had been refused by the Dutch courts. This social pressure forced the government to grant them permanent residence. In France and Belgium there have been hunger strikes by illegal workers demanding the right to stay.

There is a contradiction in democratic societies which claim to uphold civil liberties and humanitarian values to hunt down and deport people who have worked, brought up their families, been law-abiding and maintained themselves independently of the state, in some cases for many years. European countries should consider the principle of regularisation for illegal workers and their families after a specific period of work and residence. This would recognise that they have contributed economically and culturally to society, that they have shown a positive commitment, despite hardship and exploitation, and that, in spite of the fact they have broken the immigration rules, they are not criminals deserving of the exemplary punishment that deportation often involves. The counter-argument that most governments accept is that an automatic amnesty or periodic amnesties would encourage a substantial rise in illegal immigration by migrants hoping to evade capture until they can apply for legalisation. As we have seen, immigration is very difficult to control and a regular policy of amnesty would make this even more difficult. Thus governments generally prefer to make the granting of amnesties entirely discretionary.

Notes

1   Cf. 'Immigrés: Partout on Verrouille', *Le Point*, no. 785, 5–11 Oct. 1987: 75–85.
2   Zamir had got married after gaining permission to enter the UK but before exercising this right.

References

Ardill, N. and N. Cross (1987) *Undocumented Lives: British Unauthorized Migrant Workers.* London: The Runnymede Trust.

Cealis, R., C. Marie and X. Jansolin (1983) 'Immigration clandestine, la régularisation des travailleurs sans papiers 1981–82', *Bulletin Mensuel des Statistiques du Travail,* Supplément no. 106.

Costa-Lascoux, J. and C. de Wenden, (1984) 'Immigration reform in France and the United States: Reflections and Documentation', *International Migration Review,* 17: 613–22.

Groenendael, T. van (1982) 'Illegal immigrants in the Netherlands – a survey', Utrecht: Nederlands Centrum Buitenlanders.

Groenendael, T. van (1983) 'Legalising illegal aliens', *Nieuwsbrief voor Nederlandstalige Rechtssociologen,-Antropologen en-Psychologen (NNR)* 2: 347–60.

Groenendael, T. van (1986) *'Dilemma's van Regelgeving. De Regularisatie van Illegale Buitenlandse Werknemers 1975–1983'.* Alphen aan den Rijn: Samsom H.D. Tjeenk Willink/Utrecht: Nederlands Centrum Buitenlanders

Hansard (1974) House of Commons Official Report, cols 637–8, 11 April.

Hansard (1977) House of Commons Official Report, cols 125–8, 29 Nov.

Home Office (1965) *Immigration From the Commonwealth,* Cmnd 2739. London: HMSO.

Moulier-Boutang, Y., J.P. Garson and R. Silberman (1986) *Economie Politique des Migrations clandestines de main d'oeuvre: Comparaisons internationales et exemple français.* Paris: p.276.

OECD (1986) 'The Future of Migration', Conference of National Representatives, 13–15 May.

Tribune de Genève (1987) '10,000 travailleurs au noir à Genève', 26 Nov.

Walraff, G. (1986) *Tête de Turc.* Paris: La Découverte, p. 309.

3

Industrial Rights

Jan Vranken

This chapter is concerned with the industrial rights of migrants, which means that it is not about all migrants but about migrant workers. The distinction is crucial. Whereas migrants who are not workers have virtually no means to act upon the power structures of the countries they are living in – except where they have been given political rights – migrant workers have always had the opportunity to influence their job, environment and working conditions, even before any industrial rights were assigned to them. They could, for example, join in strikes, and thus contribute to their success, or disregard calls for strike action and assist their failure. Once they become members of trade unions, they can participate in their activities and are eligible to stand for work councils and shop stewardship positions – that is, they have obtained industrial rights – and their economic and social role becomes more significant. In some countries, industrial rights have constituted a first step towards political participation, but they do not derive their significance from this 'stepping-stone' position alone. Industrial rights are important in themselves, as they are for native workers who already enjoy full political rights.

However, the identification of immigration with one of its specific forms, the immigration of labour, remains pertinent. In Germany, Belgium and Switzerland most post-war immigration consisted of unskilled or low-skilled workers from Mediterranean countries, and in the other four countries such immigrant workers accounted for a high enough proportion of immigrants, at least for a certain period, to attract the attention of the general public and policy-makers alike. Their concentration in specific geographical areas – mainly in or near industrial centres – increased awareness of their presence and contributed to its being seen as a problem.

It is because of this identification of 'migrants' with 'migrant workers' that trade unions have been concerned with all migrants and their problems. They were often the first 'welfare agency' for migrants and their first 'political' organisation, defending their basic social and economic rights. Even now that immigration has virtually stopped and the structure of the migrant population is gradually changing, trade unions are still seen by large groups of migrants as the main defenders of their interests. The unions themselves are still assuming this responsibility, but increasingly in conjunction with other organisations. For example, churches and other voluntary associations have gradually taken over much of the trade unions' role regarding immigration problems and migrants, particularly those concerned with the improvement of migrants' living conditions and with the introduction and defence of legal and political rights either for all migrants or for specific groups such as political refugees and illegal immigrants. This development has been aptly described by Schmitter Heisler (Heisler and Schmitter Heisler, 1986: 82):

> When migrant workers first arrived, little contact between them and the host society's institutions was expected except that entailed by the employment situation itself. In retrospect, such expectations seem to have ignored the near impossibility, in advanced industrial welfare states, of maintaining strict separation between employment and such social institutions. From the onset, immigrants had some contact with union representatives, health officials, and social workers. With increased length of residence and family migration, the institutional contacts expanded to include non-work-related institutions such as churches, local housing authorities, and school systems.

The Context

The role of trade unions with respect to migrants has not been the same in all the seven countries being compared in this book. The differences are produced by two factors: the *type of immigration* and the *position of the trade unions* in that particular society. The combination of the two variables – type of immigration and position of the trade unions – can be summarised in the typology set out in Table 3.1. This provides both a synthesis of the discussion of the two variables and a set of guidelines for the points considered next.

Table 3.1   *Seven-country typology of trade-union position versus type of immigration*

Position of trade unions/Type of immigration	Predominantly foreign, 'migrant workers'	Predominantly migrants from quasi-colonial regions
Rather strong	Belgium Germany	Sweden UK
Rather weak	Switzerland	Netherlands France

The type of immigration is an important variable, since the organised import of unskilled labour is not a characteristic of

immigration common to all seven countries. Some had no urgent need
to set up immigration offices in Southern Europe and North Africa,
because they already had a labour reserve of their own – for example,
in their colonies or former colonies. The second factor – the position of
trade unions – varies according to structural and cyclical factors – for
example, the decision-making structure – and economic or political
developments such as economic crises or changes in government.

The nature of immigration
The nature of immigration is an important variable explaining the
introduction and level of industrial rights of migrant workers in the
seven countries covered in this study. To a large extent, this is related to
the presence or absence of a colonial past.

In the Netherlands, France and the UK, large-scale organised
importation of foreign labour was for a long time unnecessary because
of the immigration of migrant workers and political refugees from
their colonies. These immigrants differed from the foreign workers
recruited by other European countries in that they possessed a number
of political and other rights based upon the former colonial relationship. They also had a number of other advantages over the labour force
imported from other countries: their knowledge of the language and
the 'culture' of the host country, and the feeling that the former
colonial power had some duty to fulfil towards them – a feeling not
altogether absent from the conscience of political leaders and governments of the receiving countries.

In the case of Sweden, immigration has for a long time been mainly
from other Nordic countries which are culturally and geographically
very close and whose citizens were not subject to entrance restrictions.
We therefore place Sweden under the same heading as the colonial
powers, although the colonial relationship between Sweden and
Finland ended in the nineteenth century.

Belgium, although also an important colonial power until 1960,
never had large-scale immigration from its former colony: immigrants
from Zaire were and still are mostly students and political refugees. In
terms of migration type we thus classify Belgium with non-colonial
powers such as Switzerland and Germany.

However, not all immigration to the seven countries can be class-
ified as either the colonial or the labour-force type. Demographic
considerations have played an important role in France and Belgium,
and a large proportion of German immigrants were 'Heimatvertrie-
benen' and refugees from the German Democratic Republic. But since
neither demographic considerations nor the refugees from the East
were ever part of the public or political discourse on migrant workers
in the respective countries, they are not taken into account in the

typology set out in Table 3.1, which combines consideration of the nature of immigration with the other variable, the position of the trade unions.

But in spite of these differences, the majority of immigrants were, and usually still are, employed in two main types of occupation: as industrial workers (mainly in mining, building, mechanical and engineering jobs), and as marginal workers in jobs rejected by native people (such as personal services, hotels and catering). And for most migrant workers, their position in the labour market has developed from 'restricted' labour to 'free' labour – even though a large number had to acquire even 'restricted' status, having entered the country illegally. Sometimes they were repatriated upon discovery, sometimes they were allowed to stay – usually in cases of collective regularisation.

We now go on to examine the second variable influencing the role of trade unions regarding migrants – namely, the position and role of trade unions in the seven countries, their attitudes towards immigration and their actions on behalf of immigrant workers, the position of migrant workers in the trade unions, and the industrial rights which migrant workers have obtained largely through the trade unions' actions. Information on specific points is sometimes unavailable for one or more countries, and it is therefore difficult to make consistent comparisons and draw firm conclusions. Nevertheless, the available information should produce an overall picture.

The position of trade unions in society
The position and role of trade unions in a particular society are important variables in explaining the extent of migrant workers' industrial rights.

Recent studies have often described the position and role of the trade unions as 'corporate democracy'; that is, 'an institutionalised pattern of policy formation in which large interest organisations co-operate with each other and with public authorities not only in the articulation (or even "intermediation") of interests, but – in its developed forms – in the "authoritative allocation of values" and in the implementation of such policies' (Lehmbruch, 1977: 94). However, according to Miller (1981: 148), 'associational participation' is only one of the ways in which trade unions acquire importance as political actors. The others are:

1   through their close alliance with political parties, especially in cases of broad-based, socialist-oriented trade unions of which 'socialist parties are outgrowths, almost organic appendages';
2   through having become political actors in their own right, engaging themselves in a broad range of conflicts and issues from

nuclear weapons to environmental questions, and influencing the outcome by using important non-institutional means such as their press facilities, strikes and demonstrations;

3 by their 'politicising of the non-political', making it possible for foreign workers to influence their immediate working environment through trade-union affiliation.

In describing the position and role of trade unions in political decision-making, relevant indicators are their size (membership), relative importance (degree of unionisation), number (one confederation or a number of small local or craft unions), and relationship with political parties and national authorities. According to their score on each and all of these variables, trade unions will have a larger or smaller say in such diverse matters as the regulation of immigration, the distribution of work permits, the definition of industrial rights and the participation of migrant workers in decision-making.

In examining the position of migrant workers, it is of course not only the current situation of trade unions which is important; industrial rights for migrant workers had already been introduced by the 1950s, and in the main have been the basis for developments in the following decades. Moreover, the position of trade unions has undoubtedly weakened during the 1980s because of economic recession and government initiatives in a number of countries to curb their power.

The first element of variation between the seven countries is in the number of trade unions. In Germany, Sweden and the UK, there is one co-ordinating organisation for virtually all trade unions: the Deutsche Gewerkschafts Bund (DGB), Landesorganizationen, or National Federation of Workers/Tjänstemännens Centralorganisation (Central Organisation of Employees) (LO/TCO) and Trades Union Congress (TUC) respectively (see below). All three are thus the sole representatives of workers in industrial relations, and this strong position is enhanced by their special relationship with the major left-of-centre party – at least when this party is in power.

The Swedish situation is most unequivocal. Trade unions are the strongest of all the interest groups in a society whose decision-making structure is very much based on the existence of interest groups. In particular the LO, which organises 2 million manual workers – a 90 percent membership – is politically very influential, largely because of its close relationship with the Social Democratic Party, which has been in power virtually without interruption since the early 1930s. The TCO organises some 70 percent of all lower-grade office workers and civil servants.

In the UK, there were 371 unions in 1984, the largest of which were affiliated to the TUC. Total union membership is 10.7 million, and

TUC membership represents 9.5 million workers, or 88 percent of all trade unionists. Unionisation is just under 45 percent. To a large extent, unions are still craft unions, although some have developed into multi-industrial unions with a membership of about a million – for example, the Transport and General Workers Union (1.4 million) and the Amalgamated Engineering Union (975,000). The main industrial unions are officially affiliated to the Labour Party, and even constitute its main source of income. Both Conservative and Labour governments consult with the trade unions. However, their political influence declined dramatically after 1979, when the first Thatcher government was elected, and more recent government legislation has imposed a number of restrictions on trade-union activities. Nevertheless, they are still represented on a number of national bodies.

German unions are the largest in Europe, and are very well organised. Sixteen industrial unions, of which the Metalworkers' Union is the largest, are grouped under the DGB which has some 7 million members. Some other small unions outside the DGB have about 200,000 members, making the overall unionisation level about 34 percent of the employed population. Social Democrats and Christian Democrats co-operate as individuals inside the trade unions, which as organisations, however, are very close to the SPD. Their influence declined somewhat after the 1983 elections, when a Christian Democrat–Liberal coalition came to power, but they still play an important role in German society.

In the other countries covered by the project, a number of trade-union federations compete to organise employees, with variable degrees of success. They are divided on political and religious grounds, as is the whole society. Most typical examples are the Netherlands, Belgium and, to a certain extent, Switzerland. This means that there is no exclusive link between the unions and the left in these countries, since Christian Democrats (and even the conservative Liberal Party in Belgium) also have 'their' union.

In the Netherlands, trade unions have for a long time reflected the division of political parties into three 'pillars': Socialist, Protestant and Catholic. However, since 1976, when the Catholic NKV and the Socialist NVV merged into the FNV (the Federation of Dutch Trade Unions), the FNV has dominated the scene, with 60 percent of total union membership. It is still strongly linked with the Social Democratic Party, just as the other federation, the CNV (Christian National Union), is linked with the Christian Democratic Party. There is a third union federation, the (Raad van Overleg van) Middelbaar en Hoger Personeel, which organises mainly senior officials. It represents 7 percent of union members. Total membership in 1986 represented 29 percent of the employed population – a sharp decline since the 1970s and early 1980s, when it was around 40 percent. All unions are consulted by the political decision-makers on social matters.

The Belgian situation is very much like the Dutch, although *pillarisation* is perhaps even more significant as an organising force, especially in Flanders. Three unions – two larger ones, Socialist and Christian-Democrat, and one smaller one, Liberal – have a total membership of about 2.5 million, representing a very high unionisation level of 70 percent of the employed population. For manual workers it is even higher, at 90 percent. The Belgian labour movement is an alliance between cooperatives, trade union and political party, there are substantial numbers of trade-union members in the Belgian parliament, and many trade-union leaders have had governmental responsibilities. These personal bonds, together with the highly developed collective bargaining system, explain the huge influence of trade unions on Belgian politics in the period between 1945 and 1980, although the Conservative Martens governments have reduced union influence in the decision-making process.

The French trade-union movement is anything but a strong political force. It is split into three main union federations: the Confédération Générale du Travail (CGT), the Confédération Française Démocratique du Travail (CFDT) (before 1964 the CFTC) and the Force Ouvrière (FO). In addition there are several smaller unions, such as the Confédération Générale des Cadres (CGC) and the FEN (Fédération de l'Education Nationale) – the teachers' union – which perhaps is the best organised trade union in France. Unionisation is very low, at around 20 percent. The major trade-union federation, the CGT, has very close links with the Communist Party (PCF), which has never participated in government except for a short period between 1981 and 1984. The CFDT on the other hand 'probably comes closest to resembling a political party' (Miller, 1981: 153), although in electoral matters it generally supports the Parti Socialiste (PS), and it influences its programme. Thus the idea of 'autogestion' (self-management by the workers) has become an important idea in the political programme of the PS under the CFDT's influence. French trade unions can be fairly well described as 'permanent opposition organisations', mainly because of their weak structural position and perhaps also because of their ideological stance. Their successes often come as the result of dramatic events such as the Front Populaire in 1936 and the students' revolt in 1968.

In Switzerland there are three main federations of wage-earners' associations, but only two consider themselves as trade unions. Of these, the Schweizerischer Gewerkschaftsbund/Union Syndicale Suisse is by far the largest, representing over 70 percent of organised workers. Politically it is close to the Social Democratic Party, while the other 'trade-union' federation, the Christnationaler Gewerkschaftsbund/

Confédération des Syndicats Chrétiens is close to the Christian Democratic party. For fifty years both have followed a policy of 'peaceful' industrial relations based on collective agreements, and both have refrained from the use of strikes as a means of industrial action. Together they represent 20.6 percent of the employed population, but the total membership of all wage-earners' associations is only 31.8 percent. The federations are active as pressure groups in the political arena, where they occupy an important position, together with employers' and farmers' associations, and they can propose legislation; but collective bargaining, and especially wage policy, are matters for the affiliated trade unions. Trade-union membership has varied during recent decades, and these variations are partly related to the degree of unionisation of foreign workers.

A summary of the comparative strength and of the trade unions of the seven countries is set out in Table 3.2.

Table 3.2   *Seven-country comparison of trade-union strength*

Country	Number of main union federations	Relative size of 2 largest federations	Unionisation (% of employed)	Political influence
Sweden	1	95:–	90/70	Very strong
Germany	1	95:–	34	Strong
UK	1	87:–	45	Medium
Netherlands	2	60:40	29	Medium
Switzerland	2	70:15	20	Medium
Belgium	3	50:45	70	Strong
France	3	55:25	20	Weak

Trade Unions and Labour Migration

In this section we examine the position of migrant workers in a number of dimensions of the employment sector, including their participation in trade unions, their degree of involvement, organisation and militancy, their opportunities for influence, their participation in works councils, shop stewards committees and industrial councils, and the relations between unions and migrant workers.

Until 1973–4, all major European host countries, with the exceptions of Sweden and Switzerland, had liberal immigration policies in spite of the opposition of trade unions to unrestricted labour immigration. Indeed, they were not the only interested party. How far were the demands of each major economic interest group taken into account by national governments in designing and implementing these liberal immigration policies?

Clearly, employers have had greater influence than unions. They need foreign labour when it becomes difficult or even impossible to recruit national workers for less well-paid, unsocial jobs, while unions have always favoured a system of immigration control and regulation. Nevertheless, in all countries to a greater or lesser extent unions have agreed to the recruitment of foreign labour for some industries during certain periods.

Trade-union opposition to unrestricted labour immigration is explained by the disadvantageous effects on the position of the national labour force and on the specific group which each union represents. Immigrants have often been used by employers as a means to change the balance of power in their favour, weakening the position of the trade unions in collective bargaining and industrial conflicts with a surplus of cheap labour. Furthermore, migrant workers often lack trade-union experience because they come from countries with a low level of industrialisation and no trade-union tradition. They are less inclined to join a union upon their entry and, even if they eventually do so, they are less inclined to become involved in its activities, especially if they have foreign citizenship.

Trade unions' opposition to immigration has not been very successful, for a number of reasons. First, rising living standards, better schooling and subsequent higher expectations among national workers made them increasingly reluctant to take low-paid, dirty, heavy, low-status jobs in mining, cleaning and catering. Employers urgently needed cheap labour for these jobs, which were not subject to automation, in order to cope with international competition, so they pressed very hard for liberal immigration policies so that they could recruit workers. Bilateral agreements guaranteeing equality of treatment and pay for foreign workers eventually reduced trade-union opposition; they also reflected the prevailing assumption that the importation of foreign labour would be temporary.

Once large numbers of foreign workers had entered the country, the unions were obliged to abandon their reservations in order to integrate the migrant workers into their organisations. The strong relationship between the degree of unionisation and the union's bargaining power has often been demonstrated, both in action and in empirical research, and solidarity between national and foreign workers in the labour market is in the union's interests, as it is in the interests of both national and foreign workers. Recent figures on migrant workers' union membership suggest that the policy of integrating them into the unions has been relatively successful, except in the Netherlands.

However, although this sequence of 'opposition – acceptance – integration' can be found in all seven national situations, there are still significant differences between the project countries. The attitude of the trade unions has not been the same, either throughout the post-war period, or in all countries.

Between 1948 and 1957, the two main French union federations – the CGT and the CFTC (now the CFDT) – paid particular attention to the Algerian workforce, which was very badly treated by the police. There was undoubtedly some political motive behind this attention; indeed, immediately after the Evian Agreement, which granted independence to Algeria in 1962, both federations began to reconsider their position on migration. A number of common demands were formulated and common actions were undertaken, a process which culminated in the Declaration of June 1974. In this document both federations stated that the employers and right-wing parties exploit the problem of immigration to divide the working class; they also proclaimed their intention to continue their action for equal rights for both French and foreign workers, and for an improvement in the working and living conditions of migrant workers. This programme of demands clearly rested upon a perception of the migrant workers' presence as temporary – an approach which changed profoundly in the early 1970s, when migrant workers started playing an important role in a number of industrial conflicts. In fact, the CGT now regards migrant workers as one of the most 'combative' elements of the working class in France, whereas before they were seen more as a threat to the working class (Miller, 1981: 150; Castles and Kosack, 1973: 134). In spite of ideological differences, all trade unions are in favour of programmes to promote family reunification, job and residency security, and equality of social and economic rights, although it was mainly the CFDT who between 1978 and 1983 engaged in conflicts concerning housing or illegal immigrants. However, they differ most consistently on the subject of political rights: the CGT does not support the demand for local election voting rights for immigrants, whereas the CFDT does favour equal political rights, including the right to vote in elections.

At the beginning of the post-war wave of immigration, Swiss unions considered the presence of migrant workers as temporary, tied to a phase of economic reconstruction and boom. But gradually, as the additional labour supply had a negative impact on the growth of wages, they began to criticise the government's and the employers' liberal immigration policy and, from the mid-fifties until the seventies, the SGB took the lead in the campaign against immigration. The warnings it issued on the danger of further entries of foreign workers were so ill-worded that it gained notoriety as a chauvinistic trade-union federation. It called for the strengthening of the restrictive measures introduced by government from 1963 onwards, with the aim of reducing the numbers of foreign workers to a maximum of 500,000 by 1972. It warned against 'Ueberfremdung', arguing that a further increase in the number of foreigners would upset the traditional balance between the various religious and language groups and would have adverse consequences upon Swiss institutions such as the 'social pact'. It is therefore not surprising that, in its campaign to reduce the number of foreigners, the SGB came very close to right-wing groups such as the Zurich Democrat Party and the 'Nationale Aktion gegen die Ueberfremdung von Volk und Heimat', led by James Schwarzenbach. The SGB has expressed its opposition to these groups but, according to Castles and Kosack (1973: 146-8), it does not disagree in principle with their aims, a point of view contested by Miller (1981: 161). After 1970 (the defeat of the anti-foreigners initiative), governmental immigration policy was based on the two principles of stopping immigration and promoting integration. Both union federations approved this policy and continued their activities in favour of real equality for migrant workers already in Switzerland. The affiliated unions in the building industry have repeatedly spoken out in favour of abolishing the seasonal worker status. CNG and most SGB-affiliated unions (with the noticeable exception of its metal workers' union) supported the 'Solidarity Initiative' (Mitenand Initiative/Initiative Etre Solidaires'), pleading a unique and equitable status for migrants together with a strict quantitative limitation; however, this initiative was heavily defeated in a referendum in 1981. Through the influence of mainly building workers and civil servants' unions, this line of equal economic and social rights for migrant workers has overcome the former protectionist line. A greater openness can also be seen in relation to the sensitive question of asylum-seekers, although in the political debate these are becoming the new scapegoats in place of migrant workers.

In Germany, even before immigration from Turkey started, German unions had a decisive influence on migration matters. Thanks to their action, the first migrant workers – Italian farm workers in 1954 – already received equal pay and social security rights. Furthermore, a number of government initiatives were taken to guarantee acceptable living conditions for migrant workers. Beyond this, little was done to promote integration of migrant workers into German society, since, as in other European countries, the prevailing view was that migration was a temporary phenomenon. But in the early 1960s this view slowly changed, leading to the eventual publication of *Deutsche Gewerkschaften und Fremdarbeiter* (German Trade Unions and Foreign Workers). In this document, the DGB stressed the need for social integration of migrant workers and their families, who were now accepted as a permanent component of the German economy. This integration was to be realised by opening up works councils and shop steward positions to all migrant workers, by integrating migrant children into the German school system, by providing more social services, and by ending all forms of discrimination against migrant workers. Some time later, under the pressure of migrant workers' strikes and the threat of a parallel organisation being formed to represent migrant workers, the DGB even incorporated into its official policy such demands as a revision of the foreigners law to provide better protection of migrants' freedoms and rights, to assist family reunification and to allow migrant worker representation on governmental advisory boards.

This position has since been modified, because of economic and public opinion developments, and since 1983 the DGB's migration policy has been based on three main ideas: social integration of long-resident foreigners, strict control of further immigration (especially with respect to family reunification) and the promotion of return. These three ideas were also the basic principles of the migration policy of the national government. This consensus on the federation level, however, covers up many internal differences between the industrial unions belonging to the DGB.

In Belgium, the response to the immigration of foreign workers depended mainly upon the economic situation and has never been the result of a debate. A very strict immigration policy was favoured in times of economic recession and high unemployment, and a liberal attitude was taken in times of full employment. The employers' and the government's labour market policy was accepted by the trade unions on condition that it did not interfere with the interest of Belgian workers. Since it did not do so, as long as the migrants were confined to the secondary labour market, work permits became the main instrument of labour policy during these periods. Once immigration had stopped, trade unions began to pay more attention to non-economic issues such as general living conditions of the migrants, discrimination and racism and, in the contemporary political context, they are the only large social organisations which consistently promote and defend the rights of the migrant population.

In Britain, the trade unions have traditionally been suspicious of, and hostile towards, high levels of immigration. After the Second World War, strict conditions were imposed on the employment of European volunteer workers before the unions would agree to their recruitment. In some industries such as mining, the employment of foreign labour proved to be impossible because of union opposition. However, the reaction of the trade unions to New Commonwealth immigration round the mid-fifties was surprisingly positive, at least at the national level. Union leaders felt an obligation towards immigrants who, they believed, had been forced to come to Britain as a result of colonial exploitation. But at the local level, many workers were concerned about the recruitment of black workers, partly from racial prejudice and partly from fear of job competition. Therefore in 1965 the trade unions which were affiliated to the Labour Party supported the very tough immigration controls introduced by the Labour government. The TUC and its member unions have opposed any form of discrimination against Commonwealth immigrant workers, but their policy has always been one of *laissez-faire*, based on the assumption that immigrants would sooner or later become integrated into the labour force and the trade unions. In the 1970s the national leadership became more aware of the problems of racism, especially within the unions, but despite their more positive stance there has been a move towards the creation of black caucuses within the unions.

Until the mid 1960s, the Dutch unions' attitude towards immigration has been characterised by *ad hoc* policies without any specific attention to migrant workers, and only recently have they taken an interest in the consequences of large-scale immigration. In 1971 they formulated two major principles for an immigration policy: immigration policy should be restrictive (and return promoted), and migrants should have the same rights and duties as Dutch employees. The contemporary period begins in 1979, when the idea was introduced that the Netherlands had become a multi-ethnic society and that any policy towards ethnic minorities should be based upon the principles of emancipation, reduction of social and economic disadvantages, and the prevention of discrimination.

After the Second World War, the Swedish trade unions did not interfere to stop the corporate decision to allow the immigration of non-Nordic workers (Nordic workers were not subject to entrance restrictions). However, with the huge spontaneous immigration which occurred after 1964, the unions felt they had lost control and asked for stricter regulation of non-Nordic immigration. The government adopted the trade-union view and in 1967 ruled that employment, work permits and housing had to be arranged before entrance into the country. Integration of migrant workers in Swedish society became a part of trade-union policy in 1970, but it was another decade before the social and cultural needs of immigrant workers were fully recognised by the LO (Knocke, 1986).

The main conclusion to be drawn from this review of the seven national situations is that the unions' attitude towards migration and migrant workers varied according to the state of the economy – that is, according to the state of the labour market. There is a striking parallel between immigration policies and the business cycle (Martens, 1973), and this has led to remarkable similarities between most countries included in this study in terms of the development of union attitudes at different periods.

Participation in Trade Unions

Union membership

Most barriers to migrant worker unionisation are the same in the seven
countries: they include their legal status, language and cultural
differences, their relatively lower standard of schooling, their
occupational position and immobility, their lack of familiarity with
unions, tensions between migrant and indigenous workers, and
restrictions on trade-union participation. The importance of these
barriers varies from country to country.

Although union activities are not usually seen as political activities
which might lead to expulsion – for example, when 'public order and
security are threatened' – many migrant workers fear that involvement
in union activities might cause problems with the national authorities.
When they join a union, it is often because union membership is
'compulsory' or because the union is seen as a welfare agency or as a
means to promote individual professional interests. This attitude can
partly be explained by the dissimilarities between trade unions.
Migrants tend to transfer to their new country what they have learnt
about unions in their mother country.

Differences between foreign nationalities in terms of union membership can also be explained by their degree of integration into the host
country: knowledge of the local language, and access to information
about the legal, social and economic organisation progressively
increase the degree of integration, while the idea of returning to the
mother country ceases to be a guiding principle dominating life and
work. This factor helps to explain the higher unionisation rates among
'older' and 'culturally related' immigrant populations.

Perhaps the biggest single factor accounting for the different
unionisation levels is that migrant workers are imported for employment in low-skilled and low-paid jobs which are concentrated in the
traditional industrial sectors and some service industries such as
cleaning and catering. In these sectors unionisation is often (but not
always) much lower than in those better-organised sectors where
sometimes even a 'closed shop' exists and where migrant workers are
often under-represented, as illustrated by the following review of some
national situations.

In Sweden, from the beginning of labour immigration, the trade
unions made agreements with some employers that they should
recommend foreign workers to join the union. Even where these
agreements were not concluded, there was a strong 'moral obligation'
to do so. Figures on trade union membership in Sweden show that in
1981, 90 percent of employed Southern European citizens (concentrated in manufacturing and mining) were unionised, compared with 79

percent of Swedish citizens born in Sweden. However, migrant workers' union membership is determined by their occupational sector, not by their position in the job hierarchy, nor by their socio-economic background. Membership in such sectors as contract cleaning and catering is low (40–50 percent), but this is irrespective of nationality. 'Part-time jobs, isolated jobs, unsocial work hours and marginality to the labour market is the reason for low union organisation for all persons working in these low hierarchy job sectors' (Knocke, 1986: 223).

In the UK, the unions' concept of non-discrimination meant that no figures on migrant membership used to be kept, and only recently has information on their unionisation become available. This reveals that Afro-Caribbean and Asian workers have higher rates of union membership than native white workers (56 percent compared with 47 percent in 1982), a difference accounted for largely by the fact that a far higher proportion of whites are in non-manual occupations, which are less likely to be unionised. This is especially true for women, among whom the proportion of part-time workers is very much higher for whites, which also contributes to lower unionisation. Because of the small, even local, scale of British trade unions, there are wide variations; much seems to depend on the local situation and on the personalities and attitudes of local officials. Opposition to black workers seems especially strong in craft unions, which can effectively bar migrant workers from certain jobs, because they frequently control access to employment in skilled trades.

In Germany, the degree of unionisation among migrant workers is on the whole comparable to that among native workers. In 1984, 35.8 percent (30.8 percent in 1980) of foreign employees were members of one of the DGB's trade unions, compared with 33.4 percent in 1980 for the total population employed, unionisation of workers being highest among Turks (49 percent), Greeks (46.6 percent) and Spaniards (43.7 percent), and lowest among Yugoslavs (although still 34.5 percent). Migrant workers are over-represented in some trade unions: textiles and clothing (15.4 percent), steel (13.0 percent), chemicals, paper and ceramics (11.2 percent) and leather (10.6 percent). They are under-represented in other areas, such as education and research (0.5 percent), and in trade, banking and insurance (0.9 percent). Union-isation among migrant workers is particularly high in the mining industry (over 98 percent) and high in the metal industry (around 60 percent). In a number of industries, (market gardening, farming and forestry, and the food, hotel and catering industry) few employed migrants are union members, but unionisation in these industries is low for German workers too, because of the small size of companies, the high rates of job mobility and the importance of temporary employment (Suhrkemper, 1983: 84).

The Swiss picture is similar. The proportion of foreign workers belonging to a trade union is 23.1 percent, which is somewhat higher than the overall rate. The situation has thus changed since Castles and Kosack (1973: 149) concluded that 'the Swiss unions do not appear to have been very successful in organising foreign workers'. The incorporation by the SGB of most of the demands put forward by foreign workers' organisations has led these organisations to urge their members to join the SGB, with a consequent noticeable increase in the numbers of foreign workers who join (Miller, 1981: 163). Migrant workers are concentrated in the traditionally better-organised industrial sectors, and so the main unions to which they belong are the Building Workers' Union, (where they form a large majority of about three-quarters) and the Metal Workers' Union (where they represent about a quarter of the total membership). Unions seem to have been more successful in organising foreign workers in the French-speaking and Italian-speaking parts of Switzerland than in the German-speaking part, a fact which is attributed to the different traditions in these regions. However, given the high proportion of foreign workers in the traditional industries which are better organised by the unions than other sectors, one would expect more foreigners to be union members. Trade unionists suggest a number of reasons to explain their unwillingness to join, such as the high contributions and the temporary nature of their stay, but Castles and Kosack (1973: 149–50) attach more importance to the feeling among foreign workers that the unions do not represent their interests, and to the bad relationship with Swiss workers.

In Belgium and France, the situation is quite the opposite, with the degree of unionisation among migrant workers lower than that of native workers. For Belgium there is an obvious explanation, in that the very high unionisation of native employees (70 percent for all employees, but 90 percent for manual workers) makes it unlikely that foreigners will achieve higher membership rates. But this explanation hardly applies in France, where only 20 percent of the native French workers are unionised, and the figure for migrant workers is even lower, at only 15 percent (although there have been considerable variations at various times). This is in spite of the internationalist tradition of French unions and 'their extensive networks of special structures designed to facilitate the articulation of foreign workers' problems' (Miller, 1981: 149). The reasons for the weakness of migrant unionisation in France are the concentration of foreign workers in industrial sectors where union organisation is very weak or even non-existent (such as construction), the importance of sub-contracting from the underground economy, and the overall weakness of unions. French trade unions are also less of a 'welfare agency' than the unions in the other six countries, and preoccupation with political issues probably has less appeal for migrant workers. Another factor inhibiting them from joining unions may be the encouragement of 'illegal' immigration in France.

In the Netherlands, no reliable national figures are available, because many unions refuse on principle to register their members' nationality or ethnic group. According to a recent survey in Rotterdam, 24 percent of Spaniards, 21 percent of the Moroccans, 18 percent of Turks and 14 percent of Italians are union members; the overall degree of unionisation of ethnic minorities is around 16 percent, which is significantly below the 29 percent of the wage-earning population as a whole.

Schmitter (1981: 317–34) has advanced the hypothesis that trade-union participation among immigrants is always lower than among native workers, but that there is a difference between countries where trade-union organisations are strong and where they are weak; in the former countries, the migrants' participation tends to be only slightly lower. The situation in the seven countries which are subject to our analysis does not confirm this statement. Indeed, unionisation is significantly higher among migrants than among natives in Sweden; in the UK, Switzerland and Germany, it is about the same for both population groups (with a slight tendency in favour of the migrant workers for the former two countries); and only in France, Belgium and the Netherlands is it significantly behind that of native workers.

The organisation of migrant workers within trade unions
In considering the organisational position of migrant workers within trade unions, two models can be contrasted. The first excludes any organisation of workers along national or ethnic lines because of ideological beliefs ('internationalism'), and because autonomous organisations would only stimulate the division of foreign and indigenous workers. The alternative model accepts the specificity of the immigrant workers' position, and allows and even stimulates the establishment of their own associations within the trade union. In most countries with several trade unions, Socialist and Communist trade unions follow the first policy, and Christian Democrat unions take the second stance; this is, for instance, the case in Belgium and France. In countries with one trade-union federation, the 'internationalist' model is more likely to inspire its organisational philosophy than the pluralist model.

In France, the CGT opposes any autonomous migrant worker organisation outside the regular factory and local union structure, although it has its language groups at the factory and departmental level, and a Commission Nationale de Travail Immigré at the national level. In the CFDT, on the other hand, local and departmental unions with large numbers of migrant workers can undertake autonomous action in favour of foreign workers. This autonomy, undoubtedly inspired by its Christian tradition, has increased the popularity of the CFDT with foreign workers because their trade-union membership thus gives them at the same time the organisational means and the legal protection to become involved in quasi-political action.

In Belgium too there is a clear difference between both major federations as regards the organisational position of migrant workers. Apart from a National Advisory Commission for Immigration, whose task is limited to information and research and some local initiatives, the Socialist trade-union federation ABVV/FGTB has no specific organisation for migrant workers, although initiatives in this direction have been announced. The Christian union federation, on the other hand, has a very elaborate structure for migrant workers, with even its own press.

The two major unions of the Swiss SGB – the Swiss Steel and Clockworkers' Union and the Construction Workers' Union – have always had foreign language groups to encourage migrant worker membership by promoting the articulation of specific migrant worker problems within the union. The Construction Workers' Union, whose membership is 75 percent foreign, has gone furthest in this respect, by changing union by-laws to allow the unrestricted election of migrant workers to leading positions.

The Swedish LO has established a special consultative structure. It has established a central immigrant council in its administration, and immigrant district committees in about half the 232 districts in which migrant workers make up the majority. The same attitude is taken by the German DGB, which established a special section for migrant workers on the level of its managing committee. Migrant shop stewards and foreign language groups have the opportunity to organise meetings parallel to regularly scheduled ones. The DGB also puts at the disposal of its members a number of counselling centres which serve as forums for the articulation of foreign workers' problems both towards the DGB and towards public authorities. The IG Bergbau und Energie and the IG Metall (IndustrieGewerkschaft, or industrial unions) have set up mixed working groups to discuss problems concerning co-operation at factory level, and to make recommendations to the unions' decision-making bodies.

In the UK, most unions have no special arrangements for immigrant or foreign workers, maintaining a colour-blind approach, and arguing that all their members are encouraged to be active and that no special attention ought to be paid to black members. The general position has recently changed with TUC initiatives in the areas of positive action, contract compliance, ethnic monitoring and equal opportunities policy, but these initiatives have so far had little impact. Some unions – for example, teachers, journalists, and cinema and TV technicians – have reserved or co-opted seats on advisory committees or working parties for black members. NALGO, a major white-collar union, has positive action policies including black members co-opted to its national executive committee. But the widespread trade-union view that the trade-union movement is concerned with a man or woman as a worker and that the colour of a man's skin has no relevance whatever to his work is not accepted by black workers, and gradually black caucuses have grown within unions and black workers' groups have been formed. This has put pressure on trade unions and the TUC to give a higher priority to the interests of black workers, and some white-collar unions with a significant black membership have responded to this pressure positively.

The degree of activity and involvement, militancy and
opportunities for influence
Although 'passive participation' can easily be measured on the basis of unionisation figures, it is much more difficult to evaluate the level of active participation, let alone to compare it between countries. Let us first take a closer look at the presence of migrant workers in union executive positions.

In the beginning, few non-Nordic migrants were elected as union representatives in Sweden and, although the number of immigrants has increased year by year among elected representatives, the odds are still two to one that Swedish citizens born in Sweden are more likely than Southern European citizens to become union delegates. This corresponds with union members' subjective evaluations; 20 percent of Swedish members consider themselves to be active members, but this figure drops to a low 8 percent for Southern European citizens.

In Germany too there are few migrant workers in leading positions in the trade unions. In 1979, 12.3 percent of the members of IG Metall were migrant workers, but only 7.4 percent of the Vertrauensleute (mediators) were foreigners. The situation in the IG Chemie Papier und Keramik was even worse: 13.4 percent of its members are migrant workers, whereas only 6.4 percent of the Vertrauensleute are of foreign nationality. In both unions, however, there has been a significant increase (from 2.3 percent in 1970 to 7.4 percent in 1979 in the Metall, and from 5.2 percent in 1975 to 6.4 percent in 1979 in the Chemie). This increase in the DGB's attention to the problems of migrant workers is often considered as a response to the threat of a largely migrant workers' union developing outside the established unions. Foreign Vertrauensleute are to be found mainly in large companies, in companies with a high quota of migrant workers, and in those with relatively few female employees. Union leaders explain the discrepancy by pointing to the lack of suitable candidates.

In the UK, rates of attendance at union meetings are similar for white and Asian men, but somewhat lower for West Indian men (40 percent against 36 percent). For West Indian women, the figure was higher than for white or Asian women (33 percent against 26 percent). More male white union members hold a union position than do Asians or West Indians (11 percent against 4 percent). Of white female union members, 6 percent hold a union position, as compared with 3 percent of Asians and West Indians (Brown, 1984).

In France, the Act of 11 July 1975 (Article 4) granted the right to become a member of the board to every foreign union member in the country, providing he has not been convicted of a criminal offence and has been working in France for at least five years at the date of his election. However, few non-EC citizens achieve this position, and nowhere does their number reach the maximum of the one-third that they have been allotted. As part of the campaign to increase migrant worker membership, the CGT considers the promotion of militant migrants into leading positions to be a priority.

Another aspect of active participation is involvement in industrial action such as strikes. During the wildcat strike period in Sweden, which started in the late 1970s and lasted until well into the 1980s, it was often rumoured that foreign workers were deeply involved in starting these conflicts. Although this was true in the automobile industry, it was never proved that they remained influential throughout these events, and these fairly spontaneous industrial conflicts had only ephemeral consequences. Similar events took place in Germany, where migrant workers started some wildcat strikes in 1973, in Belgium (the Limbourg miners' strike of 1970), in Switzerland (the 1970s) and in France in 1982–3 (Peugeot, Talbot, Citroen and Renault). The main result of these actions was to change the position taken by trade unions regarding the role of migrant workers in industrial action and union activities, not least because of the symbolic importance of the industries where these strikes took place, because of the perceived threats to 'social peace' (for example, in Switzerland) and because of the role played by Islam in the mobilisation of migrant workers, especially in France. Meanwhile, it has been demonstrated that extremism and moderation as such do not play an important role, but that the CGT and the CFDT use charismatic leaders to mobilise migrant workers during industrial conflicts, especially in large companies (Wihtol de Wenden et al., 1986).

In contrast, it is often said that migrant workers are used as strike breakers, but the evidence suggests otherwise. As Castles and Kosack (1973: 177) state,

> the fear that immigrants would act as strike-breakers has proved unjustified. On the contrary, they have participated actively in picketing and demonstrations. The employers and authorities have attempted to exploit the weak legal and economic position of immigrants during such disputes.

Migrant workers thus have at their disposal several means of influencing the trade unions, and they frequently make use of them. They include withholding union membership, threatening to do so, effectively withdrawing from union membership, disrupting the unions-supported industrial harmony, and appealing to homeland and to international labour organisations for support in respect of their rights.

Workers' Participation

Some form of workers' participation exists in all European countries, although its importance and specific organisational arrangements differ from country to country.

Workers' participation is usually organised through one or more of a number of institutions: works councils, shop stewards' committees ('union delegates') and industrial councils ('joint industrial committees' and so on). Because of their relative importance in organising migrant workers, our description and analysis will focus on works councils.

Whether these institutions are important in the decision-making process depends on the position of trade unions in the particular society. The fact that migrant workers play a role in these councils, even in countries where they have no voting rights, is probably because they came as an imported labour force – which the unions tried to integrate as quickly as possible – and this approach, in the end, appears to have received approval even from the employers.

Works councils exist under different names and have different powers. They are called 'Betriebsrate' in Germany, 'comités d'entreprise' in France, 'conseils d'entreprise/ondernemingsraden' in Belgium, and 'Ondernemingsraden' in the Netherlands. They have been introduced by law or by collective agreements in all countries except Switzerland and the UK. Swiss law permits employers to create factory committees, but there is much ambiguity about their role and how they should be constituted.

Works councils as such exist in only a minority of industries, particularly in heavy industry. They rarely do more than supply information; consultation happens only sporadically and control is non-existent. In the UK there is no legislation on works councils nor do collective agreements generally deal with them; in a number of companies a works council or an equivalent body operates, but they vary widely in both membership and structure. Only in the nationalised industries has consultation been made statutory.

In Germany, France, Belgium and the Netherlands they are compulsory in private companies which employ a certain number of workers (5 in Germany, 50 in France and Belgium, 100 in the Netherlands). Their size depends on the number of employees. In some countries non-profit-making establishments are included within the legislation, while in others the existence of works councils is restricted to industrial companies. Public companies are nearly always excluded; and although in France some public firms have works councils, they do not perform the full range of functions provided in the private sector. In most cases there are separate councils for manual workers and for clerical workers, and sometimes executive staff members have their own council – for example, in Belgium and France.

The functions of works councils are mainly of a consultative and advisory nature. Decision-making and supervision are usually limited to social and welfare matters such as specifying the period of annual holidays and supervising social works. Only in Germany do works councils have an equal say with management on relatively important matters such as job evaluation, piece rates and wage structure, working hours, overtime arrangements, break and holiday schedules, recruitment policies, dismissal of workers, training, allocation of company housing and occupational safety. In Belgium and France specific councils have been established to take care of safety and health matters: the 'comités d'hygiène et de securité' in France, and the 'comités de securité, d'hygiène et d'embellissement des lieux de travail/comites voor veiligheid, gezondheid en verfraaiing van de werkplaatsen' in Belgium.

In France and Belgium, the list for each of the councils is established by the 'representative' unions but, in France, non-union lists of candidates may be proposed for the second ballot. In the UK, the existing works councils are either union-based or not union-based; in the Netherlands and in Germany the right to present candidates is not limited to the unions. In no country is the union officially represented in the works council, and at the most they are allowed as observers. This may be explained by their lack of legal status – they are *de facto* organisations.

In all the project countries, foreign workers have the right to qualify as electors for the works council, or to stand for election, provided they meet the general requirements. In Belgium in 1971, and in France and Germany in 1972, the last legal restrictions on foreign participation were removed. However, both France and Belgium have general rules which may indirectly discriminate against foreign workers: these are the requirements to have worked in the company for a specific period of time and also to have a good knowledge of the language of the country. Other factors which may reduce foreign worker participation are the practice of the trade unions and the willingness of foreign workers to participate. Union representatives may be unwilling to put migrant workers, especially foreign nationals, on the voting lists. Furthermore, lack of industrial experience, lack of confidence in their new environment, and uncertainly about their future commitment may make migrant workers reluctant to vote and stand for election. They may feel that participation is the prerogative of native workers, and this view may be encouraged by their home governments, some of whom discourage their citizens from participating in industrial or political activities in their country of temporary residence.

As migrant workers become more integrated into the labour market and more established in particular companies, participation is likely to rise. The more militant they become, the more attention trade unions will pay to their needs, and the more effort they will make to ensure that they are represented within the union and on works councils. At present, the representation of migrant workers is generally very low on these bodies.

Although the number of foreign 'Betriebs- und Personalraete' (elected representatives of the employees within the special German system of co-determination – Mittbestimmung) is increasing, the share of foreign Betriebsraete is still lower than that of foreign Vertrauensleute (see above). Indeed, since full participation in the elections was made possible in Germany in 1972, the number of Betriebsraete rose from 3,800 in 1972 to about 5,000 in 1974, about 6,000 in 1978, and about 6,600 in 1981; but their share in the total number of works council members remained very low (3.3 percent in 1981). In many companies with a high number of migrant workers (over 70 percent), no 'Betriebsratmitglied' of foreign nationality was elected.

In Switzerland, migrant worker participation within factory committees has always been low because of discrimination against foreigners, and this is facilitated by the obscure nature of those committees. But both government and the SGB have encouraged their participation as a first step towards integration in Swiss society. In the Netherlands it appears that Mediterranean and Surinamese migrants take part as much as Dutch workers in elections to works councils. However, Mediterranean workers are much less likely to be candidates for such councils than either Dutch or Surinamese workers. In Belgium, migrant workers are clearly under-represented in works councils. Whereas their share in the workforce of companies with a works council was 10 percent in 1975, 9 percent in 1979 and 8.4 percent in 1983, migrant workers constituted 5.4 percent of works council members in 1975, 5.7 percent in 1979, and 6.4 percent in 1983. The explanation most often put forward is the decreasing importance of industrial sectors with high numbers of migrant workers.

Shop stewards (or union delegates) are workers who are sometimes elected, but are usually designated by union secretaries. They should not be confused with workers' delegates (in France) who are elected workers who represent their fellow workers in an establishment in order to inform the employer of the individual rights of the worker which have not been met by the employer, and which relate to wages, trade classifications, protective legislation, hygiene and social security. Most countries give some form of legal protection to shop stewards, but in all countries the best guarantee is the strength of the unions themselves, which then can deal with such issues on a formal or informal basis. This protection is more effective in a period of boom than in times of depression. Migrant worker participation in shop steward elections is subject to the same barriers as those affecting their participation in work council elections, particularly in countries where there is some relation between both positions, as in France. In Germany, the number of shop stewards is steadily growing.

Conclusion

As the large majority of post-war immigrants came to Western Europe as migrant workers, industrial rights constituted an important element in the range of legal, social and political rights which were immediately available to migrants. Membership of trade unions, participation in union activities, eligibility for works councils and shop stewards' positions were important ways in which migrants could participate in their new society. The gains that could be made through industrial action could benefit the whole migrant community.

It might be expected that the position and role of trade unions in society would be an important variable determining differences in the development and extent of migrants' industrial rights. Trade unions have a relatively powerful position in Sweden, Belgium, Germany and Britain compared with France, the Netherlands and Switzerland. But the strength or weakness of trade-union organisation has not, for example, had a consistent effect on immigration policy in the project countries. All major European receiving countries had liberal immigration policies until 1973–4, with the exception of Sweden and Switzerland. Trade unions were generally opposed to liberal immigration policies so one might have expected more restrictive policies in the first four countries and more liberal policies in the latter three.

However, only in Sweden, France and the Netherlands was the expected relationship achieved.

In Belgium, Germany and Switzerland, this could be explained by the fact that other more powerful groups – namely, the employers and the government – were able to overcome the restrictive proposals of the trade unions. This position would change after the deep recession of 1973, which caused all the receiving countries to impose tough controls on immigration. In Britain, relations with colonial and Commonwealth countries were important in maintaining liberal immigration policies until the 1960s.

In none of the seven project countries are foreign workers denied the right to participate in trade unions and works councils. Participation by migrant workers as members or activists in trade unions is related to the degree of unionisation in the sector of the labour market they occupy and the encouragement of union officials. The esteem and influence of the trade unions in society is also important; thus in Sweden and Belgium where the unions are well organised and politically influential, a high proportion of both native and migrant workers belong to unions. In Britain, the higher rates of union membership among such groups as Afro-Caribbeans and Asian workers is explained by their higher proportion in manual occupations. This is also true for migrant workers in Germany and Switzerland, where migrant workers are concentrated in the better-organised industrial sectors. However, in Switzerland one would expect a much higher rate of unionisation among foreign workers. The low esteem of unions in Switzerland, the high membership contributions, the hostility between Swiss and foreign workers and feelings that unions represent only native workers all contribute to low rates of union membership. In France, the incidence of illegal immigration, the concentration of migrant workers in sectors where the unions are poorly organised, and the lack of a welfare role for unions may all contribute to the low membership of trade unions among migrant workers. Nationally, the unions are weak and divided in France, which may also contribute to their lack of success.

Two models can be contrasted with respect to the organisational position of migrant workers within trade unions; the 'internationalist' model and the pluralist model. The first excludes any organisation of workers along national or ethnic lines; this still dominates in Socialist and Communist trade unions, and it is most important in Sweden, the UK and Germany. The 'diversity' model, which allows and even encourages the establishment of migrant workers' associations within trade unions, is typical of Christian Democratic unions.

Even in countries where migrant workers have a higher degree of unionisation than natives, such as in Sweden, they are under-represented in the leading positions in the trade unions. Their relative newness and inexperience, lack of linguistic facility in the language of their country of residence and lack of support from native workers may all contribute to this absence from higher positions. However, as migrant workers become more integrated into the labour market and more securely established in particular companies, their participation and success are likely to increase. The threat in some countries of autonomous militant industrial action by migrant workers has caused unions to be more responsive to their needs.

Another aspect of industrial participation is involvement in industrial action such as strikes. It is often argued that foreign workers are heavily involved in initiating such conflicts, which would not be too surprising, given their position in the labour market, but this has been proved in only a few cases, and not as a general rule. The opposing view that migrant workers are often used as strike breakers has little evidence to support it.

As migrant workers become more established, they do attempt to play a greater role in influencing trade-union policy, and the trade unions in turn are more likely to take up migrants' grievances both in the industrial sphere and on other issues relating to immigration controls and deportations of illegal workers.

Industrial rights can be seen as a first step towards political integration and involvement in the host society. However, they do not derive their importance from this alone. Industrial rights are important in themselves to protect the working conditions, health, safety and income of all workers, both native and foreign.

References

Balfour, Campbell (1972) *Industrial Relations in the Common Market*. London: Routledge & Kegan Paul.

Bernard, P.J. (ed.) (1976) *Les Travailleurs Étrangers en Europe Occidentale*. Paris/The Hague: Mouton.

Brown, C. (1984) *Black and White Britain*. London: Heinemann Educational Books.

Carby-Hall, J.R. (1977) *Worker Participation in Europe*. London: Croom Helm.

Castles, S. and G. Kosack (1973) *Immigrant Workers and Class Structure in Western Europe*. London: Oxford University Press.

De Jongh, R., M. van der Laan and J. Rath (1984) *FNV'ers aan het woord over buitenlandse werknemers*. Leiden: COMT.

Giner, S. and J. Salcedo (1978) 'Migrant Workers in European Social Structures', in S. Giner and M.S. Archer, *Contemporary Europe, Social Structures and Cultural Patterns*. London: Routledge & Kegan Paul.

Heisler, M.O. and B. Schmitter Heisler (1986) 'From Foreign Workers to Settlers? Transnational Migration and the Emergence of New Minorities', in *The Annals of the American Academy of Political and Social Science*, 485 (May).

Knocke, W. (1986) 'Swedish Trade Unions and Immigrant Workers', in J. Fry (ed.), *Towards a Democratic Rationality*. Aldershot: Gower House, pp. 219–30.

Lehmbruch, G. (1977) 'Liberal Corporatism and Party Government', in *Comparative Political Studies*, 10 (1): 91–126.

Martens, A. (1973) *25 jaar Wegwerparbeiders. Het Belgisch Immigratiebeleid na 1945.* Leuven: Sociologische Onderzoeksinstituut.

Miller, M.J. (1981) *Foreign Workers in Western Europe: An Emerging Political Force.* New York: Praeger.

Mouriaux, R. and C. Wihtol de Wenden (1987) 'Syndicalisme Français et Islam', in *Revue Française de Science Politque*, 37 (6) (Dec.): 794–819.

Schmitter, B. (1981) 'Trade Unions and Immigration Politics in West Germany and Switzerland', in *Politics and Society*, 10 (3) (Spring): 317–34.

Suhrkemper, K.P. (1983) 'Deutsche Gewerkschaften und auslaendische Arbeitnehmer', in F. Hamburger, M.-E. Karsten, H.-U. Otto, and H. Richter, (eds), *Sozialarbeit und Auslaenderpolitik*, Neuwied und Darmstadt: Luchterhand, pp. 78–94.

Wihtol de Wenden, C., J. Barou, M. Diop, N. Kerschen, E. de Saint-Blanquat and T. Subhi (1986) *Analyse des conflits récents survenus aux usines Renault de Billancourt depuis 1981 au sein de la population immigrée*, Contrat de connaissance CNRS/RNUR.

4

The Civil Rights of Aliens

Tomas Hammar

There are two principal aims of any aliens Act: first, to regulate the flow of immigration of foreign citizens into a country; and second, to establish the legal position of those foreign citizens who have been admitted to the country as residents. The first aim, control and regulation, has been emphasised everywhere, but the second is often neglected and, in several West European countries with large foreign populations, the rights of those foreign citizens who are legal residents are today becoming a matter of increasing concern.

Of great interest in this context is a recent Norwegian debate that arose during preparations for a bill presented to the Norwegian Storting in 1987. The Commission on Aliens made serious attempts to draft legislation specifying not only the conditions required for exclusion or deportation from the country, but also the legal conditions of residence in Norway.

In response, a well-known professor of international law, Atle Grahl-Madsen, produced an alternative text to that proposed by the government commission. In this text he suggests a number of substantial amendments aimed at giving foreign citizens an even stronger legal position in relation to the police, the courts and the government (Grahl-Madsen, 1985). He argues that the traditional distinction between citizen and non-citizen is no longer valid in many immigration countries where many people have established intense and close relations with the country, even though they are not citizens. Indeed, they may in some cases have lived in this country all their lives, having been born there to parents of foreign citizenship. They may own property in the host country, and some may perhaps be influential businessmen, while others may be civil servants. They may have permanent resident permits, or even have the right of permanent residence, but for various reasons they have remained foreign citizens and perhaps also for good reasons prefer to do so.

In German and in Scandinavian languages, the word for foreigner is 'Ausländer' or 'utlänning', where 'Aus' or 'ut' mean from the outside, while 'Inländer' or 'inlänning' could perhaps be used to refer to persons who are permanent residents. Grahl-Madsen suggests that any future aliens act should distinguish not merely between citizens and foreigners, but also between two types of non-citizen, giving three categories of persons in all:

1   foreigners (Ausländer, utlänningar, étrangers);
2   permanent residents (Inländer, denizens or persons with full residential rights);
3   citizens.

This idea provides a useful starting point for a discussion of civil rights of foreign citizens in West European countries, as it can help us to understand better the need for more secure legal protection for those who belong to Category 2 – those who are neither complete foreigners nor citizens of the country in which they reside.

Civil Rights and Human Rights

In examining the relationship between civil rights and human rights, we look first at the historical development of human rights, and show that civil rights may be seen as the rights developed during one specific stage of this process. Some significant differences between human rights and civil rights are then discussed.

R.P. Claude distinguished four stages in the development of human rights and liberties, each of which enhances the meaning and standards of human rights (Claude, 1976; Marshall, 1964). These four stages are:

1   political freedom, or the establishment of legitimate limits to political authority;
2   declaration of rights which establishes between the individual and the government a relationship which is regulated by rights and duties;
3   democratic rights establishing equality of political rights and participation; and
4   positive rights establishing distribution of resources and membership in a social welfare state.

The civil rights that we discuss here are mainly those of the first and second stages of this model. They cannot function well if there are no limits to political authority – as in an absolute monarchy or in a totalitarian state – and stage 1 is therefore a prerequisite. But democracy – stage 3 – need not be fully developed. In the nineteenth century, after the French Revolution, political freedom and civil rights were increasingly bestowed upon everyone – not only upon those who were entitled to participate in political life as voters or candidates and politicians. Then, in the beginning of the twentieth century, when political democracy emerged and all adult citizens were granted voting rights, the extension of full civil rights to all citizens became an absolute requirement. Finally, mainly during the second half of the twentieth century, positive social rights – stage 4 – were developed in the welfare states. Thus human rights and liberties were enlarged to include legal and political as well as social rights, and all these rights were granted to every adult citizen of the society.

However, the direct consequence was that the demarcation line between citizens and foreigners became more and more crucial. Foreign citizens were not granted full rights and freedoms, but instead often found their political freedom severely limited. They had, in fact, only those rights specifically granted to them by the state – even the right to stay and the right to work. Even then, when it was deemed necessary, the state could decide to cancel their permits and compel them to leave its territory. Democratic rights to vote and to stand for election were regarded as the exclusive privilege of those who were citizens of the state, and were never accorded to foreign citizens except for those with dual nationality which included citizenship of the state. These restrictions applied to all foreign citizens irrespective of their ties to the host country; in other words, the principle was applied just as rigorously to those inländers who were permanent residents in the country as it was to those who were newly arrived or staying only temporarily.

The United Nations Declaration of Human Rights

In the Universal Declaration of Human Rights proclaimed by the United Nations in December 1948, a number of fundamental rights are accorded to all individuals as members of the human race, regardless of national origin or present citizenship. But in the matter of political rights, discrimination against aliens is accepted – or at least not forbidden. When Article 2 starts by declaring that 'Everyone is entitled to all the rights and freedoms set forth in this Declaration, without distinction of any kind', this at first seems to imply that all political rights too will be granted to everyone, regardless of citizenship, but it soon becomes evident that this is not so. The Article continues: 'without distinction of any kind such as race, colour, sex, language, religion, political or other opinion, national or social origin, property, birth or other status' – without mentioning citizenship. The second part of the Article states that no distinction shall be made on the basis of the status of the country or the territory 'to which a person belongs', but this is no help in the matter of political rights, for it refers only to the status of the country or territory, and says nothing about the status of the individual. The Declaration therefore implicitly accepts that citizenship may be the basis of particular treatment or discrimination.

The subsequent Articles stipulate the right to life, liberty and security of person, the right to recognition as a person before the law, and the right to protection against slavery, torture, arbitrary arrest and exile. Article 13 guarantees freedom of movement and residence within the borders of each state as well as a person's right to leave any country (including his own) and to return there. However, this Article is not interpreted as advocating a person's right to take up residence in a country other than the one where he holds citizenship.

The absence of the word 'citizen' in the Universal Declaration does cause some ambiguity on this specific point, for the Declaration tacitly accepts discrimination based on citizenship, but it does not explicitly acknowledge this fact. This ambiguity may provide an opening for future reinterpretations of the expressions actually used: namely, 'his country' and 'people'.

There have been debates about political rights of aliens in several immigration countries. For example, in West Germany and in Sweden it has been argued that the term 'people' as used in these countries' constitutional texts could refer to the permanently resident population – the people living in the country – and can therefore include not only citizens but also those in 'Category 2' the denizens or inländers. These foreign citizens with legal rights to stay permanently in the country may be said to hold 'informal membership' of the country in several important respects, and it might therefore have some future significance that the word 'citizen' is not mentioned in the Declaration of 1948.

The International Covenant on Civil and Political Rights that was adopted by the General Assembly of the United Nations in December 1966 does mention the word 'citizen'. In Article 25 it states that 'every citizen' shall have the right and the opportunity to take part in the conduct of public affairs, to vote and to be elected, and to have access to public service in his country. Foreign citizens are accordingly not guaranteed the same rights (Claude, 1976).

These and further limitations exist in the provisions of the European Convention on Human Rights of 1953. Article 16 not only exempts the contracting states from granting aliens voting rights, but also permits restrictions on freedom of expression, of assembly and of association.

Changing Perspectives in the 1970s

The 1948 Universal Declaration of Human Rights signified a break with previous principles which completely excluded foreign citizens from political life in their country of residence; everyone was granted political freedoms without discrimination against non-citizens. As we shall see, this innovation caused most Western European states to re-examine their policies and change their previous restrictions. The process started early in some countries and late in others, but the direction was everywhere the same: in accordance with the Declaration and the United Nations Covenant. It is not always easy to show that this change in the legal perspectives in each country was directly influenced by the development of international law at the time, but in general terms these new international instruments pointed the way (Madra, 1984).

In recent years, there has been a tendency in Europe to give foreign citizens more access to the political system. In 1977, the Parliamentary Assembly of the Council of Europe urged the Committee of Ministers to consider voting rights for aliens at the level of local authorities. In October 1983, the General Secretary of the Council of Europe, in co-operation with the Portuguese government, organised a 'Colloquy on "Human Rights of Aliens in Europe" '. Reports presented to this colloquy included material of direct significance for the subject of voting rights for aliens – in particular, a report by a Turkish lawyer, E. Ozsunay.

Before, during and immediately after the Second World War, the tradition in most countries was to forbid foreign citizens to take part in political activity. The reason was probably concern about the danger of external conflicts entering the domestic political scene, and about the risk of external interference organised by other states. Given how quickly this strongly negative attitude has changed, it is interesting to trace the origins of this development.

Sweden and West Germany provide good examples. In 1936, the Swedish Aliens Act laid down one indispensable condition for humanitarian treatment of political refugees, 'namely that foreign residents remain totally neutral. Political activities may not take place' (Björling and Lindencrona, 1955; Records of the Swedish Riksdag, 1936). During the war years, 1939–45, the police in Sweden were given a free hand to arrest, imprison or put into long-term work camps any foreigners who were politically active or could endanger Swedish security – for instance, because of their extreme political views. As late as 1953, refugees and deserters from the war in Algeria were forbidden to take part in any political activities. Even in 1965, when a change was already apparent, foreigners were admonished not to forget that a prolongation of their permits might be refused on grounds of political activities. Today, the Swedish government can still deport foreign citizens for political reasons, although this power of political deportation has been very little used. In 1973 legislation was passed against international terrorism, directed at members of organisations known for their use of violence and threats of force for political purposes. However, few resident foreign citizens are involved in this kind of political activity, and criticism of the legislation has related not so much to its intentions as to its potential for improper usage.

In West Germany, similar developments have taken place (Dohse, 1981). In 1953, foreign citizens residing there were granted the right to take part in assemblies and demonstrations. In 1964, they were also given the right to establish their own associations, and three years later, in 1967, membership of political parties was allowed. However, the parties were free to decide whether they wanted to admit foreign citizens, and the Bavarian CSU decided not to do so. In all political parties, foreign citizens were excluded from the procedure of nominating candidates for public elections, and the majority of the members of any political party had to be German citizens. Separate parties of foreigners were not allowed. Today, although an extension of the political rights of foreign citizens has taken place, some of the restrictions remain. In principle, the law still allows the German administration to forbid foreign citizens to take part in political activities when important national interests are endangered. The relevant conditions are – as we will discuss below – not exactly defined, and this means that there is wide scope for discretionary decisions.

In France prior to May 1981, activists in trade unions could be expelled on the grounds that they had not 'respected the political neutrality to which any foreigner residing on French territory is bound' (Wihtol de Wenden, 1984; Verbunt, 1985). The basis for this is a general principle, still valid, that foreign citizens can be deported if they threaten public order. However, 'public order' is not precisely defined and, because the juridical notion is imprecise and subject to many possible interpretations, foreigners never know what kind of political activity, in what situations, may be considered a threat to public order. Therefore the best they can do, if they wish to secure a future in France, is to abstain completely from all forms of political participation. The French law of 9 October 1981 replaced a law-decree of 1939, requiring that foreign associations in France should obtain an authorisation from the Minister of the Interior, in case foreign citizens had a substantial influence through the association. The new law made foreign associations equal to all other associations, subject only to a notification to the minister. But even if some political rights are granted, such as freedom of expression and freedom of assembly and demonstration, and from 1981 also freedom of association, these rights have to be utilised in such a way that the obligation of political neutrality is respected.

As can be seen, a change in perspectives has taken place in France, as in Sweden and West Germany, although in France more remains dependent on administrative decisions and therefore on the political intentions of the incumbent government, and much less has been guaranteed by means of constitutional and legal rights. As a result, more political activities have been allowed under one political regime than under another. Although the Socialist government in 1981-6 extended the political freedom of aliens, not only by new legislation but also by a more liberal interpretation of what public order demands, the Conservative government in 1986-8 turned out to be more restrictive. It is therefore likely that, to protect their own interests, many foreign citizens in France abstain from political activities in both liberal and conservative periods, as they cannot feel sure that their activities will not be held against them at some time in the future.

The trend has been the same everywhere in Europe. A general broadening of political freedom is being extended to foreign residents too, but at the same time most states make use of their discretionary powers defining the grounds for expulsion of foreign citizens. This is done in the national interest, for the national security, or just to protect public order. According to the still valid Swiss Federal Law of Abode and Settlement of Foreigners 1931, any foreigner can be expelled if condemned by a penal court or 'if his behaviour and actions lead to the conclusion that he is not willing or able to fit into the established order of the host country' (Article 10).

The Right of Permanent Residence

The examples quoted from France, West Germany and Switzerland with regard to expulsion in the interest of public order clearly show that the right to reside permanently in the host country is a basic prerequisite for political activities. Those who fear that political participation may cause them problems, and may perhaps lead to refusals when they apply for extended permits, will often refrain from politics. On the other hand, if there is little risk of such consequences, foreigners will make more use of the rights given to them. We must therefore also consider to what extent foreign citizens are granted the status of permanent residents.

In the 1980s, the situation has become much better. Many more foreign residents have obtained the privileged position of a permanent resident, and in several countries new kinds of permits have been introduced which allow longer residence periods and easier renewals. As a consequence, the legal status of foreign citizens has improved, and they are now for the first time able to make realistic plans for their future stay in the host country, even if they are not granted its citizenship, or do not wish to acquire it.

In 1986, about 78 percent of foreign citizens in Switzerland had obtained a permit of permanent resident (Niederlassungsrecht), which was unlimited in duration and guaranteed freedom of movement within the Swiss Confederation as well as freedom of speech (as compared with foreigners with only an annual residence permit who are, as we shall see, not allowed to make unauthorised political speeches).

In West Germany, the proportion of permanent residents has also risen rapidly, and 69 percent of the population of legally resident foreign citizens had obtained this status by 1986. However, a large part of the foreign population holds only temporary permits, or permits based on discretionary decision, after more than ten years of legal residence, and they have not obtained a new or prolonged permit (Aufenthaltsrecht) as a matter of right. However, the trend is positive: more foreign citizens are getting permanent permits as a matter of right, and more are making use of the political freedom which increasingly is being extended to them. Since 1986, foreign workers have received unrestricted work permits if they have worked legally in West Germany for five of the last eight years, and practically all of them meet this requirement.

It is probable that the second generation that has grown up in West Germany will not be as patient as their parents have been. Their position is stronger and more secure, because they were born there, went to school there and are fluent in the German language. Official policy is to place prime emphasis on measures that integrate members of this second generation. But still, with the United Nations Universal Declaration in mind, they well might ask if they should not be included among those who can say that the FRG is 'their country'.

In France, according to a new law of 1984, there are only two types of residence permit – one valid for not more than a year, and one valid for ten years. The latter is granted to foreigners who have been resident in France for three years, and may be renewed almost automatically. Those who have obtained the ten-year residence permit – and they make up the major part of the legal foreign population in France – enjoy a relatively secure status, although of course they may, just like other foreigners be expelled on the grounds that their activities are a threat to public order.

In Sweden, permanent residence permits are given to all foreign residents after one year's legal stay in the country. Applications for the first residence permit must be made before arriving in Sweden and cannot be made, for instance, on the basis of a tourist visit. Only political refugees asking for asylum may apply while already in Sweden. As we have seen, the Minister can expel foreign citizens on political grounds in accordance with the Aliens Act, but this power is used extremely rarely. Normal political activities, even in favour of extreme political views, are not seen as a reason for expulsion or refusal to grant permanent residence. There are thus few legal obstacles to foreigners who want to make use of political rights in Sweden although the Aliens Act includes, as mentioned, a special provision concerning the expulsion of international terrorists.

Constitutional Rights and Judicial Review

In some democratic states, and especially in federations formed by a number of states, politics is to a large extent a matter of law and constitution. In others, it is mainly a pragmatic matter of majority rule in a system of representation. Human rights as well as civil and political rights are of greater importance in the former countries, where these rights may be upheld by decisions of the courts based on their interpretation of constitutional acts and precedents.

Several countries have declarations of rights, either as separate documents or as part of the constitution itself. Judicial interpretation of these rights, given by the supreme court of the country, can have great political significance. Federal states, such as West Germany and Switzerland, usually attach more importance to the constitution and to its judicial interpretation, as this is the basis of the division of power between the federation and the states. Unitary states, on the other hand, such as Belgium, France, the Netherlands, Sweden and Britain, do not have the same need of constitutional interpretations, and this may also have consequences for those civil and political rights which are given in these countries' constitutions. But after both world wars, the trend has been to include at least some type of declaration of rights in new constitutions, and this is true of all the countries in this study except Switzerland and Britain, where such new constitutions do not exist.

In Britain, general freedoms and rights as discussed here exist under common law, reinforced by custom and practice. All those who are legally resident, both citizens and non-citizens, have the same rights and duties and are subject to the same laws, unless these are specifically limited by an Act of parliament. In the Netherlands, the same holds true, but the basis is here the written constitution, revised in 1983. According to Article 1 of this constitution, all residents of whatever citizenship shall be treated equally, and exceptions can be made by law only. In fact, many exceptions have been made, but efforts are made to identify these discriminatory regulations and to check whether they are based solely on tradition or on good reasons that are still valid. In both the Netherlands and in Sweden, catalogues have been recently published documenting the regulations which make distinctions between the way citizens and foreigners are treated (Beune and Hessels, 1983; Diskrimineringsutredningen, 1984).

The German Grund Gesetz, or Basic Law, and the Belgian

constitution make most rights and freedoms valid for everyone, and not just German and Belgian citizens. A few are valid for citizens only – in West Germany, for example, the freedom to hold public meetings and the freedom to form associations – but these freedoms have been given to foreign citizens by legislation, the only difference being that they are not as strongly protected as if they were part of the constitution.

In 1976, the Swedish constitution included the following positive policy declaration on minorities: 'Ethnic, linguistic and religious minorities shall be given an opportunity to preserve and develop their own cultural and associational life' (Chapter 1, Article 2.4 of the Regeringsform). A principle established only a year before in a unanimous decision of the Riksdag was hereby elevated to the rank of a core value in the Swedish democratic ideology. When the Riksdag proclaimed in 1975 that Swedish immigration and minority policy aimed at giving immigrant groups a 'freedom of choice' in the matter of preserving and developing their own culture and language in Sweden, this gave rise to many activities such as more associations of immigrants, new publications and improved schooling for immigrant children, all in an effort to promote ethnic pluralism. It is important to note, however, that the right given in the constitution is interpreted as a right for individual members of a minority group and not as rights for the minority groups themselves.

Civil Rights

As mentioned, a prerequisite for political participation of aliens is the legal protection of life and personal freedom, as well as a protection against inhuman and degrading treatment or punishment. In all seven European countries that are the subject of this study, foreign citizens have the right to liberty and security of the person. They are equal before the courts and enjoy the minimum guarantees given every citizen charged with a criminal offence. Residence and work permits with short duration, and discretionary decisions about prolongation of permits, may be major hindrances to the political mobilisation of foreign residents in the host countries, but civil rights are in general granted on an equal footing to citizens and non-citizens alike, and therefore foreigners in most countries do not encounter *legal* obstacles to their free participation in political debates, associations and political parties.

However, one major exception to their civil rights, already discussed, is found in all the seven countries. This exception is caused by the systems of aliens control that every country has established. The police are, in one way or another, empowered to arrest foreign citizens and to keep them in custody for a short time in order to check their identity and their permits, deport them, or ask for their expulsion. For the same purpose, foreign citizens may also be forbidden to move within the country's territory and from one employer or job to another, although freedom of movement is otherwise considered a fundamental right of everyone in the country. It is worth noting that these exceptions to civil rights caused by the need for an aliens control system do not usually embarrass those foreign citizens who have obtained long-term or permanent residence permits and can easily prove their identity.

In a national emergency situation – for example, when a country is in war or under the threat of an impending war – civil rights normally granted to aliens are often suspended. This may be explicitly foreseen in the law, or follow from special decisions and ordinances of the kind that were taken in most countries during the Second World War.

In most states, foreign citizens enjoy freedom of speech, expression, the press, assembly, demonstration, and association to the same extent as citizens. Ozsunay's report to the Council of Europe's colloquy on 'Human Rights of Aliens in Europe' (October 1983) gives a valuable overview. He shows that freedom of opinion, assembly and association are given without discrimination in 12 European countries: Cyprus, Denmark, France, Great Britain, Greece, Iceland, Lichtenstein, the Netherlands, Norway, Portugal, Spain and Sweden. Some restrictions are laid upon these same freedoms in seven other member states of the Council of Europe: namely, Belgium, West Germany, Ireland, Italy, Luxemburg, Switzerland and Turkey. Overall, freedom of opinion is recognised for citizens and aliens alike in most countries, with some important exceptions. Freedom of association is more often restricted, but in general the practice is more liberal than the letter of the constitution or the law. Freedom of opinion, association and assembly may in most cases be exercised by aliens, except that a 'sword of Damocles' is hanging over their heads (Ozsunay, 1983; Plender, 1983).

Freedom of Opinion

Article 7 of the constitution of the Netherlands says that 'no person shall require previous permission to publish thoughts or feelings by means of the printing press, without prejudice to every person's responsibility according to the law'. In France, too, freedom of opinion has been considered a human right since 1789, but nevertheless aliens have not always enjoyed the same freedom as citizens. In Great Britain and in Sweden aliens have the same rights as citizens, albeit with some restrictions of little practical and political significance.

The situation is different in West Germany, Switzerland and Belgium. In these countries and also, as we have seen, in France, freedom of opinion can be restricted in order to protect public order and security. The wording used in West Germany is worth quoting. Article 6.2 of the Aliens Act of 1965 reads as follows: 'The political activities of aliens can be limited or prohibited if necessary for protection against disturbance of public security and order (*öffentliche Sicherheit und Ordnung*) or against impairing the formation of the political will in the FRG or for other matters of substantial concern (*sonstige erhebliche Belange*) to the FRG.' This general, inclusive and vague definition of those disturbances that may lead to restriction would in practice need further clarification. The interpretation might change according to circumstances, according to the political values of the incumbent government or according to the position of those aliens or that category of aliens that may cause disturbances. In particular, the words '*sonstige erhebliche Belange*' or 'other matters of substantial concern' leave wide room for political discretion and value judgements as to what matters are in the interests of West Germany. According to some authors, the interests of the state shall be interpreted in a wide sense, to include all political, social and economic interests. It is not deemed necessary to specify what the danger might be: any kind of harm to the interests of West Germany might be said to satisfy this article. We must add, however, that this interpretation is far from generally accepted in West Germany, and the significance of Article 6.2 is not that it has been frequently used, but the fear that it might be.

Foreign citizens residing in Switzerland are not allowed to speak on a political issue at an open or private meeting of an association unless they have prior authorisation from the cantonal government. And even when this authorisation has been given, speakers must refrain from saying anything that might be interpreted as interference in internal Swiss political affairs. However, most cantonal constitutions recognise freedom of opinion, association and assembly, not only for their citizens but also for aliens. Enforcement of these restrictions is likely to vary from one canton to another within Switzerland, as well as from time to time.

In Belgium, freedom of opinion is explicitly recognised for everyone (Article 14 of the constitution), but freedom of association and assembly are guaranteed only for Belgian citizens. In practice, however, and according to the Aliens Act of 1980 (Article 20.3), these freedoms are also recognised for aliens.

Freedom of Assembly and Demonstration, and of Association

Freedom of peaceful assembly and of association is guaranteed in international declarations – for example, in the United Nations Universal Declaration, Article 20, and in the European Convention of

Human Rights, Article 11. The latter includes also the negative right of not belonging to an association.

However, the freedoms of assembly and association are circumscribed even more than freedom of opinion. In the Netherlands, they are given in the constitution to every resident, including all resident aliens, but the 'exercise of this right shall, in the interests of public order, be regulated and limited by law' (Article 9). This means that the Dutch authorities may, for instance, forbid meetings if they expect riots. Such actions have been rare, and appeals may be lodged against them, but they have taken place, as when the Mayor of Amsterdam, at the request of left-wing Moroccans and Dutchmen, prohibited a meeting of a right-wing Moroccan association called 'Amicales'.

Article 9 of the Dutch constitution is reminiscent of the French and German clauses permitting their governments wide discretion over restrictions. As already mentioned, a French statute of 1981 put associations directed by aliens on the same footing as other French associations, but in West Germany associations of aliens can be forbidden when they engage in politicial activities, violate or jeopardise internal or external security, or threaten public order or other matters of substantial national concern. Foreigners residing in Switzerland can form their own associations but, as we have seen, there are restrictions on their activities.

Have Foreigners Voiced Their Demands?

How are civil rights utilised by foreign citizens? This is a much more difficult question to answer, because it requires analysis of the political participation of foreigners in the European host countries. Several studies have been undertaken in this field, but the results serve only to whet our appetite (Ozsunay, 1983; Plender, 1983).

First of all, we must not assume that political activities exist only when civil rights are granted. It is obvious that foreign citizens can be members of political parties even when they are not allowed to vote in local elections. If they are barred from forming their own associations, they may join existing associations in the host country and play a role in them, raise their demands there and find representation for their interests through them. If they are forbidden to publish their own periodicals, they may publish articles in domestic magazines or give interviews to newspapers. Thus in these and many other ways foreign citizens have played an active part in the processes of influencing political opinion in many countries where political and civil rights have been strictly limited.

Taking a broader historical perspective, we might say that foreign citizens could not be treated otherwise in European democracies, because these states are influenced by change in the political climates of other countries in Europe. In the future, the rapid development of the international mass media may make this intra-European dependence even more pronounced.

However, we must also avoid the other extreme of believing that an extension of civil rights to resident aliens does not have an impact on their attitudes and behaviour. As we have emphatically pointed out, a lack of civil rights increases the obstacles and risks involved in any kind of political participation. Many foreign citizens accept being excluded from the political life of the host society as a manifestation of the treatment traditionally accorded to temporarily resident foreigners but, if and when civil rights are accorded to them, many are ready to make use of these rights.

Thus some foreign residents take part in the political life of the host country without civil rights, while others do not, but would like to do so if such rights were extended to them. There is of course also a third category: namely, those who for one reason or another remain inactive even when they are legally invited to take part. We cannot here discuss extensively all the many reasons for this non-participation, but we will return to them in a later chapter of this book when we discuss the voting behaviour of foreign citizens. We must, however, briefly mention Albert Hirschman's 'Exit–voice–loyalty' theory, which has been utilised in this context by Roger Ko-Chih Tung. We shall then also refer to Mark Miller's thesis that it is wrong to talk about the political quiescence of foreign workers in Europe who, even early in the 1970s, had developed a rich and intense political life.

According to Hirschman (1970) and Tung (1981), emigration may be seen as a political act. Instead of trying to achieve improvements within the political system of their origin, emigrants leave their country, hoping to find individual solutions in other countries. The choice of Exit or Voice (either emigration or raising political demands and engaging in activities) may be explained by a multitude of factors, several of which are of a political nature, such as political interest and competence or political efficacy, and loyalty to or support for the political system (Easton, 1965). In other words, we would expect emigrants to give evidence of low efficacy and low loyalty, to exhibit the same characteristics in relation to the political system of the country of immigration, and therefore to show low levels of political interest and activity.

Other factors reinforce this tendency towards low political participation. During the first few years, immigrants' political efficacy may be low because they do not yet know enough about the host country's political culture, or even its language. Even after several years, many foreign citizens may view their stay in the host country as temporary and therefore have little interest in politics. As a result, most immigrants are relatively passive in terms of political participation as compared with citizens.

However, among them there are always activists, and their number has been on the increase. In Castle and Kosack's early work on *Immigrant Workers and the Class Structure in Western Europe* (1973), foreign workers were seen as powerless and voiceless, but change was already under way, as shown in Mark Miller's rich presentation of the process of politicisation and mobilisation of foreign workers in France, Switzerland and the Federal Republic of Germany (Miller, 1978). He gives numerous examples of protests in various forms by foreign workers: protests against unacceptable housing, against deportations of foreigners who have taken part in protests, against discrimination in employment, and against unequal working conditions. They have also taken part in more direct political demonstrations – for example, protests against the war in Vietnam, demonstrations on homeland affairs, or participation in regular May Day parades. In France in particular, but also in Switzerland and Germany, they have usually protested together with nationals of the host country, thereby legitimising their demonstrations, strikes and sit-ins as lawful domestic extra-parliamentary opposition in which some foreign citizens also happened to take part. The authorities have thus been unable to ban these protests, and it has been difficult for them to prevent immigrants from joining in, even if such immigrant activities under other circumstances would have been seen as a threat to public order. Thus alliances between native and foreign protesters have helped to protect the protesting immigrants.

The Turkish wildcat strike in Cologne in 1973 is an example of foreign workers successfully using illegal actions to gain increased support for demands to extend civil and political rights. The German trade union IG Metall openly denounced the wildcat strike as illegal and political in nature, but this, and several other foreign worker actions that followed soon afterwards, shocked the unions, for it gave clear evidence that the Turkish workers in Germany did not feel that the German unions represented their interests. As a result, a drive to improve representation for foreign workers started within the unions (Castles and Kosack, 1973).

These illegal political activities showed that immigrants' demands were not being heard by the regular political parties or interest organisations, and that this lack of voice and representation for foreign workers and residents had led to 'revolts' which were unacceptable to the host society. Unions therefore had to move to increase foreign worker representation. The same pressures may force political parties to open up channels to foreign residents, and lead to alliances being established between native associations and immigrant groups.

In France, where extra-parliamentary opposition has been even stronger than in West Germany, successful strikes in 1971 and thereafter signalled growing militancy by foreign workers. The French trade unions were, like those of the Germans, forced to improve the representation of foreign workers in order to avoid an autonomous movement of foreign workers in France. In the same period, numerous racist incidents led to demonstrations in the streets of major French cities. Several of these were organised by the Mouvement des Travailleurs Arabes (MTA), a Marxist-Leninist organisation with a widespread following (Miller, 1978). Participants in these street demonstrations, as well as participants in hunger strikes against deportation of illegal immigrants, were often themselves illegally residing in France, 'les sans-papiers'. They clearly risked deportation, and some of them in fact were expelled.

In West Germany, an association called the IAF, or Interessengemeinschaft der mit Ausländern verheirateten deutschen Frauen, has been formed by German women married to foreign citizens. German citizens cannot be deported, so these women feel free to organise and fight on behalf of their husbands and families, while their husbands, as foreign citizens, fear there would be negative consequences if they themselves were to organise and protest. However, the objectives of this association include a broad spectrum of issues of direct interest to all foreign citizens in the country and not only to the foreign husbands of German women. Thus the IAF has circumvented official policy of either not granting foreign citizens civil rights or inhibiting their use of such rights. This illustrates both the problem of those foreign citizens whose civil rights are severely limited, and at the same time the problem of a state that attempts to implement such a policy. There are too many loopholes to make a toughly applied restrictive policy effective in the long run.

In conclusion we can therefore agree with Mark Miller that foreign citizens and foreign workers in the European host countries have not been silent and inactive. They have from the beginning of the 1970s taken part in a variety of political actions and protests aimed at improving both their status and their working and living conditions. As foreign citizens, they have not been granted voting rights and representation except in a few cases at the local level, but they have made use of the civil rights that have been given to them. Some have even been prepared to take illegal action, with all its attendant risks, when there were no alternatives.

As may be seen in other chapters of this book, foreign citizens have also joined trade unions and other organisations and associations.

They have become members of political parties and they have taken part in electoral campaigns. But what access to information do they have through the press, radio and television? This form of political articulation is one of the most important factors in the actual use of the freedom of opinion. What opportunities do immigrants and foreign citizens have to disseminate their demands and hopes, and to discuss their proposals and ideas, through these media in the host country?

In most countries, the minority press has had substantial economic problems. Small language groups can barely afford the cost of publishing a daily newspaper or even a weekly periodical. And these publications have to compete both with papers imported from the country of origin and with the press of the host country. Subsidies to the minority press have been given by some host governments. For instance, from 1976 to 1987 the Swedish parliament gave a total of about SEK 5 million a year to 35 periodicals published in foreign languages by minority associations, and to some 15 periodicals about immigrants and ethnic minority cultures, published in Swedish. Most of these periodicals were issued by associations of immigrants from one country or at least from one language area, and they played a significant role in mobilising support for these associations and providing a basis for their representation in relation to the Swedish authorities.

The television and radio networks in all the host countries have allocated time to special programmes for the major immigrant groups, such as the Turks, Yugoslavs and Moroccans. Special staffs have been employed to produce these programmes. They have been very popular, but they have been short of broadcasting time and many of their programmes have to a large extent been imported from the countries of origin. These programmes have thus not expressed the views or demands of the foreign residents and, even if they did, they would rarely have reached the decision-makers in the host countries. Daily newspapers have been imported and distributed on a large scale, and some of these have even appeared as special issues for foreign immigrants; for example, a special issue of a Turkish newspaper is printed in West Germany. The many periodicals produced by foreign residents are probably even more significant in forming opinion among immigrants in Europe.

At the end of the 1970s there were radio programmes in ten European countries for some 18 different language groups. In Belgium there were programmes in 11 languages, and in Sweden 8. At the same time, six countries had television programmes in nine languages, West Germany had programmes in eight, and Sweden in four (Council of Europe, 1979). Several of these programmes, especially those broadcast by local radio stations, offer good opportunities to raise issues of direct interest to the foreign resident population, to start political discussions and to publicise demands. But the national programmes, especially national television programmes, offer many fewer such opportunities; they either give more emphasis, and thus influence, to homeland matters – for instance, in the form of imported programmes – or they offer host country programmes translated into a minority language.

Minority Rights

Ethnic, religious and cultural pluralism has been developing in West European immigration countries, although not to the same degree everywhere, and nowhere has it meant acknowledging that the new immigrant minorities have specific rights.

The Versailles peace treaties of 1919 made the nations' right of self-determination a basic principle, and a system of minority rights was established in order to protect national minorities, especially in Eastern Europe, which could not form their own nation states. But ethnic and religious minorities in Western Europe were never covered by this system, and it has never been accepted that minorities that were not indigenous could be regarded as minorities holding specific rights. Therefore neither immigrants to Western Europe, nor their second- or third-generation descendants could be regarded as minorities in this sense. Just as in the classic immigration countries – the USA, Canada and Australia – immigrant ethnic groups were allowed and even encouraged to develop their own language and culture, but they were not granted the status of minorities.

During the 1980s, the Netherlands and Sweden have encouraged ethnic pluralism more than other European countries, and the Netherlands' immigration policy is officially called a 'minorities' policy. In Sweden an extensive system of mother-tongue instruction has already become part of the regular school curriculum, although, as has been already mentioned, this is in the interests of the individual members of the ethnic minorities only, not in their collective interest as groups. A policy change towards the end of the 1980s seems to move away from ethnic pluralism and towards what is considered to be more realistic: namely, slow and voluntary integration into the majority.

Conclusions

During the 1970s, civil rights have gradually been extended to foreign citizens legally residing in the European immigration countries. They still lack full political rights, but they have come to enjoy improved status as foreign residents, protection of their personal freedom, and the right to take part in the formation of public opinion through freedom of speech, press, association and demonstration. These rights are not usually guaranteed in constitutions, only in the regular laws, but they are respected under normal conditions. Consequently, the position of foreign residents in Europe in the political life of the host countries is like that of those nineteenth-century 'citizens' who had not yet been granted suffrage in general elections but who in most other respects possessed full legal rights.

The extension of foreign residents' and foreign workers' civil rights that has taken place in all the project countries has been influenced by their political participation in legal and illegal actions as well as by their basic associational work. But it is evident that democratic systems cannot allow the prolonged political segregation of large groups of permanent residents who are employees, taxpayers and neighbours – in other words, people who are integrated with the rest of the resident population in so many other respects.

Miller's view that the political actions of foreign workers in Europe in 1973 and 1974 actually led to decisions to stop the recruitment of foreign workers to West Germany and France seems to be an over-simplification. Many factors have to be taken into account in the complex economic and political context, especially the almost total lack of long-term planning to integrate the millions of foreign workers who had already settled in these countries.

It took a very long time for policy-makers to become aware of the need to integrate large, permanently settled minority populations, but, by the mid 1970s, a new period had started in European immigration history. Individuals and minority groups have acquired stronger motivations for political action, and they are now admitted at least to the ante-rooms of political life – the rooms where political articulation of interests takes place. Of course, this partial access to political life has not immediately led to a high degree of political participation. Many obstacles other than the legal ones remain, and these keep the level of such activity among foreign citizens far below the average of the indigenous population.

References

Bäck, H. (1983) *Invandrarnas riksorganisationer* (The National Federations of Immigrants), Commission on Immigration Research (EIFO), no. 24, Stockholm.

Beune, H.H.M. and A.J.J. Hessels (1983) *Minderheid – Minder recht* (Minorities – Limited Rights?). The Hague: Staatsuitgeverij.

Bjorling, J. and G. Lindencrona (1955) *Utlänningslagen jämte dithörande författningar* (Aliens Act and Decrees). Stockholm.

Castles, S. and G. Kosack (1973) *Immigrant Workers and Class Structure in Western Europe*. London: Oxford University Press.

Claude, R.P. (1976) *Comparative Human Rights*. Baltimore, Md.: Johns Hopkins University Press.

Council of Europe (1979) *The Mass Media at the Service of Migrant Workers' Cultural Identity*. Strasbourg: Council of Europe.

Diskrimineringsutredningen (1984) *Om utlänningars rättsliga ställning* (The Legal Position of Aliens), DsA (6). Stockholm.

Dohse, K. (1981) *Auslandische Arbeiter und Buergerlicher Staat*. Konigstein Taunus: Anton Hain.

Easton, D. (1965) *A Systems Analysis of Political Life*. New York: John Wiley.

Grahl-Madsen, A. (1985) *Norsk fremmedret i stöpeskjeen. Et bidrag till debatten om ny fremmedlov* (Norwegian Aliens Legislation under Debate). Bergen: Universitets-forlaget.

Hirschman, A.O. (1970) *Exit, Voice and Loyalty*. Cambridge, Mass: Harvard University Press.

International Migration Review (1985) *Civil Rights and the Sociopolitical Participation of Migrants*, special issue (Autumn).

Jaakkola, M. (1983) *Sverigefinländarnas etniska organisationer* (The Ethnic Associations of Swedish-Speaking Finns), Commission on Immigration Research (EIFO), 22, Stockholm.

Madra, O. (1984) *Migrant Workers and International Law*, report to the General Secretary of the Council of Europe, Istanbul.

Marshall, T.H. (1964) *Class, Citizenship and Social Development*. New York: Chicago University Press.

Miller, M.J. (1978) *Foreign Workers in Western Europe: An Emerging Political Force*. New York: Praeger.

Ozsunay, E. (1983) *The Participation of the Alien in Public Affairs*. Strasbourg: Council of Europe.

Plender, R. (1983) *Introductory Report on 'Human Rights of Aliens in Europe'*. Strasbourg: Council of Europe.

Swedish Riksdag, Second Law Committee (1936) *Records of the Swedish Riksdag*, 53.

Tung, R.K. (1981) *Exit–Voice Catastrophes: Dilemma between Immigration and Participation*. Stockholm: Department of Political Science, Stockholm University.

Verbunt, G. (1985) 'France', in T. Hammar (ed.), *European Immigration Policy*. Cambridge: Cambridge University Press.

Wihtol de Wenden, C. (1984) 'The Evolution of French Immigration Policy', GRAMI working paper mimeo, Paris.

5

Immigrant Associations

Zig Layton-Henry

Studies of migrant workers have tended to concentrate on their lack of political rights and resources in the receiving countries of Western Europe. However, the ability to organise in autonomous associations to protect their interests, to mobilise support over issues of concern and to make representations to political authorities is an important political right and resource. The large-scale post-war migration to Western Europe has led to the creation of a plethora of immigrant associations in all the receiving European countries, and these have become important vehicles by which migrant workers participate in the political process. In some countries there is considerable concern that the creation of 'foreign' enclaves or ghettos in European states with their own organisational infrastructure will create unassimilable minorities which will cause unmanageable conflict in society. However, in spite of the fact that immigrant associations are founded in order to preserve the ethnic identity and culture of their members, inevitably they play a major role assisting in the contented settlement of their members, and encouraging active involvement in the host society. This apparent paradox of associations committed to the defence of ethnic culture and identity, at the same time contributing to security, involvement and integration in the wider host community, was one of the major findings of Eisenstadt's analysis of immigrant organisations in Israel (Eisenstadt, 1956). This paradox will be explained later in the chapter.

Most West European societies recognise the right of free speech and association for both citizens and non-citizens. In Britain these rights are unrestricted and are recognised both by custom and practice and in the common law. In most European countries custom and practice is reinforced by constitutional guarantees, as is the case, for example, in the Netherlands, Sweden and Germany. Only in Belgium and France have the rights of foreigners to organise been restricted, and in both cases these laws have recently been repealed. In France, before 1981, associations of foreigners had to have the permission of the Minister of the Interior before they could be established. French associations only needed to inform the ministry of their existence. In Belgium, before

1984, foreign citizens did not have the right to organise in associations, as three-fifths of the founding and active members of associations had to have Belgian nationality. This law was changed in July 1984, and now non-citizens can establish associations providing that three-fifths of the founding or active members reside in Belgium, have a residence permit and are registered on the population register.

The scale of post-war migration to the advanced industrial countries of Europe has been so great that some countries on the European periphery and the Third World lost significant proportions of their populations. Almost a tenth of the Portuguese population now live in France, a quarter of the Surinamese population live in the Netherlands and a seventh of the Cypriot population live in Britain. European countries now accommodate large populations of Caribbeans, Indians, Pakistanis, Africans, Arabs and other people particularly from Southern Europe and the Third World. The large numbers of migrants, their frequent lack of linguistic facility in the language of the receiving countries and their different customs and religions, encouraged them to create havens or enclaves in the host societies where they could relax, obtain assistance and continue the customs and practices of their own culture. Pakistani migrants to Britain in the 1950s and 1960s, for example, often had a poor command of the English language, difficulties in finding accommodation, practising their religion, finding traditional food, (especially halal meat) and even in obtaining up-to-date information about their home country. A network of associations and institutions was gradually established to serve the needs of a population which has now reached 397,000, of whom some 167,000 have been born in Britain (*Population Trends*, 1988). Restaurants, mosques, banks, newspapers, Qur'anic schools and cultural associations have been established in areas of Pakistani settlement, which to some extent reproduces in Britain the social context which used to shape their lives in Pakistan. In Birmingham, for example, there are 38 mosques serving a Pakistani population of 45,000. The Bank of Pakistan has established branches to handle accounts and arrange for remittances to be sent back to relatives in Pakistan. These institutions and associations have been expanded, reinforced and modified as migrant workers have become more settled and established and as family reunions occurred. Extended family and village networks have developed in Britain through chain migration (Anwar, 1979) and have been strengthened by the practice of the arranged marriage (Bhachu, 1985).

Similar processes have occurred in all the European countries where immigration has taken place. A plethora of immigrant associations have been established performing a wide range of functions and, directly or indirectly, contributing to the vitality, viability and resources of the various immigrant communities.

The range, scope and number of immigrant associations can be gauged by a few examples. A Swedish study of immigrant associations in 1973 found 846 such associations with an estimated membership of 75,000 (Jaakkola, 1987). These included 216 local Finnish societies with 54,000 members. By 1985 this had grown to 1,200 associations with a membership of 170,000 in a population which includes 400,000 aliens and an additional 350,000 naturalised Swedes. In 1982 it was estimated that there were 769 Portuguese associations in France and 322 Italian associations. The Italian associations were organised into 50 groups based on different regions in Italy. There were also 48 Italian radio stations. The membership of these local Italian associations was not high, being 30–45,000 in total (Campani et al. 1987). A survey of Spanish associations in Switzerland and the Netherlands found 177 associations among 100,000 Spanish immigrants in Switzerland and 124 associations among 24,000 Spanish immigrants in the Netherlands (Verdork et al., 1987).

In Britain the Commission for Racial Equality found 892 ethnic minority organisations in the Midlands and Wales (CRE, 1982). Sawyer and Fraser found 750 ethnic associations in Greater London (1988), while Coventry City Council found 132 in Coventry in 1986. If we consider the Muslim population in Britain there are 50 Muslim associations organised in a National Liaison Committee. Different Muslim groups are organised on an ethnic or national basis such as Pakistanis, Bangladeshis, Yemenis, Iranians, Kurds or Kashmiris. There are at least 143 mosques in Britain (Joly, 1987). Josephides found 70 Greek Cypriot associations in London serving a population of 90,000. These included seven Greek Orthodox churches, two private radio stations and a newspaper. Most associations were cultural or village-based, with youth clubs, community schools and community centres being the most important (Josephides, 1987). These examples only scratch the surface of a rich and thriving network of associations organised by numerous ethnic and national immigrant communities in the major immigration countries.

The First Phase of Migration: Temporary Labour Recruitment

The functions and activities of immigrant associations are strongly related to the phases of the migration process. In the first phase of migration most migrants are usually young male workers. These migrants have close ties with their homeland and are often supporting family and relatives there. They tend to work and live together with fellow nationals often from the same part of their country of origin.

Their needs are limited, as their main objective is to earn and save as much as possible and then to return home. The institutions they most patronise are cafés and social clubs. They are often very interested and involved in homeland political activities. It is not surprising therefore that homeland parties often make great efforts to organise such workers and play a prominent role in organising their leisure and social activities.

The Italian Communist, Socialist and Christian Democratic parties have all been active among Italian migrant workers and have established numerous branches in areas of Italian settlement abroad. Presumably the main aim of the parties is to maintain and expand their support on the assumption that the migrant workers will return and play an active role in homeland politics. The ability and willingness of Italian migrants to return home to vote in elections is an added incentive for the parties to organise and canvass their support.

In Britain similar activities can be found. The Greek Cypriot Communist Party has been very active amongst the large Greek Cypriot population in London. It organises a wide range of activities and is much more successful than its major competitor, the Conservative Democratic Party. It has its own centre and restaurant. Its social events are well supported and visiting Cypriot politicians are often entertained. However, the Cypriot Communist Party has only tenuous links with the British Communist Party and seems to perform social rather than political functions. Cypriot businessmen, for example, who employ non-union labour are prominent members (Josephides, 1987).

Homeland parties and politics have also been a strong feature of the Asian communities in Britain. Post-war migration rapidly created the largest overseas communities of Sikhs, Pakistanis and Bangladeshis in Britain and these communities provide considerable financial support for their homeland parties and are actively courted by politicians from the Indian sub-continent. All the major Indian parties have branches in Britain.

Major problems can arise between the sending and receiving countries when opposition groups mobilise support among migrant workers. Early Spanish migrant workers were often anti-Franco or influenced by refugees from Franco Spain. Spanish associations in France and Switzerland were often strongly opposed to the authoritarian regime in their homeland (Verdork et al., 1987). Miller cites several examples where revolutionary organisations committed to the violent overthrow of homeland regimes were active among foreign worker communities (Miller, 1981). There are many such organisations among Turkish migrant worker communities in Germany, both of the far right and the far left. Turkish groups, such as the extreme right-wing National Movement and its para-military youth section, 'the Grey Wolves', have been responsible for many violent attacks against Turkish leftists in Germany. The Croatian Oustachi has a long history of violent opposition to the Yugoslav state and has attempted to mobilise support among foreign worker communities. This has led to violent clashes within overseas Yugoslav communities as well as acts of terrorism against Yugoslav diplomats.

The activities of homeland opposition groups in the receiving countries is a major source of strain between the governments of the sending and receiving countries. Sending governments have made constant representations about opposition and terrorist activity organised among migrant workers in Western Europe. The Indian government, for example, has made many complaints to the British government about the activities of Sikh separatists in Britain. Also in 1984 an Indian diplomat was murdered in Birmingham by Kashmiri migrant workers who were members of the Kashmiri Liberation Front. Such activities cause some European governments to insist on the political neutrality of foreign citizens on their territory, but this is hard to enforce. It also leads homeland governments to take a strong interest in the communities established by their citizens overseas.

A number of governments have established homeland fraternal organisations among their citizens overseas, in addition to the extensive diplomatic and consular presence they maintain in the host countries. These fraternal organisations, like the Amicale de Algériens en Europe, perform a number of functions: they promote the homeland identity of migrants, publicise the policies of the homeland government, provide a vehicle for migrant workers to lobby their homeland governments and they may be recognised as the legitimate representative of the migrant community by the host state. Many sending governments fund these fraternal organisations for their emigrants overseas. Some of these, like the Moroccan Amicale, function almost as a kind of overseas political police force controlling the activities of Moroccan migrant workers and preventing the development of opposition political activity. At the other extreme the Italian government funds a wide range of Italian emigrant organisations, including trade union branches, party organisations and cultural associations. Some sending governments send teachers to receiving countries to encourage the development of the homeland national identity in the children of emigrant workers.

Another important influence among migrant workers is the influence of religious organisations from the homeland country. The Catholic Church has a widespread network of missions among migrant workers, and missionary priests have often sponsored thriving immigrant associations – for example, among the Italians, Portuguese and Spaniards in France, Italians, Croats and Spaniards in Germany and the Spanish and Italians in Switzerland. Similarly, wherever Turks, North Africans, Pakistanis and other Muslims have migrated, mosques and Qur'anic schools have been established. The Greek Orthodox Church has been active among Greeks in Germany and Greek Cypriots in Britain. Churches and other religious groups are not only active in the first phase of migration but when the second phase, that of family reunion, gets under way, they come to play an even more important role in establishing community schools, youth clubs and religious classes for the second generation. They may become important agencies for teaching the language and culture, as well as the religion of their community.

The Second Phase of Migration: Family Settlement

As temporary labour recruitment turns into permanent settlement under the impact of such factors as family reunion, immigration controls and the growth of a second generation born and educated in the host country, the functions and activities of immigrant associations change. While maintaining their interest in the home country and defending its language, religion and culture, they are forced to cater to the needs of an established and expanding community which is more settled and is establishing more links with the host community. In fact, the defence of the homeland culture and identity requires greater resources to be devoted to the second generation.

An increasing priority for the community as it becomes established is the education of the second generation. All European countries insist that all children must go to school once they reach five or six years of age, and for most immigrant parents this means the local state primary and secondary schools. Parents thus lose control of their children to an institution dedicated to teaching them another language, culture and value system. Inevitably, they acquire another identity which competes with the identity learnt at home. The younger generation may thus move away from the moral and cultural influence of their parents towards that of the host society and become less sure of their national identity.

Immigrant communities respond to this situation by establishing part-time community schools which attempt to preserve the language and culture of the immigrant community by teaching them to the second generation. The function of these schools is not only to preserve the language and national identity of the children but also to preserve the ethnic identity of the immigrant community itself. The transmission of the language is rightly regarded as crucially important. To have command of one's mother tongue proves one belongs to a national group and confers the ability to return to one's native country and to be reintegrated.

In all European countries immigrant communities have established Saturday schools or evening classes to teach the second generation, but these schools are only successful with children already fluent and at ease in their parents' mother tongue. The others cannot keep up and usually drop out. A good example of such problems is provided by the Qur'anic schools associated with mosques in Britain. Pakistani children were taught the tenets of Islam in Urdu, and only if their Urdu was poor was language teaching given too. However, recently Qur'anic schools have begun to teach Islam in English as young Britons of Pakistani origin are so much more at ease and literate in English. The burden of teaching both Urdu and Islam to the second generation is considered to be too great.

These sorts of problems have made mother-tongue teaching a major issue among immigrant groups. Parents face the danger that their children may lose their mother tongue or know both their mother tongue and language of the host community less than fluently. However, they may be worried that efforts to maintain the mother tongue will hold their children back academically at school. The wishes of the parents in respect of mother-tongue education may be crucially influenced by their views of themselves as either temporary migrants or permanent settlers. If they see themselves as temporary migrants, they may encourage immigrant associations to pressure homeland governments to send teachers to teach their children in their mother tongue. They may also campaign for mother-tongue education to be allowed in the regular state schools. To illustrate the importance of education in the mother-tongue for immigrant groups, it may be useful to examine the campaign by Finns in Sweden for this facility and to contrast this campaign with the dilemmas which have caused other immigrant groups to oppose it.

The Issue of Mother-tongue Education in Sweden

The lack of competence of Finns in the Swedish language has been a factor limiting the opportunities of Finns in Sweden. This has troubled Swedish policy-makers, who have been committed to the principle of equal opportunities for all, including non-citizens. In 1976 parents with a mother tongue other than Swedish received the right to request that their children be taught in their mother tongue. Since 1979 the mother tongue of immigrant groups has been increasingly used as the language of instruction for Finnish, Turkish and other ethnic minority children where the numbers of such children made the formation of such classes possible.

During 1981–2 Finnish societies all over Sweden were increasingly mobilising over the language issue. Some 63 Finnish societies delivered proposals to the authorities in different municipalities to improve the position of the Finnish language. When the budget cuts in 1982 threatened to limit the teaching of Finnish, a large demonstration was arranged in Sergel Square in Stockholm, and within a week more than 10,000 Finns had signed a petition supporting the teaching of Finnish. In addition there were school strikes in many areas organised by Finnish parents, the most notable being a two-month strike by schoolchildren in Stockholm. These strikes and the language campaign received considerable publicity in the media. The matter was even discussed at ministerial level between Sweden and Finland.

Finns in Sweden are in a particularly strong position to obtain concessions from the Swedish government on issues like multi-cultural education and instruction through the mother tongue. The Finns are by far the largest minority group in Sweden, and before 1809 Sweden and Finland were united in one country. Swedish is still an official language in Finland due to the existence of a small Swedish-speaking minority. Moreover, both countries are members of the Nordic Union, and Finns in Sweden are protected by the Nordic Cultural Agreement (1971), the free Nordic Labour Market and the Nordic Language Agreement (1981).

Finland is geographically close to Sweden, and travel between the two countries is efficient and cheap. This makes it easier for Finns in Sweden to regard themselves as temporary labour migrants rather than as permanent settlers. Moreover, the progressive policies of the Swedish government towards all immigrants under its immigration policy of 1975, and as shown by the granting of local and regional voting rights to foreign citizens, has given immigrant groups the political space and confidence to campaign for their rights and wishes. This confidence and these campaigns are not always welcomed by the political authorities who have encouraged this development. The Finnish parents' actions in organising the schools strikes were strongly condemned by Swedish politicians (Jaakkola, 1987).

The issue of mother-tongue education is being fiercely debated in all host countries in Western Europe. In France 40 percent of children of Portuguese migrants learn Portuguese at primary school with the help of teachers from Portugal. This falls to 20 percent for Portuguese secondary school children. Yugoslavia, Spain and Turkey send teachers to help educate the children of their overseas citizens. In Britain immigrant parents are divided and confused about the impact of mother-tongue teaching on the educational success of their children. In areas of recent settlement, instruction through the mother tongue might ease the transition from home and community to school and the wider society. Many surveys have shown that because Asians in Britain regard themselves as settlers and not as temporary migrants, fluency in English is highly valued. Nevertheless, the Commission for Racial Equality is favourably disposed towards teaching in the mother tongue.

Greek Cypriots in Britain provide an unexpected example of an immigrant group opposed to instruction in the mother tongue (Josephides, 1987). They are strongly attached to their community schools and are worried that mother-tongue teaching in state schools would undermine the *raison d'être* of their community schools. They fear that if this occurred their children would become even more quickly assimilated into British society. This is because community schools play an important role in reinforcing Cypriot identity for the second generation. The Cypriot High Commission in London supports the majority of Cypriot parents in their opposition to mother-tongue teaching for this reason.

It is clear that in the struggle to preserve the ethnic identity, language and culture of their children, immigrant parents are forced to become politically active in the host society. They have to organise community schools, lobby for mother-tongue teaching and specialist teachers from their home country. Thus, paradoxically, the desire to defend their ethnic identity and community forces them to participate more in the policy-making processes of the host community.

This process also occurs in other areas of community life. Immigrant associations quickly respond to requests from their members for help in solving accommodation, health and welfare problems. Advice centres are established to advise on taxation problems, entitlements to state benefits and problems relating to the immigration of relatives and friends. As the community becomes more settled, temporary arrangements become more permanent and legal. Planning permission is obtained for mosques, temples and churches which replace rooms in immigrant houses. Licences and legal status are obtained for businesses and clubs, and grants are sought for community centres and welfare agencies.

The Mediating and Bridging Roles of Associations

The success of migrant workers in establishing communities and developing an infrastructure of institutions and associations has helped to create the conditions for successful settlement and integration in the receiving societies. Associations initially established to preserve the culture, religion, language and ethnic identity of migrant groups, are inevitably, over time, drawn into closer contact with the institutions and authorities of the country of settlement.

This process can be illustrated by way of the typology shown in Figure 5.1.

Figure 5.1 *Typology of immigrant associations by orientation to country of origin and country of residence*

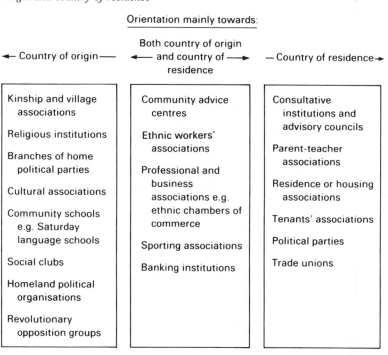

Orientation mainly towards:

← Country of origin —   ← Both country of origin and country of → residence   — Country of residence →

Kinship and village associations	Community advice centres	Consultative institutions and advisory councils
Religious institutions	Ethnic workers' associations	Parent-teacher associations
Branches of home political parties	Professional and business associations e.g. ethnic chambers of commerce	Residence or housing associations
Cultural associations		Tenants' associations
Community schools e.g. Saturday language schools	Sporting associations	Political parties
Social clubs	Banking institutions	Trade unions
Homeland political organisations		
Revolutionary opposition groups		

——————————————— Trend over time ———————————————→

The struggle by Finns in Sweden over the issue of the mother tongue illustrates how a campaign of cultural defence resulted in a high level of participation in Swedish politics by Finnish groups. In Britain, as the second generation enters the school rolls in ever-increasing numbers, immigrant parents are drawn into parent–teacher associations with non-immigrant members and are involved in campaigns and general education issues as well as lobbying local authorities over educational issues through their own associations. Issues such as the wearing of turbans in schools, the right of female Muslim pupils to wear modified uniforms and sports clothes and the need for multi-cultural education have mobilised immigrant parents. Muslim parents in particular have been concerned about religious education and single-sex schools.

The provision of welfare services is another area where closer contact and co-operation develops between immigrant associations and the national and local authorities. In most countries it is the municipal authorities which provide welfare services, and they provide a standard service to all residents which is well funded and professionally staffed. Immigrant associations initially provide an amateur voluntary service but gradually may demand some recognition and grants for their services. The local authorities may be willing to agree to this in order that a service is provided which is acceptable culturally and linguistically to the immigrant community. Cheetham argues that ethnic associations may now provide the only decent help available to some minority groups (1988).

In Britain, the Netherlands and Sweden where immigrant groups are able to vote in local elections there is a political pay-off for local authorities in providing subsidies to immigrant associations. The Greater London Council, before its abolition in 1984, made support for immigrant associations a major part of its political programme. Since 1984 similar policies have been pursued by London boroughs with large immigrant communities. In the Netherlands, before the local elections of 1986 a number of parties promised subsidies to Muslim organisations.

In Germany, autonomous migrant associations have to compete with three powerful German institutions which have traditionally provided welfare services for migrants. The secular/socialist Arbeiterwohlfahrt has concentrated on helping the Turks and Yugoslavs, the Protestant Innere Mission has helped the Greeks and the Catholic Caritas has provided welfare facilities for Catholic migrants such as the Italians, Spaniards, Portuguese and Catholic Yugoslavs. However, these migrant groups have gradually resisted this paternalistic arrangement and struggled to control the financial resources and provision of services themselves. Migrant representatives on local consultative institutions have increasingly been elected by migrant associations rather than being the selected nominees of the German welfare associations.

One consequence of official recognition and subsidies for immigrant welfare associations is increased co-operation with and regulation by local authorities. Grants and subsidies must be accounted for and the associations must provide a professionally acceptable service. The associations will be able to influence local authority policies but in turn become part of local authority provision. To some extent they are thus integrated into the local political system.

The Role of the State

The numbers, form and effectiveness of immigrant associations are greatly influenced by the laws, institutions and policy-making processes of the host society. Belgium and Sweden can be taken as contrasting cases. Until recently in Belgium foreign migrants were unable to establish autonomous associations, and this has limited the organisation and participation of migrants. Migrants have had to belong either to mixed associations such as church groups or welfare agencies or to Belgian-dominated associations like trade unions. This legacy has depressed membership in associations, with the exception of trade unions. An example of a mixed association aimed at encouraging integration is the Flemish Co-ordinating Committee on Migration which has an equal number of migrant representatives and Belgians. There is also a Flemish High Council for Migrants.

The Flemish and Walloon Regional governments subsidise migrant associations, especially those catering for the needs of the second generation. There are immigrant newspapers, which are dominated by the conservative Christian Labour Union. There have been two attempts to form national federations: (1) the Committee for the Co-ordination of the Organisations of Immigrant Workers, which covers the Brussels region; and (2) the Platform for Immigrant Associations which operates in Flanders and is subsidized by the Flemish Regional government. It has good access to decision-making institutions in Flanders.

Due to the tradition of restricting immigrant associations in Belgium the interests of migrant workers have been protected and promoted, to a greater extent than elsewhere, by the institutions of the homeland countries. Homeland parties, for example, have been active among migrant groups. However, the most important role has been taken by embassies.

By contrast, in Sweden the recognition that immigration was permanent led to the introduction of the New Immigration Policy in 1975. Since then the Swedish authorities have encouraged the formation of immigrant associations and their organisation into national federations. In the corporatist Swedish polity immigrant associations are not only seen as having an important role in protecting and promoting the interests of their members but also in giving legitimacy to policies which influence their members. Immigrant associations are consulted in the policy-making process in the same way as other representative groups in Swedish society. In the Swedish system relevant groups and associations must be consulted before legitimate policies can be formulated. The Swedish government has thus stimulated the formation of immigrant associations and provided them with funds partly in order to have representative immigrant associations to consult, bargain with and approve their policies. This encouragement has led to the creation of a large number of associations and greater political activity as immigrants have realised the importance of their role in the political process. The crisis over mother-tongue education has shown how the encouragement of immigrant political activity can have unexpected consequences.

   Considerable state funding at the local and national level has been made available to immigrant associations in Sweden, providing that they fulfil certain conditions. They must be democratically organised with a written constitution, have an elected governing board and an annual general meeting. Thirty national federations receive some SEK 18.4 million. They also receive an additional SEK 1.1 million from their homeland countries and raise about SEK 3.3 million themselves. Local immigrant associations receive subsidies of about SEK 13.5 million per year. This high level of subsidy has several dangers. It gives considerable resources to the leaders of immigrant associations without their having to involve their membership in fund-raising activities or without the need to recruit a large membership. Associations may be formed by a few people primarily in order to gain state subventions. There are complaints that these associations are top-heavy and also that local, regional and national associations have little contact with one another. There is also a considerable gulf between those who are members and the rest of the ethnic minority communities.

   At the local level, associations are organised on the basis of ethnicity or nationality, but at the national level there are three multi-national federations: the Immigrant Cultural Centre, the Immigrant National Federation and the International Federation of Immigrant Women. There are also two alliances of national federations: the Co-operating Immigrant Federation in Sweden, and the East European Alliance which is dominated by refugees from the Baltic states.

   The Dutch, like the Swedes, have encouraged the formation of autonomous immigrant associations. The Dutch government produced a Minorities Report in 1983 which argued that the activities of immigrant organisations played a valuable role in improving the position of ethnic minorities in the Netherlands. The Dutch government is responsible for encouraging and subsidising activities promoting ethnic minority interest and disseminating information about them. Ethnic minority associations, especially women's groups, are encouraged. Both the government and local authorities provide grants to immigrant associations. As foreign residents are now able to vote in local elections there is some competition between the parties to support and encourage immigrant associations.

   Some immigrant organisations have reacted to this official encouragement by seizing the opportunities to engage in politics on behalf of themselves and their communities. Turkish Muslim organisations in the Netherlands have gained considerable influence in a relatively short period. The Muslim leaders at national level are intelligent, fluent Dutch speakers and respected by their community. Dutch politicians are therefore willing to consult and negotiate with them. They are thus able to promote the interests of their community with considerable effectiveness.

There are a large number of national federations of immigrant groups in the Netherlands. Examples include the Federations of Surinamese Hindu organisations, Afro-Caribbean organisations, Antillean organisations and Democratic Mediterranean organisations. The Turks have three national federations covering sports organisations, socio-cultural organisations and Muslim organisations. The Moluccans are a very well-organised group in the Netherlands and they have an Advisory Council for Moluccans. Each of the major Moluccan organisations sends its own delegates to this council. At the local level Moluccan organisations have not been successful in influencing local government policies but the national body has been highly successful, so much so that the government wished to absorb it into a larger Minorities Advisory Council, but parliament vetoed this in 1985. The Minister of the Interior has now agreed to the formation of eight national Advisory Committees.

In Britain the state has reluctantly become involved in combating racial discrimination and disadvantage. The reasons for this are largely to do with the need to preserve social harmony and maintain law and order. The urban riots of 1981 and 1985 have encouraged both central and local government to provide resources, in addition to mainstream provision, for ethnic minority organisations and projects. Most of these funds are channelled through local authorities or government agencies like the Manpower Services Commission and the Commission for Racial Equality. In recent years many local authorities in areas of immigrant settlement have established posts for race relations officers to advise the authority on race relations, monitor equal opportunity policies and liaise with immigrant associations and groups. In London and other major cities a growing number of ethnic minority councillors have been elected to local authorities (Anwar, 1986).

There are a number of schemes which provide funds for ethnic minority organisations and projects: for example, the Urban Programme and the Inner City Partnership schemes. The Urban Programme involves an arrangement by which central government reimburses local authorities for 75 percent of their expenditure on approved projects. In 1981–2 there was £8 million available for the Urban Programme. This rose to £15 million in 1982–3 and £27 million in 1983–4. The money is available for a wide range of projects including Youth and Community Centres, support and advice groups, cultural and recreation projects, welfare centres, women's refuges and education and training projects for young people. Supplementary schools and training workshops run by minority groups have received grants. Also, although local authorities are reluctant to give money to religious groups, grants have been made to Hindu Community Centres, Sikh temples and Islamic Centres (CRE, 1979; Department of the Environment, 1984).

The Greater London Council was particularly active in making grants to ethnic minority organisations and in publicising its anti-racist policies. By defining ethnic minorities broadly – for example, by including the Irish – the Labour leadership in the GLC wished to raise its already high electoral support among these groups but in particular to raise their turn-out at elections. The abolition of the GLC means that support for ethnic minority associations will devolve on the London boroughs and, although they will have less resources, there will be political pressure in areas of immigrant settlement for the funding to continue, albeit at a reduced level.

One pressure on local parties and authorities to take account of ethnic minority needs is the fear that they might create their own political organisations outside the mainstream political traditions. There is plenty of evidence of a thriving network of organisations among immigrant communities, many of which are strongly political. Second-generation Bangladeshis in the East End of London, for example, have organised the Bangladesh Youth Movement, the Progressive Youth Organisation, the Bangladesh Youth Front and the Young Muslim Organisation. They have been joined by the Bangladesh Youth Approach and the Weavers Youth Forum in a Federation of Bangladeshi Youth Organisations to lobby over issues like housing, education, police accountability and racial attacks. In practice these organisations act as campaigning groups within the local political system rather than apart from it. They lobby for resources and changes in policy and work with the local Labour Party and the local authority, at the same time urging them to adopt more positive policies towards the Bangladeshi community (Carey and Shukur, 1986).

Ethnic minority associations in Britain tend to be less prominent at the national level. But organisations like the West Indian Standing Conference and the various Indian Worker Associations present evidence to parliamentary Select Committees, lobby government departments and enlist the political support of government agencies like the Commission for Racial Equality or the various organisations concerned with immigration matters. Now that four black members of parliament have been elected, these organisations may feel more confident about lobbying parliament.

Conclusion

Most states are concerned about the organisation and activities of non-citizens within their territory. This is primarily for reasons of security. Governments feel that the loyalties of non-citizens are primarily to other states and that in times of crisis well-organised groups of aliens may pose a threat to national unity and the national interest. Governments are also concerned that aliens may import the politics of their countries of origin into their countries of residence with damaging consequences to national security and international relations. Immigrants may be political refugees who wish to organise against the government of their home country. Traditional political loyalties and divisions may persist among immigrant communities and may lead to violence on the territory of the host country. Terrorism is also an ever-present threat in the contemporary world, and most governments fear that foreign nationals and perhaps members of immigrant communities are more likely to be involved in such activities than their own nationals, whose activities they can control more easily. For these reasons the ability of foreigners to organise in many European states has been subject to government regulation and licence.

However, as post-war immigration to Western Europe has turned into permanent settlement, governmental concerns about security have receded and the ability of foreigners to organise without restriction has become more widely accepted. This has in part been a recognition of what has actually happened. Post-war migration to Western Europe has resulted in the establishment of myriad immigrant associations which have emphasised the multi-cultural reality of contemporary European society. Concern has shifted to the role that immigrant associations play in delaying or preventing the integration and assimilation of immigrants into their new country of work and residence.

It has been the argument of this chapter that the long-term trend is for immigrant associations to play a positive role in assisting integration and aiding the contented settlement of immigrants. Gradually, as settlement takes place, immigrant associations are transformed from isolationist havens of ethnic and national cultures to active participants in the political processes of the host countries. The initial concerns with homeland politics and news, and preserving the religion and other cultural traditions of their members, are gradually widened to help members adjust to and be successful in their new country of residence. Immigrant associations play an important role in protecting the rights of their members in their new society. This will also assist their adjustment and integration.

The growth of the second generation of young people descended from immigrant parents exposes the dilemma facing immigrant associations. They wish to preserve the cultural, linguistic and national identities of the second generation, but this can only be achieved by increased involvement in the host society, especially in the political process, and will result in the associations and their members becoming more integrated. In order to influence the education of the second generation, to obtain grants for advice centres and planning permission for religious and community buildings, immigrant associations have become active participants in local and national politics. This involvement has often been encouraged by host society governments who wish to consult these associations about the implementation of policy and obtain their endorsement to legitimise their policies towards immigrant communities. They may also wish to use these associations to help in the administration of policy such as health and social welfare provision.

Organisations established by the second generation indicate this shift from an isolationist enclave to intense involvement. Youth associations often take the lead in demanding equal treatment, fair policing policies and grants for sporting and recreational facilities for immigrant communities. In Britain youth organisations have been prominent in resisting racial harassment and attacks.

Schoeneberg argues that whether ethnic associations have a predominantly segregationist or integrative effect will depend in large measure on the basic orientations and activities they offer to their members and on the position they take towards the rest of society (1985). This formulation underemphasises the crucial role of the state authorities and the attitude of the receiving society as a whole. Our survey of the role and activities of immigrant associations in Western Europe suggests that, whatever their attitudes and activities, whether positive or negative towards the host society, they assist in the contented integration and settlement of their members (Eisenstadt, 1956). The major factor which could lead to segregation and isolation would be discrimination and rejection by the authorities and population of the host society. However, even rejection and conflict may mobilise the immigrant population, force them to seek out allies in the host population and cause them to organise politically to defend their rights. They may be able to gain resources and support from their homeland government in their campaign. Conflict may force local and central government to intervene to restore social harmony. This is likely to involve some recognition of the rights of ethnic minorities and their associations. Paradoxically then, even associations which are opposed to integration and assimilation contribute in the long term to the integration of their members in the host society.

References

Anwar, M. (1979) *The Myth of Return: Pakistanis in Britain*. London: Heinemann.

Anwar, M. (1986) *Race and Politics: Ethnic Minorities and the British Political System*. London: Tavistock Publications.

Bhachu, P. (1985) *Twice Migrants: East African Sikh Settlers in Britain*. London: Tavistock Publications.

Campani, G., M. Cantani and S. Palidda (1987) 'Italian Immigrant Associations in France', in J. Rex, D. Joly and C. Wilpert (eds), *Immigrant Associations in Europe*. Aldershot: Gower.

Carey, S. and A. Shukur (1986) 'A Profile of the Bangladeshi Community in East London', New Community, 12, (3): 405–17.

Cheetham, J. (1988) 'Ethnic Associations in Britain', in S. Jenkins (ed.), *Ethnic Associations and the Welfare State*. New York: Columbia University Press.

Commission for Racial Equality (1979) 'Fund Raising: A Handbook for Minority Groups'. London: CRE.

Commission for Racial Equality (1982) *A Directory of Ethnic Minority Organisations in the Midlands and Wales*. London: CRE.

Coventry City Council (1986) 'Ethnic Minority Groups Register', Coventry City Council.

Department of the Environment (1984) *The Urban Programme: Tackling Racial Disadvantage*. London: HMSO.

Eisenstadt, S.N. (1956) 'The Social Conditions of the Development of Voluntary Associations: The Case of Israel', in R. Bachi (ed.), *Scripta Hierosolumitana*, 3: 104–25, Jerusalem, The Hebrew University.

Gitmey, A. and C. Wilpert (1987) 'A Micro-Society or an Ethnic Community? Social Organisation and Ethnicity among Turkish Migrants in Berlin', in J. Rex, D. Joly and C. Wilpert (eds), *Immigrant Associations in Europe*. Aldershot: Gower.

Hily, M. and M. Poinard (1987) 'Portuguese Associations in France', in J. Rex, D. Joly and C. Wilpert (eds), *Immigrant Associations in Europe*. Aldershot: Gower.

Jaakkola, M. (1987) 'Informal Networks and Formal Associations of Finnish Immigrants in Sweden', in J. Rex, D. Joly and C. Wilpert (eds), *Immigrant Associations in Europe*. Aldershot: Gower.

Jenkins, S. (ed.) (1988) *Ethnic Associations and the Welfare State: Services to Immigrants in Five Countries*. New York: Columbia University Press.

Joly, D. (1987) 'Associations among the Pakistani Population in Britain', in J. Rex, D. Joly and C. Wilpert (eds), *Immigrant Associations in Europe*. Aldershot: Gower.

Josephides, S. (1987) 'Associations among the Greek Cypriot Population in Britain', in J. Rex, D. Joly and C. Wilpert (eds), *Immigrant Associations in Europe*. Aldershot: Gower.

Miller, M.J. (1981) *Foreign Workers in Western Europe: An Emerging Political Force*. New York: Praeger.

Population Trends (1988). *Population Trends*, 46 (Winter 1986). London, HMSO.

Rex, J., D. Joly. and C. Wilpert (eds) (1987) *Immigrant Associations in Europe*. Aldershot: Gower.

Sawyer, P., and J. Fraser (1988) *Bridges: A Directory of African, Caribbean, Asian, Latin American and Mediterranean Community Groups in Greater London*. London Voluntary Services Council.

Schmitter, B.E. (1980) 'Immigrants and Associations: Their Role in the Socio-Political Process of Immigrant Worker Integration in West Germany', *International Migration Review*, 19 (3): 416–35.

Schoeneberg, U. (1985) 'Participation in Ethnic Associations: The Case in West Germany', *International Migration Review*, 19 (3): 416–37.

Verdork, A., S. Mancho, C. Peredo, M.A. de Prada, J.L. Recio, L. Seoane and R. van Soest, (1987) 'Spanish Immigrant Associations in the Netherlands and Switzerland and the Problem of Ethnic Identity', in J. Rex, D. Joly and C. Wilpert (eds), *Immigrant Associations in Europe*. Aldershot: Gower.

6

Consultative Institutions for Migrant Workers

Uwe Andersen

The Role and Significance of Consultative Institutions

If one considers the wide range of possible forms of political participation for migrant workers, then consultative institutions are a very special case. They are similar to voting rights in the sense that migrant workers may be able to elect representatives to a formally constituted body which can then press their views on policy-makers. However, they are not part of the normal democratic process, and while they have some legitimacy they have no power – only influence through argument and the size of their constituent groups. Further-more, because they are formally organised by local or regional authorities, who lay down the terms of reference and provide the finance and administrative facilities, consultative institutions are not as independent and unconstrained as the associations and organi-sations established by migrant workers themselves.

The term 'consultative institution' emphasises the two basic dimensions of these arrangements. First, they are a means by which decision-makers can take into account the views of people formally excluded from the democratic process because of their foreign nationality. They are also a means by which the special interests of particular groups, perhaps groups that are seen as articulate or disadvantaged, can be given due weight in the policy-making process.

However, as the term 'consultative' implies, the views or opinions expressed by these bodies are only advisory and do not have any legal or political force. Consultative institutions are thus a form of limited but guaranteed access to the political process. The term 'institution' implies that formal arrangements are necessary to ensure that migrant workers or ethnic minorities are consulted so that their particular problems can reach the policy-makers. The creation of a formal institution provides a recognised and legitimate channel for the groups to press their opinions and demands. They provide a formal or privileged channel to the decision-making process.

The role and value of consultative institutions are highly controversial both in the arena of public debate and in the academic literature. These debates vary between different European countries and within countries over time, but on the whole five major positions can be distinguished, three in favour of consultative institutions and two against. These are summarised in Figure 6.1.

Figure 6.1   *Attitudes towards consultative institutions*

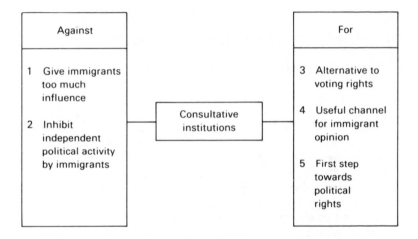

Those who oppose consultative institutions from positions 1 and 2 do so for very different reasons. Adherents of position 1, often those on the right, are strongly opposed to the granting of special facilities either to foreign migrant workers or to ethnic minorities. They insist that no political rights should be granted to non-citizens and that if they deserve to participate in political decision-making, they should become naturalised citizens. They are also opposed to special arrangements for ethnic minorities, whom they argue should be treated on the same basis as the majority and should not have the benefit of positive discrimination.

Supporters of position 2 argue that consultative institutions are a gift without value for migrant workers. They provide the appearance of political participation but in reality it is a privilege without substance as migrant workers have not had to struggle to establish these institutions. They are a means of co-opting and stifling migrant workers' demands, and they inhibit the establishment of independent organisations and genuine political activity. In Katznelson's terms (1973), they are a form of buffer institution that deflects migrant workers' demands away from the major arenas of political decision-making. The leaders of immigrant communities are co-opted into institutions financed and controlled by local authorities and are thus deflected from direct political action to less important forms of political activity.

The opponents of consultative institutions tend to be in the minority. On the whole, they are considered to be worthwhile arrangements, but their supporters also disagree about why they are valuable. The most controversial area is their relationship to voting rights. But one can view consultative institutions as a valuable political arrangement quite independently of voting rights, as in position 4. Consultative institutions may also be seen as useful for groups with particular problems even when they have the vote. For example, they have been used for groups with special needs such as elderly or disabled people, and in West Germany they were established for displaced persons from the former German eastern territories after the Second World War. In Britain they have been used to articulate the views of ethnic minority communities, even though these recent immigrants did have voting rights.

A common feature seems to be that they are set up on behalf of groups that are regarded as poorly organised or powerless so that they need special arrangements if they are to influence the decision-making process. Consultative institutions can thus be seen as a form of positive discrimination or compensation for lack of power.

On the other hand, consultative institutions may be seen as necessary to allow foreign citizens access to policy-making arenas precisely because they are excluded from voting in local and national elections. In this case, they are an alternative to voting rights that are not necessary for citizens. It is the growth of large communities of non-citizens in European countries that has brought about the need for special arrangements for consultation.

In contrast to this view, supporters of position 5 see consultative institutions as a means of encouraging migrants to participate in the political process as a step on the way to full participation through voting. It is thus important to distinguish the *raison d'être* for establishing consultative institutions when analysing their functions and effectiveness. These questions will be considered again in the conclusion.

Consultative Institutions in the Seven Project Countries

Although all the countries included in our study use consultative institutions for the participation of migrant workers in some form, the situation varies very markedly between one country and another.

Moreover, since most consultative institutions function at the level of the local community, there may be important differences even within these countries, despite the common political and constitutional arrangements. While on the one hand this situation offers good opportunities for comparative research, on the the other hand it makes it difficult to collect all the available information about the diverse nature of consultative arrangements. This chapter will therefore provide an outline of the various arrangements and the functions in the project countries, in order to provide a basis for further analysis.

The countries most strongly identified with consultative institutions for the participation of migrant workers are Belgium and West Germany. Belgium was the first country to establish municipal advisory councils. In 1968, two Walloon communities, Cheratte and Flemalle-Haute, established advisory councils for migrant workers, and by 1975 the number had risen to 29. By then, however, a debate had begun which challenged the functions and value of these institutions. In the wake of this debate, many of these advisory councils were abolished. Ironically, the first to be closed down was the advisory council in Cheratte, the first to be established. There is now considerable disillusionment surrounding the few consultative institutions which still function at local community level.

Belgium has also experimented with consultative institutions at the regional and national levels. Since 1982, there have been two regional consultative institutions. These are the Vlamse Hoge Raad voor Migranten in Flanders, and the Conseil Consultatif des Immigrés de la Communauté Française for Wallonia and Brussels. These were preceded by national consultative arrangements, the latest of which, the Counseil Consultatif de l'Immigration, was established in 1973.

In West Germany, consultative institutions for the participation of migrant workers have become very common at the local level. According to a survey in 1983, nearly 40 percent of local communities had some form of advisory councils and the total number can be estimated at about 300. There were two periods when large numbers of consultative institutions were established – 1972–5 and 1980–1. In contrast to some other countries, there is no consultative institution for migrant workers at the federal level in West Germany. The Ausländerbeauftragte, a kind of benevolent ombudsman for migrant workers, is appointed by the federal government without the involvement of migrant workers. Even at the state level, there is only one very weak consultative body in Bavaria, although some states have duplicated the Auslanderbeauftragte at the regional level. West Germany therefore combines extensive use of consultative institutions for migrant workers at the local level with almost none at regional or national levels. This arrangement considerably weakens the influence of migrant workers.

In Switzerland, with its very high percentage of foreign migrant workers, there is extensive use of consultative institutions, especially in the larger cities, and there are about 20 consultative bodies in existence. These function at local, cantonal and federal levels. At the federal level, the Eidgenossische Kommission fur Auslanderprobleme was created in 1970.

Consultative institutions have existed in some municipalities in France since 1971. These are the Conseils Consultatifs Communaux d'Immigrés (CCCI). These arrangements were encouraged in 1983 when the national government recommended that such extra-municipal bodies should be established whenever this seemed useful. At the national level, the Conseil National des Populations Immigrés was set up by the Ministry of Labour in 1984.

In contrast to the situation in the countries already discussed, most migrant workers in Great Britain, the Netherlands and Sweden have the right to vote, at least at the level of their local authorities. Nevertheless, there exist consultative institutions in these countries too. In Great Britain, local authorities had by 1967 already established 47 Community Relations Councils, and at national level had set up the Community Relations Commission. By 1985 there were 102 such bodies jointly financed by local authorities and the Commission for Racial Equality. The CRE was created in 1976 as the successor to both the Community Relations Commission and the Race Relations Board. Its main functions are to promote good race relations and to enforce the anti-discrimination provisions of the Race Relations Act (1976).

In the Netherlands, Articles 61 and 62 of the Gemeentewet enable local communities to establish consultative institutions, a facility widely used by large city authorities. In 1976, at the national level, a consultative council was established for the Moluccans, a refugee ethnic group which was having considerable difficulty in adjusting to life in the Netherlands. This was partly because of their commitment to returning to an independent republic of the South Moluccas, despite the remoteness of such an eventuality. In 1985, the Dutch parliament approved a law allowing consultative councils to be established for eight additional groups. These are mainly national or ethnic groups, although there is one for official refugees and asylum-seekers. In addition, there is an integrated council to which all the others send representatives.

A wide variety of different types of consultative institutions exist in Sweden in those communities with significant numbers of migrants.

About a third of local communities have such arrangements. There is a whole network of these consultative institutions at local, regional and national levels, and this places a considerable burden on immigrant representatives.

An examination of the position of consultative institutions in the various countries reveals that an important factor is the relationship between these institutions at different levels of government. This relationship is greatly influenced by the degree of centralisation in any particular country. Generally, consultative institutions are hierarchically organised and highly centralised. In Britain, for example, the national body, the CRE, initiates the establishment of local Community Relations Councils, provides half the funding, and supervises the appointment of full-time staff. If a local Community Relations Council acts beyond its terms of reference, then either the local authority or the CRE can close it down by withdrawing its funds. In effect, both can exercise a veto on the Community Relations Council's activities.

On the whole, consultative institutions at the local, regional and national levels are not linked closely together. The members are recruited from the main immigrant associations, although sometimes membership is so wide that individuals may be able to gain a place as a representative by establishing 'bogus' organisations. The pattern of selection tends to emphasise the ethnic orientations of the different groups and this may discourage co-operation between national or ethnic minorities. The case of the Netherlands is a good example. The Moluccans opposed the establishment of a general advisory council for all migrant workers because they were so pleased with the success of their own Advisory Council for Moluccans. The Dutch government responded to the success of the Moluccan experiment by encouraging the establishment of a general immigrant advisory council, as well as advisory councils for the major ethnic and national groups.

The system of selecting representatives would need to be changed in order to achieve a more integrated system of consultative institutions which would be more representative of ethnic and national minorities as a whole. At present, the general rule is for representatives to be nominated by immigrant associations. If they were elected on a wider basis, then the general interests of migrant workers as a whole might be better represented. In West Germany, there have been efforts to create associations, including a number of different consultative institutions, with the aim of co-ordinating their activities and exerting greater political pressure on the state and federal governments. Such amalgamations have occurred in Hesse, Lower Saxony and North-Rhine Westphalia. Such an approach might help to make migrant workers more aware of their common problems and overcome the rigid ethnic and national orientations of the various groups.

The Raison d'Etre of Consultative Institutions

How can the widespread existence of consultative institutions be explained in the seven countries that we are examining? In some countries, it seems largely to be a matter of the political culture. Sweden is a convincing example. Here, consultation with groups affected by government policy is so much a part of its 'corporatist' policy-making process that the government will encourage the establishment of groups and help to fund them where they do not already exist, so that the government can then consult them about relevant policy matters. Corporatist styles are so strong in Sweden that although local and regional voting rights have been granted to foreign residents, consultative procedures are still widely used and are seen as a necessary supplement to voting rights, rather than as an alternative form of political participation.

In other countries – for example, West Germany – it is the lack of voting rights that is used as the major justification for the establishment of immigrant consultative institutions. The existence of consultative institutions can then be used to justify opposition to granting local voting rights because, it can be argued, immigrants have an alternative means of influencing local decision-making. West Germany also has some experience of advisory councils for disadvantaged or under-privileged groups. In Britain it was widely believed that certain groups of immigrants (non-white colonials) would face racial dis-crimination, particularly in the housing and employment markets, and this justified the establishment of local committees to encourage racial harmony and provide immigrants with special access to local decision-makers.

Financial support from the government is an important factor encouraging local communities to establish consultative institutions for immigrants. This means has been used in Sweden, the Netherlands and Britain and, for a time, by the West German state government of North-Rhine Westphalia.

Two further interconnected factors associated with the creation of consultative institutions are the size of the immigrant population and the size of the community. In West Germany, the existence of consultative institutions was, not surprisingly, associated with the percentage of migrant workers within a community. However, the size of the community itself was an even more important factor, as Table 5.1 shows.

Table 6.1   *The existence of consultative institutions for migrant workers by size of community in West Germany*

Consultative institutions	All (%)	By size of community (000s)			
		10–20	20–50	50–100	Over 100
Yes	38.3	8.2	41.1	60.6	93.6
No	61.7	91.8	58.9	39.4	6.4
N=	420	147	158	66	47

This clearly demonstrates that consultative institutions for migrant workers are more widely used in the larger municipalities. This is not only because migrant workers are concentrated in these areas, but also because large municipalities have the manpower and the organisational and financial resources to encourage and negotiate with these bodies. They have greater experience of consultative institutions and a decision-making structure which enables them to deal with such bodies. The problems of migrant workers in large cities are also likely to be more acute, and the pressure to respond to them before crises arise is much greater. Thus, underlying the creation of consultative institutions is the fear that, if parts of a community are excluded from the decision-making process, then alienation and resentment may grow and this may lead to serious problems in the future, such as the inner-city riots in Britain in 1981 and 1985.

Types of Consultative Institutions

A number of basic types of consultative institution can be distinguished among the great variety of forms these arrangements can take.

Contact and co-ordination groups
The British Community Relations Councils are a good example. Their characteristics are their great flexibility of structure, the inclusion of all groups interested, both native and immigrant, their limited competence, and their broad remit to improve the relations between immigrant workers and the native population within the community.

Working and co-ordination groups
These are a variation of the first type, and occur particularly in West Germany (*Arbeits- und Koordinierungskreise*). Their distinctive feature is that their composition is highly unbalanced, with too few members who are migrant workers. Their membership consists of representatives of all administrative departments and other organisations that are involved in migrant workers' affairs. In most cases, the only migrant workers who are members are social workers nominated by their employers, the large welfare agencies. Emphasis is on sharing

information, co-ordinating activities and improving practical work
with migrants. Working and co-ordinating groups are often accused of
behaving in a paternalistic way and of assuming that they know what is
best for migrant workers.

Parliaments of migrant workers
The membership of this third type of consultative institution is
confined to migrant worker representatives. Their main function is to
articulate the interests of migrant worker communities and press for
the relevant policies to be implemented. However, they tend to be
divorced from the normal decision-making processes of the community. In West Germany, the few parliaments of migrant workers all
failed because of their political isolation, and also because of intense
conflicts between the different groups represented in the parliament.

Advisory councils
Advisory councils are the most common form of consultative body.
They exist in a variety of institutional settings and usually consist of
representatives of both migrant workers and members of the municipal
council. Sometimes representatives of other native institutions will
also be included, such as trade unions, political parties and the
churches. Advisory councils are well integrated in the decision-making
process, because they are recognised as the legitimate arena for
migrant workers' demands. Sometimes – for example, in Belgium and
also in some parts of Hesse – the position of migrant worker
representatives is strengthened by reserving voting rights in councils
for them. This allows contact and discussion between a wide variety of
organisations while ensuring that the councils primarily articulate the
interests of migrant workers. It avoids the danger of the parliamentary
form, that the advisory councils will become politically isolated. An
important feature of advisory councils is that they usually have a
formal constitution specifying their aims, functions, composition and
structure.

Committees on migrant affairs
Municipal councils may establish their own committees on migrant
affairs. These committees are different from the other consultative
institutions in that they may be able to take executive decisions. They
are thus in a potentially stronger position than is usual in the local
decision-making process. One drawback is that migrant workers on
these committees tend to be in a small minority and are dependent on
the readiness of the political parties on the municipal councils to
select them. Such committees exist in the 13 largest municipalities in
Sweden and in a few West German cities such as Wolfsburg and

Stuttgart. In West Germany, only the state laws of Baden-Wurttemberg, Lower Saxony and, since 1984, North-Rhine West-phalia, allow the co-option of expert *inhabitants* rather than expert *citizens*, thus permitting the selection of foreign migrant workers as expert advisers.

Sometimes consultative institutions differ so much that they can be used in combination. For example, the West German state government of North-Rhine Westphalia recommended that its local communities should establish both a working and co-ordinating group, and an advisory council. However, the communities felt that the suggestion was impracticable and did not act upon it. Another strategy is to combine an advisory council with a municipal committee on migrant workers' affairs, in which migrant workers participate as expert advisers who are nominated by the advisory council and provide the link between the advisory council and the municipal authority.

The Aims and Scope of Consultative Institutions

The aims of consultative arrangements are generally regarded as being, first, to improve the relationships between migrant workers and the native population, and, second, to establish a channel of communi-cation linking foreign migrants to the political system. They are expected to provide expert information about the foreign communities they represent, and expert knowledge on the views of their communities to policy initiatives. They are expected to inform local political leaders about problems worrying these communities, and to suggest remedies. Consultative institutions also act as a forum where representatives of the various immigrant associations meet so that activities and information can be co-ordinated and disseminated among the communities which otherwise may have little contact with one another.

Members of the local political system may regard consultative institutions as useful sounding boards for their policies, a means of disseminating information to the immigrant communities, and a means of discovering representatives from those communities with whom they can negotitate and whom they can integrate into the political process.

However, the value of these institutions largely depends on how representative they are of the immigrant communities. This is a matter of considerable controversy which is linked to the ways in which the members of these consultative institutions are selected. It is thus worthwhile examining in more detail the selection and composition of consultative institutions.

Selection and Representation

Among the most controversial aspects of consultative institutions are the arrangements by which the members of such bodies are chosen. These arrangements vary enormously, even within a single country. In West Germany, for example, a survey by Kevenhorster (1974) found that one-third of the advisory councils, which were supposed to represent foreign immigrants, had no foreign members at all. At the other extreme, Nuremberg allowed the direct election of foreign representatives from the local foreign population. Generally, foreign members of advisory councils are nominated because they are thought to be representatives of their communities. In West Germany, probably the commonest arrangement is for the nominations to be made by the city council, local representaties of the German trade-union federation, or organisations concerned with the social welfare of immigrants. These latter organisations, like Caritas and others, are attached to the major denominations of the Christian Church. In cities such as Stuttgart, Dortmund and Ulm, the welfare and trade-union organisations control the selection of foreign worker participants. In some German states such as Baden-Württemberg and Lower Saxony, foreign workers can be co-opted on to local government committees as expert advisers.

What is striking about advisory councils in West Germany is the wide variety of German officials who are allowed to sit on them. Even though these councils were created to facilitate foreign worker representation, the majority of council members are German (Miller, 1981). These include representatives of the local authorities, the trade unions, the churches and welfare organisations. Occasionally, voting rights may be limited to the foreign migrants' representatives, as in Wiesbaden in Hesse, but this is unusual. Normally, it is the German representatives who dominate these advisory councils, and often the mayor or a local councillor will take the chair.

At the state level, representation is similar, with representatives being included from the state government, the political parties, both sides of industry and the welfare organisations. There are very few foreign worker representatives. Sometimes officials from local consulates or embassies are invited to advise or represent foreign worker communities. At the federal level in West Germany it is the Ministry of Labour which is most involved in matters concerning foreign workers, and a number of groups have been established to co-ordinate matters relating to foreign workers.

In Switzerland, consultative institutions for foreign workers exist at local, cantonal and federal level. As in West Germany, these advisory councils include representatives from a wide variety of organisations, including Swiss political parties, churches, school officials, trade unions, employees' associations and delegates from foreign worker associations. Their role is to make policy recommendations to the cantonal governments on questions concerning foreigners, and also to act as mediators between the Swiss political authorities and the foreign worker community. Occasionally these consultative institutions become a matter of political controversy, as in Valais, when Italian diplomats were included as delegates from immigrant associations. This led to accusations by local Swiss of foreign interference in Swiss internal affairs (Miller, 1981).

There were no advisory councils or aliens' parliaments in France before 1975, as this was thought to be forbidden by the rule that foreigners should be politically neutral, but there have been many experiments since then. Most prefects have established advisory bodies on foreign labour questions, and foreign worker representatives are invited to give advice and policy recommendations to various national bodies such as the Advisory Council of the Office of National Immigration, the Social Action Fund Advisory Council, and the Socio-economic Council. Trade-union, church and welfare organisations which have full members on these bodies are expected to represent the views of foreign migrant workers.

In Belgium, the Netherlands and parts of West Germany, direct elections are often used to select foreign worker representatives on advisory councils. In West Germany, the number of cases where this occurs has grown to one-fifth of consultative institutions and is still growing. Frequent objections are the high costs of organising such elections and the low turn-out of foreign residents.

Turn-out has varied considerably in different communities – in Belgium, from an astonishing 70 percent in Cuesmes to a low of 10 percent in Courcelles. In West Germany it has ranged from 55 percent in Sindelfingen to 8 percent in Neu-Isenburg, with an average of 25 percent. In the Netherlands, turn-out has tended to be highest in the first elections, perhaps due to novelty and high expectations which fall as the advisory councils achieve only modest results. Organisation and publicity may also be higher in the first elections. Turn-out is also higher when competing factions within an ethnic community vie for representation and mobilise their supporters.

Inter-ethnic rivalry often leads to accusations by native spokesmen that 'homeland' politics are being allowed to intrude into the host country. There is great concern when groups such as the Moroccan Amicales or the Turkish 'Grey Wolves' – both of which are regarded as undemocratic and extreme organisations – attempt to get their members elected. There have been cases of such people being excluded from consultative institutions in West Germany, even though they have been elected. In the Netherlands, there has been concern about the role of undemocratic organisations mobilising support among immigrant communities. The problem of representation is at the heart of the role of consultative institutions. The dominant view is to regard them as a forum for discussion and communication between leaders of the local community and leaders of foreign worker communities, and therefore most members are co-opted, indirectly elected or even self-elected. The migrant workers who are selected are usually professional people such as teachers or social workers who mediate between the local authorities and their communities. These institutions are not allowed to become the focus for militant demands by political groups.

Conclusion

It is remarkable that all seven countries examined in this book have established consultative institutions for immigrant communities. This has been true even where the major immigrant groups have local voting rights, as in Britain, Sweden and the Netherlands. In Germany, Belgium, Switzerland and France, such consultative institutions were justified on the grounds that foreign immigrant communities were excluded from the local and national decision-making process. However, even where migrants have the vote, their influence may be limited by their minority position or because of the very limited powers of local authorities.

Evaluating the success or failure of such insititutions is extremely difficult. In some areas they may work well because of the limited aspirations of the foreign immigrant communities and the conciliatory attitude of local politicians. In Neuchâtel in Switzerland, where foreign residents have the right to vote in local elections, very few bother to do so. Swiss officials have interpreted this as an argument for regarding consultative institutions as a better means of foreign worker parti-cipation than the granting of full local voting rights (Miller, 1981). In Britain, on the other hand, Community Relations Councils have been regarded as of very limited value compared with full voting rights. Community Relations Councils have been seen as a distraction, diverting the energies of ethnic minorities into constrained, conser-vative channels and away from more influential and vigorous forms of political activity. There is much greater interest and awareness in the black community concerning the Campaign for Black Sections in the Labour Party than there is concerning the local Community Relations Councils. This does not mean that the local Community Relations Councils do not perform some valuable functions. They often do useful work in monitoring local problems such as the incidence of racial harassment, and in negotiating with local institutions – for example, the police and the local authority. They also provide a forum for local immigrant associations to come together with representatives of the local authority, local institutions and other influential groups.

Nevertheless, these local consultative institutions in all the project countries are confined to an outsider position in the local political process. They can raise issues and make requests but have limited power to pressure local parties and decision-makers. They are often confined to providing information for the local authority and legitimating its policies by being available for consultation, even though this may not result in any significant input into the context of policy. The 'rules of the game' for consultative institutions are that a modest role in the local political system requires that representatives of migrant workers accept the limited role assigned to them. Their demands are thus easily compromised or refused.

Concern about the lack of democratic selection procedures for immigrant representatives and the problems of informing immigrant communities about the work of consultative institutions has also led to a growing disillusionment about their value. This has led to a greater interest in extending to long-term foreign residents the same political rights as to the rest of the population, including voting rights. This will be the central concern of the next chapter.

References

Katznelson, I. (1973) *Black Men, White Cities.* London: Oxford University Press.
Kevenhorster, P. (1974) *Ausländische Arbeitnehmer in politischen System der Bundesrepublik.* Opladen: Westdeutscher Verlag.
Miller, M. (1981) *Foreign Workers in Western Europe: An Emerging Political Force.* New York: Praeger.

7

Voting Rights

Jan Rath

The rights to vote and to run for office are perhaps the most important of all political rights, and are considered basic prerequisites in any true democracy. But of all political rights, voting rights are also the most strictly linked to citizenship: *ipso iure*, non-citizens are excluded from the franchise in most countries. Only through naturalisation, then, can non-citizens take part in elections.

The anomalous situation that a large group of foreign residents is excluded from regular decision-making procedures creates a challenge to West European democracy since, according to its conception of democracy, policy-making should be done by people who reflect and represent the whole population.

Individual countries of Western Europe have reacted differently to this challenge. Some, such as the Netherlands, Eire and the Nordic countries, have granted foreign citizens the right to vote at the local level and sometimes (as in the Nordic case) at regional level too. In other countries, there is mounting political debate about what needs to be done. Britain, France and the Netherlands are special cases because many of their immigrants from former colonies are considered to be nationals with full voting rights.

On the other hand, some immigrants have the right to take part in elections in their homeland (Miller, 1981, 1987). Dutch, Finnish and Portuguese emigrants, for example, have the right to absentee ballots for parliamentary elections in their home countries, Moroccan emigrants can participate through consular agencies in Moroccan referendums, and Italian emigrants have special facilities to travel to their home towns to participate in Italian elections. However, although the many branches of homeland political parties are interesting phenomena that have an impact on immigrants' political life, the subject of this chapter is the debate on voting rights for immigrants in host country elections, and how immigrants, whatever their citizenship, use the rights they have.

Electoral Legislation

We examine first the situation in countries without immigrant voting rights, and then the situation in the other countries.

In most European countries – Belgium, West Germany, France, Italy, Luxemburg, Portugal, Spain and Switzerland – foreign residents do not have the right to vote or to run for office in local, regional or national elections (Commissie van de Europese Gemeenschappen, 1986), although there are minor exceptions to this general rule. For example, Brazilian immigrants in Portugal have voting rights because of the historical ties between the two countries.

Switzerland

The most peculiar exception to the general rule is perhaps Switzerland (Debely, 1986; EKA, 1982), whose federal constitution leaves the regulation of local voting rights to cantonal constitutions. In Neuchâtel canton, foreign residents have had the franchise in communal elections since 1849 (with a brief interruption between 1861 and 1874), and in the recently created Jura canton since 1979. Immigrants in both cantons must fulfil the conditions of a minimum period of stay. None of the other 23 cantons have granted voting rights to foreign residents, although a few, such as Aargau, Bern, Geneva, St Gallen, Solothurn, Vaud and Zurich, have considered but rejected the idea. The federal constitution excludes non-Swiss citizens from participation in the more important federal electoral arrangements such as referendums (Grisel, 1982) and, since constitutional amendments are decided by referendum, voting rights are unlikely to be extended. At present there is hardly any debate on the subject, although associations of Italian and Spanish immigrants have pressed for more political rights.

Belgium

In Belgium, there has been no move to extend voting rights to foreign residents, though the claim for voting rights goes back to the early 1970s, with a number of bills proposing the enfranchisement of non-national residents at the local level. The first was introduced in 1972 by the Communist member of parliament Levaux, and this was followed by at least nine other proposals from various socialist MPs over the period 1974–87, but none of these bills passed. Political pressure intensified in the early 1980s, especially before the 1982 local elections, when various organisations (particularly the trade unions) and the Belgian bishops took up the cause of immigrant voting rights. In addition, two committees – Objectif '82 for the French-speaking community and Stemrecht '82 (Voting Rights '82) for the Dutch-speaking community – began promoting the idea among the Belgian public and politicans, uniting individuals and associations (both native Belgian and immigrant organisations) in support of the campaign.

Neither the legislative initiatives in parliament nor the grassroots political campaign succeeded in introducing local voting rights. The only positive result was an increase in political consciousness, particularly among second-generation immigrants. The advocates of voting rights have not been discouraged by their lack of success; on the contrary, they have redoubled their efforts. Stemrecht '82 has become Stemrecht '88 and Objectif '82 has become Objectif '88. Initially it was mainly Belgians in sympathy with the goal of equal political rights who organised the campaign: now, second-generation immigrants have taken the lead. At the same time, the campaign is much more deeply rooted in immigrants' associations. It remains to be seen whether this has a better chance of success, as there are still many obstacles to overcome.

For a long time, the debate concerned whether or not the constitution needed to be changed. Article 4 Paragraph 2 ordains that the right to vote or to run for office is reserved for Belgian citizens only, but Article 108 of the same constitution specifying the powers of provinces and municipalities is less clear. According to one interpretation, a simple alteration of the electoral laws would do, but according to another – now the most widely accepted – a constitutional amendment is necessary.

Another important obstacle is specifically Belgian: the fear that the ethnic vote might disturb the equilibrium between the Flemish- and French-speaking communities. In particular, Flemings in Brussels are afraid that their already disadvantaged position would be further undermined because the French-speaking parties would benefit disproportionately from the enfranchisement of foreign residents.

The opinions of political parties diverge (ACV, 1986; Boukhriss 1988). The small, radical, left-wing parties and recently also the Flemish ecological party Agalev support the enfranchisement of all non-national residents. The Walloon Socialist Party (PS) and the Walloon ecological party (Ecolo) want to grant voting rights to citizens from EC member states only. In the past, the Christian Democratic parties and the Flemish Socialist Party (SP) were in favour of extending voting rights to non-citizens, but they have now changed their position: the Flemish CVP and PS have dropped the idea and the Walloon PSC at most want to grant voting rights to EC citizens. The liberal parties and the 'language parties' oppose any enfranchisement: the liberals are in favour of stimulating naturalisation. In short, there is no political majority for enfranchisement in parliament.

As regards the trade unions, both Socialist and Christian Democratic federations, ABVV and ACW, support enfranchisement. It is commonly believed that the idea of extending voting rights to foreign residents is unpopular among Belgians, and although opinion polls neither confirm nor deny this, some political parties have tried to win electoral support through anti-immigrant platforms. In such a political climate, it is unlikely that the government (currently of both Christian Democratic and Socialist parties) will introduce a bill on voting rights.

France
The political climate in France is similarly unfavourable. According to Article 3, Paragraph 4 of the constitution, only French citizens have the right to vote or to stand as candidates. This has not always been the case, as the constitution of 24 June 1793 did permit voting rights to foreigners (Verbunt, 1985), but nowadays a more restrictive constitution is in force. This was highlighted during the presidential elections of 1974 by the candidacy of the non-eligble immigrant Djelali Kamal: at the time, immigrants were still expected to respect the French tradition that aliens observe strict political neutrality.

For a short time it seemed that this situation would change. In the period before the presidential elections of May 1981, the Socialist Party (PS) promised to enfranchise immigrants in local elections and, when François Mitterrand was elected, the PS was committed to act. The government therefore introduced a bill in parliament and it was expected that immigrants would participate in the 1983 local elections. However, things turned out differently: French public opinion and the CGT unions reacted against the legislation, the conservative parties were against, the French Communist Party (PCF) refused to endorse the bill and there was no majority in the senate. The socialist government therefore dropped the idea (Miller, 1987).

During the political debate, a number of arguments were put forward. Some countries such as Algeria opposed the enfranchisement of their nationals in France because they saw it as a step towards assimilation. Some French Communists argued that the priority for immigrants was to help in the class struggle in their homelands rather than in France. Others took the view that immigrants should be granted more social rights before getting voting rights. According to some Trotskyists, immigrants should fight for their own political rights. Others feared that voting rights could make immigrant organisations redundant. Last but not least, many parties did not want to support initiatives unpopular with their own supporters. This latter point may be the most important in current French politics, especially since J.M. Le Pen and his party, the National Front, have gained support on an anti-immigrant platform.

In May and June 1981, the Socialist Deputy Minister for Immigration formally recognised immigrant associations as the representatives of their respective national groups (Verbunt, 1985). This, and the activities of the associations, is increasingly seen as an alternative to voting rights. But immigrant associations are pressing the PS to reconsider the concepts of nationality and citizenship, since they consider that some reform of the nationality and citizenship laws is necessary.

A factor that has grown in significance for immigrants is the local political arena which, in the centralised French political system, used to seem unimportant. But since 1983 a policy of decentralisation has given the local authorities more power – for instance, to control the entry of immigrants. Moreover, the 1983 local elections demonstrated that the local arena is no longer unimportant. The main issue appeared to be the alleged 'problem' of the presence of immigrants, and the National Front made significant gains. If foreign residents had had the vote, the election results would probably have been very different (Miller, 1987).

Of course, there are quite a few immigrants in France who do have French citizenship. This is partly because naturalisation is encouraged and partly due to the application of the *ius soli* principle of citizenship. The legislation is quite complicated (see Chapter 8, on naturalisation), but there are about 1.5 million Franco-Maghrébins (of whom about a million are Franco-Algerian) at present living in France who have French (or dual) citizenship, with the same political rights as indigenous French citizens.

West Germany

In West Germany, non-national immigrants have no voting rights (Franz, 1984). Politicians and legal experts disagree as to whether the federal constitution prohibits their participation. According to Article 20, Paragraph 2, 'All state authority emanates from the people', but who are 'the people'? A minority hold the broad view that they are all inhabitants of West Germany, whatever their citizenship. According to this viewpoint, the Turks, Italians and other foreign residents in West Germany should be allowed to take part in all elections. Others consider that 'the people' means German citizens only, and that foreign citizens are therefore excluded from the franchise. Some who seek the reunification of the German nation would include inhabitants of East Germany among 'the people'.

An increasing number of people hold the view that the constitution does not prohibit the granting of local voting rights to foreign citizens for, unlike the Bundestag and the Landtage (the federal and state parliaments), local councils have no legislative functions. If this interpretation is correct, the necessary alteration of the laws could be implemented at a level lower than the Bundestag.

Ultimately, the enfranchisement of foreigners is a political, not a juridical, decision. Most legal experts assert that the enfranchisement of immigrants at the federal or *Länder* level will eventually require a constitutional amendment, but the necessary two-thirds majority in both the Bundestag and in the Bundesrat cannot be secured. In fact, only the Grünen (Green Party) would support the national franchise, so at present the political debate centres on the question of local enfranchisement.

The debate developed momentum in the late seventies, and for a while it seemed that the enfranchisement of foreigners was near. In 1979 the federal government Commissioner on immigration issues, the Social Democrat Heinz Kühn, presented a memorandum on the integration of immigrant workers and their families in West Germany (Meier-Braun, 1980). He recommended that immigrants should have the right to vote or to stand for election irrespective of their citizenship, provided that they had resided in the country for at least eight to ten years. However, his recommendation was not endorsed, because it would imply that the Ausländer (foreigners) were accepted as permanent immigrants, and the federal government did not wish to admit this.

Also in June 1979, the first debate took place at lower levels; for example, in the local council of Frankfurt (Frankfurter Rundschau, 29.6.79), although the bill of the Social Democratic SPD was not endorsed. Since then, this kind of debate has been raised over and over again, at *Länder* level too; in 1982 and 1987 in Hamburg, in 1983 and 1987 in Bremen, and in 1986 in Hesse (Haug, 1984), to mention a few.

Only recently, the initiatives have been successful. In 1989 in Hamburg, EC citizens residing in the country for more than eight years were allowed to participate in the relatively unimportant neighbourhood council elections. In the same year in Schleswig-Holstein, immigrants from Denmark, Eire, the Netherlands, Norway, Sweden and Switzerland were allowed to take part in local elections. The party of the Danish minority took the initiative here too.

Of all political parties represented in the Bundestag or Landtage, the Grünen (Green Party) is most in favour of enfranchising foreign residents (Haug, 1984; Löwisch, 1984). When the party rejected the 1987 Hamburg initiative to enfranchise foreign residents at the level of neighbourhood councils, it was because the initiative did not go far enough. The small Liberal Party (FDP) also supports the idea of granting voting rights, albeit not very strongly. The position of the Social Democratic SPD is rather vague. Statements of many individual members at all party levels – particularly the lower levels – and many resolutions at party conventions indicate that it favours enfranchisement, but when it is in power it usually turns out to be more restrictive. The recent developments in the northern *Länder* may indicate a change in party policy. The conservative Christian Democratic CDU and CSU denounce the immigrant franchise passionately. In the 1984 Landtag election in Baden-Wurttemberg, a CDU candidate even campaigned with the slogan 'Wahlrecht fur Ausländer . . . Nicht mit mir!' (Voting rights for foreigners . . . Not with me). The official position of the CDU and CSU is that eventual enfranchisement should be part of a European solution. The youth section of the CDU, the Jungen Union, takes a more positive stand towards immigrant voting rights, but its influence is limited.

As support for the political parties varies from city to city and from *Land* to *Land*, so the political climate regarding immigrant voting rights also varies. In states such as Bremen, Hamburg, Hesse, Lower Saxony and North-Rhine Westphalia, where both the SPD and the Greens have relatively strong positions, the chances are clearly better than, for example, in the CSU state of Bavaria, particularly now that anti-immigrant parties are winning support. In these areas there is a growing grassroots movement of both immigrants and Germans advocating more political rights for immigrants.

Like immigrants in Belgium, immigrants in West Germany are themselves increasingly demanding a share in the political decision-making process (Arbeitsemigranten, 1979; Ozak, 1985). Their political involvement is demonstrated in many meetings where numerous immigrant associations voice these demands. Various organisations working on behalf of immigrants, such as Arbeiterwohlfahrt, Caritas, the Diakonische Werk der Evangelische Kirche, and hundreds of Initiativgruppen, advocate the enfranchisement of immigrants. The federal trade union DGB did not back enfranchisement for a long time because it was afraid of a backlash from its native members; but since 1986 it has supported the granting of local voting rights, thereby following several local branches and a number of trade unions working under the DGB umbrella, including the powerful union IG Metall. The employers' association BDA is against enfranchisement. The idea of voting rights for the Ausländer is not very popular among the German population; only about a third are in favour, mostly younger people with higher education.

Prospects for Change

To summarise, exclusionism predominates in the Swiss, Belgian, French and German legislation. In this political climate the idea of immigrant participation is not looked upon very favourably, but growing pressure can be observed coming from foreign residents and their advocates.

Those in favour of enfranchisement cite developments in other European countries such as Sweden, Norway, the Netherlands and the Irish Republic, where foreign citizens already have voting rights. Italy and Spain too – traditionally countries of emigration, but now also experiencing immigration – are likely to grant local enfranchisement (Frowein, 1982; Ozsunay, 1983). In 1989, Spain agreed with the Netherlands to grant voting rights to Dutch citizens residing for more than three years in the country. In this context, it is interesting to discuss briefly the European Community's policy of granting its citizens local voting rights. In the 1970s the EC decided to strive after European citizenship, and it recommended the enfranchisement of community citizens, to be established not later than 1980 (an aim which was not achieved). It also advocated the improvement of the inferior situation of foreign workers and their families. In the 1980s, the European parliament repeatedly discussed this matter (Boukhriss, 1988; Commissie van de Europese Gemeenschappen, 1986), and in 1987 it discussed a proposal to grant community citizens the right to vote and to stand for elections. However, this implied that major immigrant communities from Turkey and North Africa, such as Algerians and Moroccans, would be excluded from the franchise. The European parliament endorsed the proposal, but also adopted a resolution to extend local voting rights to non-community citizens. It is not yet clear whether this resolution will result in concrete action in the member states.

Nordic countries
Most immigrants in Sweden are Nordic citizens, preponderantly Finnish. In 1975, Sweden granted immigrants the right to vote and to stand for election for local and regional elections (Hammar, 1977 and 1985b). This was a remarkable decision for – unlike in the Swiss (Neuchâtel) case – the enfranchisement was clearly a result of post-war mass immigration. The decision was the more remarkable because initially the indigenous population had been against it.

The franchise was not achieved as the result of a campaign by immigrants themselves. Swedish advocates professionally working with immigrants were the first to suggest the idea. They were not immediately successful, although there was a parliamentary debate on an immigrant franchise in 1968 when a Social Democratic member of parliament presented a motion. Five years later, on 27 October 1973, the Nordic Council recommended the enfranchisement of Nordic immigrants on a reciprocal basis.

The supporters of enfranchisement met much resistance, especially from juridical specialists. Surprisingly, the Social Democrats, who had been in power for decades, did not favour enfranchisement. They saw it as conflicting with a basic idea of the prevalent electoral system, which they had invented and which they favoured: the holding of all elections (on three levels) on the same day. However, the influential Social Democratic trade-union federation LO, which is closely connected to the Social Democratic Party, did favour it. In the spring of 1974, party leader Olaf Palme suddenly changed his position. This change was due to the introduction of the new immigration policy adopted at the same time. According to Palme, the granting of voting rights exactly coincided with the new policy goals of equality, freedom of choice and partnership (Hammar, 1985a). First the Social Democratic Party, and afterwards the other parties, followed Palme's lead.

The electoral reform was enacted in 1975, and so in 1976 all Swedish immigrants residing in the country for more than three years were allowed to participate in *kommunfullmäktige* (local) and *landsting* (regional) elections. They are, however, still excluded from the most important Riksdag (parliamentary) elections. At the time of this reform the only party trying to extend immigrant voting rights to include parliamentary elections was the Communist Party. They were not supported by other parliamentary parties until 1976 when, after elections in which the Social Democrats won many immigrant votes, the Social Democratic Party promised to reconsider its position. However, shortly after this they lost power.

In 1982 they resumed office. A special committee studied the question and found that granting the Riksdag vote would require an amendment to the constitution. It rapidly became clear that enfranchisement of all immigrants would evoke much resistance from non-socialist parties, and so it was proposed to enfranchise only those from Nordic countries. But before a bill was presented to parliament, the three non-socialist parties opposed the proposal and threatened to demand a referendum. According to the traditions of Swedish politics, all parties strive after consensus when constitutional matters are concerned and so, although there was a parliamentary majority in favour of extending voting rights, the government decided not to make a formal proposal. The socialist parties made the best of a bad bargain for the same reason, and also because they knew that the idea of universal suffrage for immigrants was not yet commonly accepted. As a consequence of these political manoeuvres, the Riksdag vote is not likely to be reconsidered for a further 15 years. Today the discussion centres on the question of allowing dual nationality.

Most Swedes oppose the granting of voting rights at the national level and this is something the political parties bear in mind. In 1975 there was not much support for the local and regional franchise either but, as soon as prominent politicians began to support change, the attitude of the population changed, and now there is a firm majority endorsing the 1975 reform. However, reform at the national level proved too great a step for national politicians, particularly with the prospect of a popular referendum. Immigrants, especially the leaders of immigrant associations, are disappointed with this development (Hammar and Reinans, 1985; Tung in Zweden Vandaag, 1985).

The Swedish reform in 1975 had important consequences. The first nation to follow suit was Denmark, although it took the Danes a couple of years to get used to the idea of the immigrant franchise (Baunsgard, 1984; Frowein, 1982; Ozsunay, 1983). In 1977 Denmark enfranchised immigrants from Finland, Iceland, Norway and Sweden, thereby meeting the recommendation of the Nordic Council. There was some discusion on whether immigrants from EC countries should get the vote as well, but few MPs wanted to go as far as that, and at the time the idea was unpopular. The 1978 local elections passed off satisfactorily, and this and the Swedish experience encouraged the advocates of more drastic electoral reform. The government decided to extend the right to vote and the right to run for office, and in 1980 it introduced a bill in parliament. The socialist and social-liberal parties supported the bill, while the conservative and liberal opposition rejected the idea and tried to limit it by proposing to grant the vote only on a reciprocal basis to immigrants coming from countries that had enfranchised Danish residents. The bill was eventually endorsed by a small parliamentary majority, with numerous abstentions. Immigrants of any citizenship have thus been granted the right to vote or to run for office at the local level if they have resided in the country for at least three years.

Norway followed a similar path. On 15 December 1978, Nordic immigrants were granted the vote by a constitutional amendment (Sandvoll, 1984). When they participated for the first time in the 1979 election the government had already promised seriously to consider extending voting rights to non-Nordic immigrants, and in 1980 it published its proposals in a white paper. The radical socialist Socialistisk Ventreparti did not wait for this paper and introduced a bill proposing voting rights for all immigrants. This premature initiative was not discussed in parliament, but nevertheless in 1982 the government and all parliamentary parties did agree to enfranchise all immigrants. Opinion diverged on the prerequisites of participation. The Conservative and Centre parties wanted a minimal residence period of seven years, but the Socialist, Social Democratic and Liberal parties preferred three years, and they constituted a majority. Immigrant associations and the trade unions took a similar view.

According to a public opinion poll in April 1983, a majority of Norwegians, albeit a tiny one, supported the reform.

Finland gave voting rights to Nordic citizens in June 1981, and in Iceland Nordic citizens are permitted to vote in local elections.

The Netherlands
In an indirect way the Swedish and other reforms stimulated the granting of voting rights to foreign citizens in the Netherlands, and it encouraged the supporters of reform (Groenendijk, 1985 and 1987; Rath, 1983b and 1988b). It was clear that the process of enfranchisement would be complicated because the constitution had to be changed, but there were some favourable circumstances. First, the government had for some time been preparing a complete revision of the constitution, and a bill was introduced in 1975. The government's proposal was to take away the constitutional barriers to foreign citizens' participation in local elections. Second, it must be noted that the political representation of foreigners is not a novelty in Dutch history, as the Dutch constitution permitted it in the early years of the nineteenth century, having been influenced by the French Revolution. Another favourable circumstance was the political complexion of the government: the centre-left government was anxious to make Dutch society more egalitarian, and the bill fitted very well with this policy.

In this political climate the left-wing parties naturally supported the bill, and even wanted to extend it by proposing voting rights for the Provinciale Staten (provincial councils) and the Tweede Kamer (the second and most important chamber of parliament). The conservative parties initially opposed it, and surprisingly the Christian Democratic parties overruled their own ministers by rejecting the bill. At most, they wanted the enfranchisement of citizens of EC countries.

Gradually, the position of the opposing parties has changed, partly in reaction to the Swedish experience, but also because the bill proposed to open up merely the *possibility* of foreign citizens taking part in local elections (since Electoral Law and Local Government Law also prohibited their participation). All kinds of tactical discussions – for example, on the question of whether foreigners should or could meet special prerequisities – were avoided. A further reason for the change was that the three most important parties – the Social Democratic PvdA, the Christian Democratic CDA and the right-wing liberal VVD – were all committed to the policy. Since 1975 the Minister of Home Affairs, who has the primary responsibility for the bill, has been recruited from all three parties, although sometimes this commitment has caused tension within parties, especially within the VVD.

The change of opinion is also connected with the new Minorities

Policy towards immigrants (Entzinger, 1985). Since 1979 the government has supported equal participation for immigrants in Dutch society, including politics, and the eventual granting of voting rights to foreign immigrants became part of this policy. Many immigrants who settled in the Netherlands after the Second World War came from former colonies, and almost all Eurasians, Moluccans, Antilleans, Arubans and Surinamese living in the Netherlands are Dutch citizens and consequently entitled to vote. The enfranchisement of foreign citizens was thus in tune with the policy of equal treatment.

Finally, the parliamentary parties were encouraged by the Rotterdam and Amsterdam experiences. In both cities, systems of 'deelraden' (neighbourhood councils) have resulted from the decentralisation of power of the local councils. In anticipation of electoral reform granting local voting rights to foreign residents, both Rotterdam (in 1979) and Amsterdam (in 1981) gave immigrants resident in the cities voting rights for these neighbourhood councils, and foreign residents who want to take part in these elections do not have to conform to any specific prerequisites. The local councils were entitled to pass this measure this without the need for constitutional amendment. Left-wing parties were the initiators, as they had dominant positions in both councils, and the decisions were taken with overwhelming majorities.

In the early 1980s, parliament voted almost unanimously for the bill to extend the local franchise to foreign citizens. The subsequent amendment of the Electoral Law and the Local Government Law caused some political difficulties. Under the pressure of the Christian Democratic CDA and particularly the right-wing liberal VVD it was eventually decided that foreign immigrants could take part in local elections if they had resided in the country for at least five years, although a special check must be carried out by the Vreemdelingendienst (aliens' registration office) to prevent the possible, if highly unlikely, participation of undocumented immigrants. This latter measure provoked much protest from left-wing parties and immigrant associations.

Except for a few small but extreme Christian-orthodox parties and the racist one-man Centrumpartij, all parties supported the enfranchisement. It is interesting that unlike in Belgium, France and West Germany, the fear of a native white backlash did not really play a role in the enfranchising process – although the major parties agreed to a low-key debate in parliament to reduce the chances of a backlash occurring.

According to many opinion polls, most Dutch people, particularly the young and more highly educated ones, supported the granting of local voting rights (Rath, 1985). Recent opinion polls show a majority of supporters for the provincial franchise too, albeit a very small one.

Some think that foreign immigrants already have the parliamentary vote, perhaps confusing foreign immigrants with Surinamese and other immigrants with Netherlands citizenship.

Surprisingly, immigrants have been enfranchised without fighting for it themselves, and it has been mainly native juridical experts and politicans who have advocated extending the franchise. However, immigrants are now increasingly taking the lead in demanding national voting rights. But although the bigger trade union federations, the FNV and the CNV, the left-wing parties and virtually all immigrant associations are in favour of extending the right to vote to national elections, there is little prospect of this being granted in the immediate future.

Great Britain
In Britain the largest groups of immigrants – namely, the Asians, West Indians and Irish – all have voting rights. This is part of the colonial legacy: all are Commonwealth or British citizens and consequently entitled to vote. Although the Irish left the Commonwealth in 1949, their voting rights were allowed to continue. The enfranchisement of foreigners not coming from Commonwealth countries or Eire is highly unlikely at present, with the possible exception of reciprocal arrangements for EC nationals.

As in the Netherlands and France, there is no discussion in Britain about the voting rights of colonial immigrants. The ability of the Irish, who are foreign nationals, to vote or to stand as candidates used to be resented on the right, because most Irish vote Labour and there were no reciprocal arrangements for British citizens living in the Irish Republic. However, since 1963 all persons regardless of nationality have had the right to participate in local elections in the Republic of Ireland, and in 1984 the Irish government granted British citizens resident in Eire the right to vote in national elections, partly because of close historic ties with Britain, and perhaps also as a political manoeuvre to secure the political rights of Irish citizens resident in Britain.

The Pros and Cons of Voting Rights: the Debate

A comparison of the various countries studied enables us to draw some general conclusions about immigrants' progress towards enfranchise-ment. It appears that various arguments both for and against the immigrant franchise – some of principle and some tactical – turn up in every country, and certain conditions need to be met before immigrants can be enfranchised. We will now look at the arguments put forward, and then see what general conclusions we can draw.

The arguments

1 Human rights   Perhaps the most important argument in favour of granting voting rights is that the right to take part in the political process of one's country of residence is an essential aspect of human life.

2 No taxation without representation   For centuries this principle has been used to support the claim to political rights of those who, for example, contribute to the national economy, pay taxes, are part of the national community and participate in all institutions except for politics.

3 Voting rights and citizenship   Internationally there is a growing move towards separating the issues of citizenship and political rights. Mass media, international transport, the growth of tourism, retirement abroad and the creation of the European Community have all contributed to the blurring of international frontiers, especially in Western Europe. However, for many people citizenship has still an almost sacred meaning, and they believe that foreign immigrants should naturalise if they wish to participate politically. After all, by naturalising the newcomers prove their allegiance and solidarity with the host country. Some authors, such as Castenmiller and Brants (1984), maintain that this conviction is a mere expression of latent racism, but this is too simplistic, even if the citizenship argument is sometimes used by racists.

4 Protection of sovereignty   Some maintain that immigrants should maintain strict political neutrality. They fear their country could lose control of its domestic affairs by enfranchising foreigners: foreign powers would be able to interfere in national politics, and could develop a fifth column to undermine the nation's strength, especially in situations of international conflict. Supporters of this argument also believe that immigrant politicians cannot handle dual loyalty and should therefore have no say in foreign policy and defence matters. This rather patronising belief springs from the dubious assumptions that immigrants and natives have no common interests and that all natives are loyal. It is possible that homeland political conflicts may be introduced in regular political institutions, and immigrants may not conform to the prevailing political culture – but the latter possibility is not the sole prerogative of immigrants.

5 Voting rights and integration   One view is that immigrants should 'earn' their enfranchisement by first adopting the native way of living, with the granting of voting rights being a final step in the process of integration. Others would argue the opposite case, seeing voting rights not so much as a result of this process but as a prerequisite: immigrants with voting rights are more interested in the host society, and political parties are more interested in this specific part of the population if it forms part of the electorate. Some foreign powers oppose voting rights for their nationals for this very reason, fearing that their loyalty will decrease and that assimilation will take place.

6 Homeland politics   Some argue that immigrants should take part in homeland political affairs instead of taking part in the politics of the host land.

7 A European solution   According to this argument, the enfranchisement of foreign citizens should be the result of joint action by countries belonging to the European Community. The individual member countries should not take any separate action, but wait until the EC takes the first step. Some people maintain that such a solution would be too narrow, because it excludes Turks, Moroccans and other non-community citizens, and they point at other international developments in Europe such as the enfranchisement of all immigrants in Sweden, Denmark and the Netherlands.

8 Reciprocity   This argument is used mostly by those opposing the widening of the franchise: if German citizens have no voting rights in Turkey, why grant voting rights to Turkish citizens in West Germany?

9 No rights without duties   One argument used against enfranchisement is that enfranchised immigrants receive the benefits of citizenship without the duties: why grant voting rights to immigrants without compulsory military service? (Interestingly, in some countries such as West Germany the government is considering drafting non-German youths, since there are not enough young German men to be recruited into the army.)

10 Alternative political participation   Some argue that immigrants' interests are better served by alternative means of political participation: advisory councils in West Germany, strengthened immigrant associations in France or naturalisation in Belgium. Interestingly enough, in Britain, the Netherlands and Sweden, where immigrants do have voting rights, these alternatives are seen as complements to voting rights rather than alternatives.

11 Electoral considerations   Some are concerned that enfranchised immigrants may establish their own parties, which will compete with the existing parties. They also fear that all political parties but one's own will win immigrants' votes – especially if equilibrium among competing political groups is fragile, as in Belgium. Conversely, it may be feared that traditional supporters will withdraw their votes if a party takes a more favourable stand on immigrants' issues. Overall, the costs are expected to outweigh the benefits if immigrants are granted voting rights and the parties appeal for their votes, although some parties hope to win immigrant votes by granting voting rights to foreign citizens.

These, then are the arguments. How does it come about that in one country the arguments in favour of extending the franchise are successful, whereas in another the arguments against prevail? The answer depends upon many things – the balance of political power, the political culture, the history of immigration, and how the presence of immigrants is perceived – but several significant factors can be identified which appear to aid the cause of enfranchisement.

First, it is recognised that most foreigners are permanent immigrants. Both the Swedish and Dutch cases demonstrate that the enfranchisement process gathers momentum as soon as the permanent character of immigration is recognised. The German and Swiss cases demonstrate the very opposite: there is no need to enfranchise foreigners, since most of them are expected to return.

Second, voting rights are recognised as being not so much the final outcome of an integration process but as an important means facilitating that process. The Swedish and the Dutch governments suggest that the absence of immigrant voting rights only serves to frustrate their integration policies.

Third, left-wing parties are in power. In Sweden and in the Netherlands the bill to enfranchise foreign immigrants was introduced by left-wing governments. The Swedish and Dutch centre and right-wing parties gave their support only when the enfranchisement process was in full swing. Initiatives to grant voting rights to immigrants in Belgium, France and West Germany were also taken by the left. This may be because left-wing parties expect to win immigrant votes, but it may also relate to the ideology of international solidarity: both native and immigrant workers are part of a common proletariat suppressed by a dominant capitalist class.

Fourth, there is no political struggle for the anti-immigrant vote. As long as the main parties do not publicly clash about equal rights for immigrants, the odds favour enfranchisement. But when anti-immigrant parties are winning support and the parties become involved in a struggle for the 'anti-immigrant vote', the chances are gone. A clear example is France, where the success of the National

Front caused the other parties to take a more cautious stand on the issue of immigrants' voting rights. But even without such an overtly anti-immigrant party, politicians are concerned to heed their native white voters, as demonstrated in Belgium and Germany.

Fifth, the immigrant vote is of limited importance. The success of one party and the failure of another is not perceived as dependent on the immigrant vote and there is little or no fear that every party except one's own will profit from enfranchisement – unlike in Belgium, in particular around Brussels, where the Flemish-speaking parties assume they will be badly affected because immigrants will vote for French-speaking parties.

Sixth, the question of immigrant voting rights is seen as a political rather than a juridical matter. In every country, the enfranchisement process starts with a struggle for the 'definition of the situation', as Goffman (1959) puts it. The opponents of enfranchisement are tempted to define the situation as a juridical one, and they point out the legal difficulties, while advocates are inclined to define the situation as political, and argue that legal barriers can be overcome if there is the political will to do so. In Sweden and the Netherlands both opponents and advocates reached an accommodation in connection with the 'minorities policies' which defined voting rights as a necessary prerequisite for the integration of immigrants. In other countries, there is as yet no working consensus.

We now turn to look at the actual electoral participation of immigrants.

Turn-out

Little purpose is served by comparing the turn-out percentages of immigrants in various elections in detail, for we are dealing with different elections in different countries taking place under different circumstances. However, it is possible to identify underlying patterns of immigrant participation.

One recurrent feature is the *relatively low turn-out* of immigrant voters compared to that of native voters. In Sweden, immigrant turn-out in the first immigrant elections in 1975 was about 60 percent while that of the native Swedes was about 90 percent (Hammar, 1984). The remarkably high turn-out of Swedish voters is because three elections take place on the same day, and this involves the electorate in an intensive political campaign. However, in the following two elections the immigrant turn-out decreased to a steady 52–53 percent, and then fell again to 48 percent in the 1985 elections (Hammar and Reinans, 1985 and 1987). Levels of participation varied by ethnic group.

In the 1978 local elections in Denmark, 60 percent of the Nordic immigrants cast their votes – a percentage only a little lower than that of the total electorate (73 percent). In the 1981 local elections, when the right to vote had been granted to other non-national citizens as well, the turn-out percentage of all immigrants equalled 61 percent (Ozsunay, 1983).

In the Netherlands, the participation of immigrants with Netherlands citizenship, such as Antilleans, Moluccans and Surinamese, has been below average. This was the case in the 1982 local elections, for example – although the participation of Antilleans and Surinamese in the Hague was exceptionally high (Bovenkerk et al., 1982), exceeding even the turn-out of native whites, owing to the vigorous campaign of ethnic candidates. The turn-out of 'non-Netherlands' immigrants was very low in the 1980 and 1981 Rotterdam and Amsterdam neighbour-hood council elections: 12 percent and 20 percent compared with low native turn-out percentages of 37 percent to 50 percent (Rath, 1983a; Gemeente Amsterdam, 1982). In the next neighbourhood council elections the turn-out percentages of immigrants unexpectedly went up to 40 percent, just below the figure for the total turn-out (Pennings, 1986; Rath, 1985), but the 1986 local elections – the first real immigrant elections – reverted to the pattern of relatively low participation, although with variations according to ethnic group: few Moroccans turned out, but the percentage of Turks voting was almost as high as the percentage of Dutch (Buijs and Rath, 1986; Pennings, 1987).

In Britain, the situation is more difficult to assess. By and large a similar pattern emerges: ethnic minorities participate below average (Anwar, 1986; Fitzgerald, 1984 and 1988; Layton-Henry, 1983, 1984, 1988). In the sixties the first research projects on this indicated very low levels of turn-out, sometimes no more than 13 percent (Le Lohé, 1975), but the turn-out rate has increased ever since, especially for Asian immigrants, whose turn-out is sometimes lower than that of native whites, but at other times equals it, or is even higher. West Indian turn-out remains significantly lower than that of Asian or white voters.

Turn-out in all these countries varies not only according to ethnic groups, but also according to age and sex. Young immigrants are more likely to abstain than older ones, while the participation of female immigrants is sometimes lower, sometimes higher than that of male immigrants. In the Netherlands, the turn-out of female Turks and Moroccans is below that of males, but the turn-out of other female immigrants appears to be higher. It is interesting to note that in Sweden the participation of Turkish women was also relatively low at first, but now it equals that of men (Widgren, 1982).

At present we lack data on the turn-out of immigrants – as far as they are entitled to vote – in Finnish, Irish and Norwegian elections. The limited evidence on immigrants' electoral participation in France (Miller, 1987) and in the Swiss canton Neuchâtel (Debely, 1986) seems to confirm the patterns outlined above.

Party Preference

Although immigrants vote for many different parties, it is quite clear that they prefer Social Democratic or Socialist parties. Immigrants vote with the Socialdemokraterna in Sweden (Hammar, 1977, 1984, 1985a); with the socialist parties in Denmark (Baunsgard, 1984); with the social democratic PvdA in the Netherlands (Buijs and Rath, 1986; Rath 1983a and 1985), and with the socialist Labour Party in Britain (Layton-Henry, 1984, 1988).

An opinion poll in Switzerland indicated that many Italian immigrants would, if enfranchised, vote with left-wing parties such as the SP, POCH, Pda (Ley and Agustoni, 1976), and in West Germany, where non-national residents are not entitled to vote, the largest group of foreigners, namely the Turks, favour both the Social Democratic SPD and the *Grünen* (Esser et al., 1982; Ibrahim-Knoke, 1985). Again, there are no data available on the party preferences of immigrants in Eire, Finland, France and Norway.

Non-socialist parties do get some ethnic minority votes. In Britain, for example, the Liberals and the Conservative Party have on occasion succeeded in winning considerable support from ethnic minority voters (Anwar, 1986), but this kind of success is rare.

There are a few examples of immigrants voting *en masse* for independent immigrant parties standing for election: for example, Polish miners in the Ruhr area in Germany in the first few decades of the twentieth century. These immigrant workers were considered as German citizens with voting rights, and their vote was more or less an ethnic bloc vote for the Polen Partei (Klessmann, 1978; Murphy, 1982). More recent examples of successful immigrant parties are the Lijst Rammelaere, a list headed by a Belgian living for more than 30 years in the Dutch border town Aardenburg, and the party of the Turkish immigrant Akay in the Dutch town of Oss. Both were elected in the 1986 local elections. However, these immigrant parties are only extremely rarely successful and most win hardly any votes, because the overwhelming majority of immigrants vote for the mainstream parties.

Explanations

How can these patterns of turn-out and voting behaviour – and the exceptions – be explained? Many local or even national peculiarities may be influential, but it is impossible to discuss every factor in detail, and we therefore concentrate on more general factors determining turn-out and voting patterns.

One significant factor is the class position of ethnic minorities: they are largely part of the 'working class', since most immigrants are semi-skilled or unskilled workers, or else unemployed. In political science, it is a well-known phenomenon that politics are mainly an elite interest; persons belonging to the lower strata of a society participate less in formal politics. In short, immigrants are part of a stratum of the population with lower rates of turn-out, and they vote principally for parties that advocate the interests of the working class.

Hammar (1977) suggests that immigrants in Sweden are more inclined to vote for non-socialist parties when their period of residence is longer and their socio-economic position has improved. In other words, upward social mobility is likely to be followed by a change of party preferences. A similar phenomenon is found in Britain, where Asian immigrants show higher turn-out rates than do West Indian immigrants. Although most Asians are still part of the working class, their socio-economic position is generally slightly better than that of West Indians, and this might explain their higher participation and slightly lower inclination to vote Labour. In particular, socially mobile Asians tend to switch to the Conservatives (Layton-Henry, 1983; Studlar, 1983). For West Indians, the choice is not so much between Labour and Conservative as between voting or not voting. If they do vote, they vote for Labour. In West Germany, opinion polls show that immigrants living in areas with relatively higher socio-economic status are less likely to favour the Social Democratic SPD (Esser et al., 1982).

However, there is also evidence that class is not the main influence upon immigrants' electoral participation (Rath, 1988c). For instance, one would expect unemployed immigrants to be more alienated from the electoral system than unemployed natives, since their unemployment rates are usually much higher and their prospects worse. In the Netherlands, however, Buijs (1986) and Buijs and Rath (1986) found their turn-out rates higher. Moreover, in all the countries studied immigrants support Socialist and Socialist Democratic parties; those who are upwardly mobile may be more inclined to vote for non-socialist parties, but the majority continue to support left-wing parties (Boissevain et al., 1984).

Another important set of explanations for immigrant electoral behaviour is connected with the process of integration of the immigrants. Most immigrants have migrated from rural to industrial societies with ways of living and institutions that differ markedly from those in their home countries. Political socialisation in countries such as Bangladesh, Britain, Morocco, Sweden, Trinidad and Turkey, for example, are all markedly different: the way people treat one another, the way they perceive the administration and politicians, the way they set up organisations and the way they take care of their interests. Immigrants often face language barriers, and the fact that many hope and expect to return to their home countries may discourage their participation in the host country's politics.

However, there is evidence that after a while, when immigrants are more settled, less mobile and more familiar with the host country's way of life, they take more interest in politics. In the 1960s, turn-out rates of immigrants in Britain were very low, but in the course of time they have gradually improved (Anwar, 1986). Pieters (1984) found a similar trend among Dutch Antilleans in the Netherlands. This suggests that the longer immigrants stay in the country, the more they become adapted to and incorporated in the host country's politics. The studies of the Swedish political scientist Hammar (1977, 1984, 1985a) explicitly confirm this assumption. Hammar found the most abstentions among those immigrants who were least involved in Swedish society: predominantly young immigrant workers who were rather mobile, had been in the country a relatively short time and were still thinking of returning to their home countries. Most of these young 'guest-workers' came from adjacent Nordic countries, and Hammar found that immigrants from more distant countries such as Greece, Turkey and Yugoslavia had higher turn-out rates. He concluded that they had invested more in migrating to Sweden and that once they were settled their residence was more permanent. In the course of time they learned Swedish, widened their contacts with native Swedes, and became familiar with Swedish institutions such as political parties and elections. While the relatively high turn-out in the first immigrant elections in 1976 was probably largely influenced by the novelty and publicity, integration too may have been a factor. Furthermore, Hammar found a relationship between the length of stay in Sweden and the 'Swedishisation' of the voting pattern. As immigrants' socio-economic position improved and they became more integrated, their attitudes and behaviour changed; as a result, the older immigrants did not have such a great preference for socialist parties as that shown by the majority.

It seems likely that important explanations for the political behaviour of immigrants and the politico-cultural differences between immigrants and natives are length of stay and, more importantly, willingness to take an interest in host country's politics and adopt its traditions. It is thus quite logical that naturalised immigrants participate as frequently as natives, since their level of assimilation is likely to be the highest of all immigrants.

This reasoning can also be approached the opposite way. The low participation of immigrants is due to a low level of integration; those who cling to their own traditions and take little interest in the host country's institutions participate less in host country politics. This assumption is plausible and it has many adherents, but the consequences are far-reaching: while ignoring structural factors that relate to the host country itself, liberal adherents may argue that full electoral participation will follow only when immigrants are sufficiently 'integrated'. In the meantime, the most one can do is to foster the interest of immigrants in host country affairs – for example, by publicity and information about political institutions and the political process.

The many information campaigns directed at foreign voters are in fact largely based upon this assumption; for example, in the 1986 local elections campaign in the Netherlands. Many native Dutch, including the Dutch Home Office which initiated and paid for the campaign, believed that immigrants, being newcomers in Dutch electoral politics, badly needed information on the Dutch political system, and could not participate effectively in Dutch elections without this 'technical' information, since they had not been politically socialised in the Netherlands. However, Rath (1986) has demonstrated that this explanation is quite unsatisfactory. In spite of the extensive information campaign which accompanied the 1980 neighbourhood council election in Rotterdam, few foreign voters turned out (Rath, 1983a). In the 1984 neighbourhood council elections their turn-out was higher, but this was because the immigrants feared the electoral success of the racist Centrumpartij, and this encouraged them to vote against racism. Obviously, adequate socialisation in the host countries' political system is a necessary condition for participation, but it is not a sufficient condition; low turn-out is not simply the effect of inadequate socialisation, lack of knowledge or a defective information campaign.

In Sweden, immigrant voters found information on voting helpful in deciding whether or not to vote, but the information campaign itself was not a decisive factor for participation (Hammar, 1977). Many immigrants interpreted the right to vote as a moral duty to engage in Swedish politics. In Denmark there was no 'real' information drive owing to lack of money, yet the immigrants turned out *en masse*.

As for Britain, McAllister and Studlar (1984) doubt whether the low turn-out of immigrants is caused by inadequate political socialisation. Others such as Lawrence (1974) argue that immigrant associations and the immigrant press have all been very supportive of political participation by members of their communities. Rex (1979) argues that continuing racial discrimination against immigrants discourages them from taking part in the host country's institutions. In his view, immigrants will react by abstaining from elections and by being active in small radical organisations that demand their rights with force.

Layton-Henry and Studlar (1985) found an interesting paradox when comparing the turn-out of West Indians in British elections with that of Asians. West Indian turn-out is considerably lower, but they none the less show considerable interest in politics and in the results of elections, while Asian interest appears relatively low. The writers suggest two possible explanations. The first is that Asians are more involved in community-based organisations which promote partici-pation in elections and hence raise turn-out. The second is that alienation from established political institutions and processes discourages West Indian participation in elections. Both Asians and West Indians are faced with racial discrimination and disadvantage, but West Indians, particularly the young ones, are more frustrated and more in conflict with British society than Asians. The more individualistic behaviour of West Indians, their working-class values and their lack of strong communal organisations increase their alienation. This might stimulate their involvement in special interest groups or express itself in direct action and outbursts of violence, but is not likely to encourage electoral participation.

The lack of a more collective and mutually supportive ethos among Afro-Caribbeans has been pointed out by authors such as Pearson (1981), who maintains that the cultural heritage of West Indians contains impediments to organisation according to ethnic criteria and consequently to participation in representative political institutions. It remains to be seen, however, whether organisation according to ethnic criteria will lead to more participation. As FitzGerald (1984) argues, leaders of immigrant associations may not be as popular among the rank and file as many think they are, which reduces their capacity for mobilisation. Furthermore, according to Layton-Henry and Studlar (1985), the well-organised Asians have fewer individual contacts with party members, participate less in political campaigns and discuss political matters less. In short, despite their high turn-out, Asians are politically less active than West Indians in other forms of political activity.

Immigrants do not necessarily have to adopt a West European way of living to participate fully in politics. Glazer and Moynihan (1963), Koot and Rath (1987), Koot and Uniken Venema (1985), Rath (1988a) and Roosens (1986) point to ethnic groups acting as interest groups. Whether such 'mobilisation of ethnicity' takes place largely depends on ethnic leaders. Paradoxically the leaders must be 'assimilated' to a comparatively high degree to know how to be successful in the host society, while at the same time they emphasise aspects of their own ethnicity in order to mobilise the ethnic rank and file – and this may involve participation in elections. With this support they can then put pressure on providers and distributors of resources such as the government or political parties. It is a way of influencing the policies of the parties, securing the nomination of immigrant candidates and canvassing for immigrant support on issues which otherwise might not seem relevant to their wishes or interests.

Candidates

The right to vote usually goes with the right to run for office, and as long ago as 1892 an Asian Liberal, Dadabhai Naorji, entered the British parliament. When he left parliament in 1895, another Asian, a Conservative, became an MP; the first Asian Socialist was elected in 1922. In the same year a Communist Indonesian called Tan Malakka stood as the first immigrant candidate in the Netherlands. Despite a vigorous campaign he was unsuccessful, but in 1933 another immigrant called Rustam Effendi, also a Communist, became the Netherlands' first immigrant MP, and held his seat until 1940. In 1945 two Indonesians were appointed as members of the second chamber of the 'temporary parliament' and one Indonesian was appointed as a member of the first chamber (Poeze, 1986). In Germany there also are examples of immigrant candidates and MPs, predominantly Poles in the Ruhr area in the first few decades of this century (Klessmann, 1978; Murphy, 1982).

Not surprisingly, the number of immigrant candidates and representatives in the pre-war period was minute, but today there are quite a few. Some have even formed their own independent political parties, but most stand for mainstream parties.

A prerequisite for nomination is usually party membership, though in a few exceptional cases this is not necessary. For example, in the 1986 Dutch local elections a few radical left-wing parties allowed some places on their lists for immigrant candidates who were non-members. The parties argued that this proved their solidarity with immigrants, but it should be noted that their deeds were also inspired by the absence of immigrant party members.

Unfortunately, there are no accurate figures on ethnic minority party membership because most parties are extremely reluctant to keep such records. All but a few parties simply make themselves 'open' to immigrants. There are exceptions such as the Bavarian CSU, which has a ban on the membership of foreigners, and the Dutch Communist CPN had a ban until December 1982. As far as the other parties are concerned, all we know is that immigrants do become party members, usually of Socialist parties, but generally immigrants are significantly under-represented in the regular parties, both left-wing and right-wing, especially at levels of influence and responsibility (Decker, 1982; Drobnic, 1986; FitzGerald, 1984).

Immigrants in West Germany, and foreign citizens in France, are not permitted to start their own independent political parties, but elsewhere in Western Europe they are free to do so. In France a couple of Franco-Algerians set up a party called Sahra (*Liberation*, 19 November 1985), while in the Netherlands several parties have already participated in elections; for instance, the Turkish Hakyol or the Moroccan Vrije Marokkaanse Alliantie (Free Moroccan Alliance) in the neighbourhood council elections, and the Progressive Minderheden Partij (Progressive Minorities party) and AI'86 (Alliance of Immigrants 1986) in local elections (Rath, 1983a and 1985). In Sweden, and even in Britain with its unfavourable electoral system, independent ethnic minority parties have tried to win votes. Many natives oppose the existence of such parties, because they see them as a threat to the existing political system and to the interests of natives. However, this fear is not justified, because practically no immigrant party has ever succeeded in securing significant representation.

How have immigrants fared as candidates in elections? In France in the 1989 local elections, about 600 North Africans with French nationality took part as candidates. In the 1979 local elections in Sweden, immigrants comprised 8 percent of the total electorate and 4 percent (2,513) of the candidates (Hammar, 1982). Most occupied low positions on the lists, particularly for the non-socialist parties. Of the 13,368 councillors elected, 490 (3.7 percent) were immigrants, but only 89 of these still held their original nationalities. In the 1979 Riksdag elections two naturalised foreigners were elected: a Greek Communist and a Finnish Socialist. In the Dutch 1982 local elections, 45 Surinamese, Antillean and Moluccan immigrants were nominated as candidates out of a total of 60,000 candidates, but only seven of them were elected. In the 1986 local elections, when foreign citizens were allowed to participate, there were about 150 immigrant candidates, of which about a third – mainly Social Democrats – were elected. To date, few immigrants have stood as parliamentary candidates, but in May 1986 a Moluccan did so and was elected. In Denmark in 1981 three immigrants from Turkey and Jordan were elected to local councils. In Britain more immigrants have become local councillors, but the total is still relatively low, since most immigrants are nominated for seats they are unlikely to win (Welch and Studlar, 1987). At the national level, the situtation is little better. In the general election of 1983 there were 18 immigrant candidates, but only one was in a winnable seat, and he failed to be elected. It was not until the 1987 general election that immigrant ethnic minorities were represented in the British parliament, with the election of four Socialists. In short, immigrants are heavily under-represented both as candidates and on such elected bodies as local councils and parliament. Most immigrants who stand as candidates do so in local elections; few stand in national elections. Most run for left-wing parties, but they are seldom nominated to high positions or selected for safe seats.

One barrier to political advancement is the need to be selected and elected by the majority native electorate; another is the fact that immigrants belong overwhelmingly to the lower classes of society. Most immigrant candidates are part of an elite with a relatively high level of 'assimilation', as illustrated by the great number of naturalised foreigners among the immigrant candidates in Sweden. They are often people who are long settled and well established in the host society, and have mastery of the host country language. Often they are well-educated professional welfare workers, schoolteachers or businessmen. This elite of upwardly mobile immigrants is relatively small, which partially explains the under-representation of immigrants among candidates and elected representatives.

Another reason is the parties' lack of political commitment to immigrants. They are not yet used to the idea of giving special attention to the newcomers, especially when most of them belong to the lower classes. Furthermore, their preference for 'waiting' is sometimes related to racist attitudes among their members, who may be reluctant to deal with immigrants because they feel superior to them. On the other hand, the parties may fear a backlash from native white-voters. This fear of a backlash is a recurring theme, particularly in British literature, but it is not clear how far it is justified. Le Lohé (1983) calculates the backlash at about 3 percent of the votes, while Layton-Henry (1984) argues that a backlash occurred in the past, but now immigrant candidates are increasingly being accepted. Anwar (1986) assumes that it is merely the fear of a possible negative response which discourages the nomination of immigrant candidates. Fitz-Gerald (1984) maintains that a backlash may not have occurred at all. Finally, Welch and Studlar (1987) argue that there is little evidence of a backlash and, furthermore, that Afro-Caribbeans even have an advantage in winning, once nominated.

In other countries such as Sweden and the Netherlands there is no clear evidence of a native white backlash, and the electoral systems in these countries decrease the likelihood of its occurring. It was expected that the Dutch racist Centrumpartij would gain many votes in the 1986 local elections by drawing a great deal of attention to immigrants, but instead the party lost much of its influence and even failed to be returned to parliament at all after the 1986 parliamentary elections.

There is evidence that politicians are concerned at the possibility of a 'black backlash'. In 1984 and in 1986 some (mostly left-wing) Dutch political parties took great care not to neglect immigrant candidates-to-be (Rath, 1985). In 1984 in particular when the Centrumpartij seemed to be attracting many native white votes, the Social Democratic PvdA nominated several immigrant candidates to demonstrate that their nominations procedure had not been influenced by the fear of a white backlash. Also the party hoped to win many immigrant votes, which it succeeded in doing. In Britain too the political parties take account of the immigrant electorate as well. This is especially true in the Labour Party, where the self-styled 'black sections' of the party promote the nomination of black candidates.

Immigrant candidates may play a special role in electoral campaigns, perhaps acting as intermediaries between the parties and the immigrant communities. Their appeal to ethnic loyalty can contribute to a higher turn-out. It is less certain whether they also manage to attract immigrant voters who otherwise would not vote for that party. But there are indications that immigrant candidates do influence immigrants' party preferences, and some candidates have even produced a swing (Anwar, 1986). However, as Buijs and Rath (1986) and Le Lohé (1983) demonstrate, the appeal of immigrant candidates is often overestimated. While party executives may see immigrant candidates as representatives of their communities or even of all the immigrants together, in fact the immigrants constitute quite heterogeneous communities, and even within one immigrant group there are often many sub-groups and factions reluctant to support one another. It is therefore unlikely that Turks will vote for Moroccans, Bangladeshis for Jamaicans, or right-wing Italians for Communist Italians. Second, party loyalty is usually stronger than ethnic loyalty – although it may be partially determined by the stand of the party towards the specific interests of immigrants, which may in turn be influenced by immigrant party members.

Both ethnic loyalty to immigrant candidates and party loyalty can reinforce each other. It is anyway inevitable that all parties now have to take account of immigrants and the implications of ethnicity. This constitutes another unforeseen but increasingly important challenge to Western European politics.

References

ACV (1986) *Stemrecht voor Migranten op Niveau van de Gemeente.* Brussels: Algemeen Christelijk Vakverbond.

Anwar, M. (1986) *Race and Politics. Ethnic Minorities and the British Political System.* London: Tavistock.

Arbeitsemigranten in der Bundesrepublik (1979) *Materialien zum Projektbereich 'Ausländische Arbeiter'*, 26: 113–222.

Baunsgard, B. (1984) 'Kommunales Wahlrecht ist ein Menschenrecht – Erfahrungen in Dänemark', pp. 34–44 in H. Keskin (ed.), *Menschen ohne Rechte? Einwanderungspolitik und Kommunalwahlrecht in Europa.* Berlin: Express Edition.

Boissevain, J., A. Choenni and H. Grotenberg (1984) *Een Kleine Baas is Altijd Beter dan een Grote Knecht. Surinaamse Kleine Zelfstandige Ondernemers in Amsterdam.* Amsterdam: University of Amsterdam, Anthropology-Sociology Centre.

Boukhriss, H. (1988) 'Het "Algemeen Stemrecht". Enkel voor Belgen?', *Bareel*, 11 (41): 17-19.

Bovenkerk, F., L. Ruland and J. Rath, (1982) 'De Opkomst van een Vergeten Electoraat', *Intermediair*, 18 (35): 1-7.

Buijs, F. (1986) 'Wat doen Werklozen met hun Stem? Opkomst en Kiesgedrag van de Werkloze Kiezers bij de Deelraadsverkiezingen 1984 te Rotterdam', *Acta Politica*, 21 (1) (Jan.) 57-79.

Buijs, F. and J. Rath (1986) *De Stem van Migranten en Werklozen. De Gemeenteraadsverkiezingen van 19 Maart 1986 te Rotterdam.* Leiden: University of Leiden, Centre for the Study of Social Conflict.

Castenmiller, P. and K. Brants (1984) *(In)tolerantie ten Opzichte van Etnische Minderheden.* Amsterdam: University of Amsterdam, FSW.

Commissie van de Europese Gemeenschappen (1986) *Kiesrecht voor Burgers uit Andere Lid-staten van de Gemeenschap bij Gemeenteraadsverkiezingen,* COM(86) 487 def. Brussels.

Debely, M. (1986) *Droit de Vote des Etrangers dans la Commune de la Chaux-de-Fonds.* Geneva: Institut d'Etudes Sociales.

Decker, F. (1982) *Ausländer im Politischen Abseits, Möglichkeiten ihrer Politischen Beteiligung.* Frankfurt: Campus Verlag.

Drobnic, S. (1986) 'The Social and Political Participation of Yugoslav Immigrants in Sweden', Paper prepared for the ECPR Joint Sessions, Workshop on Migration as a National and International Challenge in European Immigration Countries, Göteborg, 1-6 April 1986.

EKA (1982) 'Teilnahme der Ausländer am öffentlichen Leben des Aufnahmelandes – ein zwischenstaatlicher Vergleich', *EKA Information*, 14 (Feb.): 49-58.

Entzinger, H. (1985) 'The Netherlands', pp. 50-88 in T. Hammar (ed.), *European Immigration Policy. A Comparative Study.* Cambridge: Cambridge University Press.

Esser, H., B. Hill and G. Von Oepen (1982) *Sozialökologische Bedingungen der Eingliederung Ausländischer Arbeitnehmer im Ruhrgebiet (am Beispiel der Stadt Duisburg).* Essen: University of Essen.

FitzGerald, M. (1984) *Political Parties and Black People. Participation, Representation and Exploitation.* London: Runnymede Trust.

FitzGerald, M. (1988) 'Afro-Caribbean Involvement in British Politics', pp. 250-66 in M. Cross and H. Entzinger (eds), *Lost Illusions.* London: Routledge.

Franz, F. (1984) 'Kommunales Wahlrecht für Einwanderer!', pp. 27-33 in H. Keskin (ed.), *Menschen ohne Rechte? Einwanderungspolitik und Kommunalwahlrecht in Europa.* Berlin: Express Edition.

Frowein, J.A. (1982) *Study of Civic Rights of Nationals of Other Member States in Local Public Life. Draft Report, October 1982.* Strasbourg: Council of Europe.

Gemeente Amsterdam (1982) *Kiezersenquête Stadsdeelraden.* Amsterdam: Gemeente Amsterdam, Bestuursinformatie.

Glazer, N. and D.P. Moynihan (1963) *Beyond the Melting Pot. The Negroes, Puerto Ricans, Jews, Italians, and the Irish of New York City,* Cambridge, Mass.: MIT Press and Harvard University Press.

Goffman, E. (1959) *The Presentation of Self in Everyday Life.* New York: Doubleday & Co.

Grisel, E. (1982) *Les Droits Politiques des Étrangers en Suisse. Les Étrangers en Suisse.* Lausanne: Faculty of Law of the University of Lausanne.

Groenendijk, C.A. (1985) 'D'étranger à Concitoyen. La Signification Symbolique du Droit de Vote pour les Immigrés aux Pays-Bas', *MRAX Information*, 40: 23–6.

Groenendijk, C.A. (1987) 'Vom Ausländer zum Mitbürger: die Symbolische und Faktische Bedeutung des Wahlrechts für Ausländische Immigranten', *Zeitschrift für Ausländerrecht und Ausländerpolitik*, 7 (1) (Feb.): 21–5.

Hammar, T. (1977) *The First Immigrant Election*. Stockholm: Ministry of Labour/EIFO.

Hammar, T. (1982) *Invandrar Kandidater: 1979 års kommunale Val*. Report No. 20, Stockholm: EIFO.

Hammar, T. (1984) 'Teilnahme der Einwanderer an der Schwedische Politik', pp. 45–55 in H. Keskin (ed.), *Menschen ohne Rechte? Einwanderungspolitik und Kommunalwahlrecht in Europa*. Berlin: Express Edition.

Hammar, T. (1985a) 'Citizenship, aliens' political rights, and politicians' concern for migrants: the case of Sweden', in R. Rogers (ed.), *Guests Come to Stay. The Effects of European Labor Migration on Sending and Receiving Countries*. Boulder, Col.: Westview Press.

Hammar, T. (1985b) *European Immigration Policy. A Comparative Study*. Cambridge: Cambridge University Press.

Hammar, T. and S.A. Reinans (1985) *SOPEMI Report Immigration to Sweden in 1984 and 1985*. Report 3. Stockholm: Stockholm University, Centre for Research in International Migration and Ethnicity.

Hammar, T. and S.A. Reinans (1987) *SOPEMI Report Immigration to Sweden in 1985 and 1986*. Report 4. Stockholm: Stockholm University, Centre for Research in International Migration and Ethnicity.

Haug, R.D. (1984) 'Kommunales Wahlrecht für Ausländer — Illusion oder Konkrete Utopie? Das Problem der Politischen Umsetzung einer Zeitgemässen Forderung', pp. 30–42 in F. Sen. and G. Jahn (eds.), *Wahlrecht für Ausländer. Stand und Entwicklung in Europa*. Frankfurt: Daĝyeli Verlag.

Ibrahim-Knoke, M. (1985) ' "Alle Staatsgewalt Geht vom Volke aus". Das Wahlrecht und die "Ausländer" ', *Kommune*, 3 (5): 15–17.

Klessman, C. (1978) *Polnische Bergarbeiter im Ruhrgebiet 1870–1945, Soziale Integration und Nationale Subkultur einer Minderheit in der Deutschen Industriegesellschaft*. Göttingen: Vandenhoeck & Ruprecht.

Koot, W. and J. Rath (1987) 'Ethnicity and Emancipation', *International Migration*, 25 (4): 426–40.

Koot, W. and P. Uniken Venema (1985) 'Etniseringen Etnische Belangenbehartiging bij Surinamers: een Nieuw Stijgingskanaal', *Migrantenstudies*, 1 (1): 4–16.

Lawrence, D. (1974) *Black Migrants, White Natives*. Cambridge: Cambridge University Press.

Layton-Henry, Z. (1983) 'Immigration and Race: Political Aspects – no. 9', *New Community*, 11 (1–2): 109–16.

Layton-Henry, Z. (1984) *The Politics of Race in Britain*, London: George Allen & Unwin.

Layton-Henry, Z. (1988) 'Black Electoral Participation: An Analysis of Recent Trends', Paper prepared for the annual conference of the Political Studies Association, Plymouth Polytechnic, 12–14 April.

Layton-Henry, Z. and D. Studlar (1985) 'The Electoral Participation of Black and Asian Britons: Integration or Alienation?', *Parliamentary Affairs*, 38 (3) (Summer): 307–18.

Le Lohé, M.J. (1975) 'Participation in Elections by Asians in Bradford', pp. 84–122 in I. Crewe (ed.), *British Political Sociology Yearbook*. Vol. 2: *The Politics of Race*. London: Croom Helm.

Le Lohé, M.J. (1983) 'Voter Discrimination against Asian and Black Candidates in the 1983 Elections', *New Community*, 11 (1–2): 101–8.

Ley, K. and S. Agustoni (1976) *Die Politische Integration von Ausländischen Arbeitneh-mern. Eine Pilotstudie zur Einbürgerungspolitik in der Schweiz.* Zurich: Sociology Institute of the University of Zurich.

Löwisch, P.C. (1984) 'Politische Mitbestimmungsmöglichkeiten in der Bundesrepublik Deutschland – eine Notwendigkeit jetzt', pp. 42–48 in F. Sen and G. Jahn (eds.), *Wahlrecht für Ausländer. Stand und Entwicklung in Europa.* Frankfurt: Dağyeli Verlag.

McAllister, I. and D. Studlar (1984) 'The Electoral Geography of Immigrant Groups in Britain', *Electoral Studies*, 3 (2): 139–50.

Meier-Braun, K.H. (1980) '*Gastarbeiter' oder Einwanderer? Anmerkungen zur Ausländer-politik in der Bundesrepublik Deutschland.* Frankfurt: Verlag Ullstein.

Miller, M.J. (1981) *Foreign Workers in Western Europe: An Emerging Political Force.* New York: Praeger.

Miller, M.J. (1987) *Forms of Alien Participation and Representation in Selected Western Democracies: An Aspect of the Transnational Politics of International Migration.* Report submitted to the German Marshall Fund of the U.S. Delaware: University of Delaware.

Murphy, R.C. (1982) *Gastarbeiter im Deutschen Reich. Polen in Bottrop 1891–1933.* Wuppertal: Peter Hammer Verlag.

Ozak, H. (1985) 'Ohne Politisches Entscheidungsrecht kann die Gesellschaftliche Integration der Ausländischen Wohnbevölkerung nicht verwirklicht Werden', *Forum*, 1: 15–28.

Özsunay, E. (1983) *Report on 'The Participation of the Alien in Public Affairs (Political and Associative Life)'.* Strasbourg: Council of Europe.

Pearson, D.G. (1981) *Race, Class and Political Activism. A Study of West Indians in Britain.* Westmead: Gower.

Pennings, P. (1986) *Migranten en de Amsterdamse Deelraadsverkiezingen van 30 October 1985.* Amsterdam: Gemeente Amsterdam: Amsterdam Municipality/University of Amsterdam, Department of Politics.

Pennings, P. (1987) *Migrantenkiesrecht in Amsterdam. Een onderzoek naar de Participatie en Mobilisatie van Etnische Groepen bij de Gemeenteraadsverkiezingen van 19 Maart 1986.* Amsterdam: Amsterdam Municipality/University of Amsterdam, Department of Politics.

Pieters, R.A.M. (1984) *Progreso di Antianonan? Een Oriënterend Onderzoek naar de Positie van Antillianen in Noord Brabant en Limburg.* Eindhoven: Stichting Progrese Antiyano.

Poeze, H. (1986) *In het Land van de Overheerser, Indonesiërs in Nederland 1600–1950.* Dordrecht: Foris Publications.

Rath, J. (1983a) 'The Enfranchisement of Immigrants in Practice. Turkish and Moroccan Islands in the Fairway of Dutch Politics', *Netherlands Journal of Sociology*, 19 (2): 151–80.

Rath, J. (1983b) 'Political Participation of Ethnic Minorities in the Netherlands', *International Migration Review*, 17 (3): 445–69.

Rath, J. (1985) *Migranten, de Centrumpartij en de Deelraadsverkiezingen van 16 Mei 1984 te Rotterdam.* Leiden: University of Leiden, Centre for the Study of Social Conflict.

Rath, J. (1986) 'Een Verwaarloosd electoraat', *Intermediair*, 22 (5): 59–63.

Rath, J. (1988a) 'Mobilization of Ethnicity in Dutch Politics', pp. 267–84 in M. Cross and H. Entzinger (eds), *Lost Illusions. Caribbean Minorities in Britain and the Netherlands.* London: Routledge.

Rath, J. (1988b) 'La Participation des Immigrés aux Élections Municipaux aux Pays-Bas', *Revue Européenne des Migrations Internationales*, 4 (3): 23–36.

Rath, J. (1988c) 'Political Action of Immigrants in the Netherlands: Class or Ethnicity?', *European Journal of Political Research*, 16 (6): 623–44.

Rex, J. (1979) 'Black Militancy and Class Conflict', pp. 72–92 in R. Miles and A. Phizacklea (eds), *Racism and Political Action in Britain*. London: Routledge & Kegan Paul.

Roosens, E. (1986) *Micronationalisme. Een Antropologie van het Etnische Reveil.* Leuven/Amersfoort: Acco.

Sandvoll, A. (1984) 'Die Einwanderungspolitik und die Einführung des Kommunalen Wahlrechts in Norwegen', pp. 71–84 in H. Keskin (ed.), *Menschen ohne Rechte? Einwanderungspolitik und Kommunalwahlrecht in Europa*. Berlin: Express Edition.

Studlar, D.T. (1983) 'The Ethnic Vote, 1983. Problems of Analysis and Interpretation', *New Community*, 11 (1–2): 92–100.

Verbunt, G. (1985) 'France', pp. 127–64 in T. Hammar (ed.), *European Immigration Policy. A Comparative Study*. Cambridge: Cambridge University Press.

Welch, S. and D.T. Studlar (1987) 'Voting for Minority Candidates in Local British and American Elections', Paper prepared for presentation at the Conference on Minorities in Advanced Industrial Societies, University of Notre Dame, Ind., 5–7 Dec.

Widgren, J. (1982) 'The Status of Immigrant Workers in Sweden', pp. 145–78 in E.J. Thomas (ed.), *Immigrant Workers in Europe: Their Legal Status. A Comparative Study*. Paris: Unesco Press.

Zweden Vandaag (1985) 3/9 Oct.:1–2.

8

Naturalisation: The Politics of Citizenship Acquisition

Gérard de Rham

The transformation of most post-war migrants from temporary residents to permanent settlers challenges the ideas and procedures for integration which had worked for previous waves of immigrants. Traditionally integration meant cultural assimilation and the acquisition of citizenship. Now the situation is more complicated due to the scale of migration, the reluctance of many migrants to naturalise, the unwillingness of some European countries to accept that permanent settlement has taken place and the refusal of some sending countries to give up their claims on their citizens (temporarily) abroad.

The problem is that in the modern world citizenship and complete equality of rights are closely tied together. On the socio-economic level, citizenship means the guarantee of fair access to the benefits of the modern welfare state (Freeman, 1986). Culturally, citizenship is often defined as sharing the dominant values of the host society. The political dimension of citizenship is the right to participate fully in the government of society, usually through voting. These three dimensions – namely, socio-economic membership, cultural belonging and political participation – can all be found in the concept of citizenship (Hammar, 1986).

In the modern world the nation state is the central organisation controlling access to the national social system. The state decides the crucial questions of admission, permanent residence, social equality, political participation and citizenship acquisition. The legitimacy of the state stems from its position as representative of the nation (historically and culturally determined) and from the election of rulers by citizens. Deciding the rules of citizenship acquisition is fundamentally important as it involves questions of political rights as well as identity: the composition and membership of the nation state.

For migrants the issue of citizenship is vitally important. The problem is that citizenship is often defined in exclusive terms as many states do not allow dual citizenship. However, large-scale international migration means that many people may wish to change their citizenship. Those who wish to acquire a new citizenship often have to prove that their ties to their new society are stronger than their ties to their society of origin. Moreover, there is generally no right to change citizenship. The granting of citizenship is entirely at the discretion of the nation state, according to international law (the Hague Convention of 12 April 1930).

In this chapter the term 'aliens' is used for describing all non-citizens and the term 'migrants' is used to describe non-citizen migrants. As this text is written in English, 'citizenship' is used to express the legal belongingness of the individual to a nation state, as a translation of such terms as French 'nationalité', German 'Staatsangehörigkeit', Dutch 'Nationaliteit' – or (in the Netherlands) 'Nederlanderschap' – and Swedish 'Medborgarskap'. This terminological use is intended to clarify the comparison between policies and debates in the different countries. In the case of current debate in France around 'citoyenneté et nationalité' (see Wihtol de Wenden, 1987), in order not to be misled, one should note that, according to this use, 'nationalité' means citizenship, whereas 'citoyenneté' has another sense near to what we called denizenship (see p.13, 194–5, this volume).

General Principles for Acquiring Citizenship

All states have established legal rules regulating the acquisition of citizenship. Basic common principles can be found underlying national regulations in spite of the differences between states. These differences are most marked in the ways *jus soli* and *jus sanguinis* principles are combined and in the political and administrative control of individual applications.

Jus soli *and* jus sanguinis

These two principles are the basis for the transmission, attribution and acquisition of citizenship. According to *jus soli* all persons born in the national territory are considered to be citizens, while *jus sanguinis* reserves citizenship to those descended from earlier citizens. One could argue that *jus soli* gives the pre-eminence to the territorial dimension in the definition of the nation state and *jus sanguinis* to the population dimension. Considered historically, *jus soli* was a feudal and monarchical rule, which stated that those born in the territory of a lord or a king were his subjects. The contrary tradition, that of the republican nation states, sought their basic legitimacy in the national community: citizenship according to *jus sanguinis* means hereditary membership of this community.

A strict application of either principle would exclude any possibility of acquiring a citizenship other than the one received at birth. One would be for one's whole life a citizen of the nation either of one's father or of one's birthplace. The descendants of immigrants would be made citizens of a new country under *jus soli* but be excluded from citizenship under *jus sanguinis*, without any choice. In practice, the regulations concerning citizenship in all countries reflect a combination of both principles, though usually with a clear preference for one or the other.

Discretionary power of the state and its limitations

As a general rule, the political authorities in each state have discretionary power over citizenship acquisition by way of individual decisions. National laws about citizenship establish the conditions and procedures for naturalisation, but the eventual power to accept or reject citizenship rests in the hands of the legally empowered political authorities.

National regulations may provide a right to acquire citizenship in situations defined in general terms, by claim, option or registration. Although controlling the procedure, political authorities cannot, in these cases, oppose citizenship acquisition, except in special cases, laid down in law.

The automatic acquisition of citizenship is similar to the possibility of registration, but without the necessity for any action by the person concerned. In this procedure, no act by the state is required to make valid an individual citizenship acquisition.

National Variations in Citizenship Acquisition

In each of the seven countries under study there exists legislation specifying the ways of acquiring, losing or transmitting citizenship. This is usually called the Nationality Act.

We are concerned with the opportunity and conditions for acquiring citizenship for foreign migrants, that is, in legal terms, for aliens legally residing within the country. We shall not consider all the rules for transmitting citizenship by descent, except for rules about the attribution of citizenship at birth for children of aliens, or at least for children at least one of whose parents is not a citizen. As far as the situation of people residing inside the country is concerned, the general principle is that children of male (and often also of female) citizens are citizens themselves. We are not studying the different rules that apply to children whose parents are unmarried or dual nationals. Nor shall we consider the rules for losing the citizenship of the host country.

This section will consider the main legal opportunities and conditions for foreign residents to acquire citizenship. Recent political debates have in several cases led to new nationality legislation in the project countries and these revisions will also be examined.

Sweden
Swedish citizenship can be acquired under relatively liberal conditions relating to age, residence, and good conduct as laid down by the Law on Citizenship (Medborgarskapslagen). The minimum age required for naturalisation is 18 years. An applicant must have resided in Sweden for five years although citizens of Nordic countries (Finns, Danes, Norwegians and Icelanders) need only two years' residence. Political refugees and people married to Swedes can apply for Swedish citizenship after four years' residence. 'Good conduct' is also a condition for all applicants. This requires that the applicant should not have been convicted of a criminal offence during his qualifying period of residence. However, only repeated criminality or very severe crimes will exclude an applicant from acquiring citizenship in the long term.

Apart from naturalisation there are two main procedures for acquiring Swedish citizenship: the first by application and the second by registration. Nordic citizens after five years' residence in Sweden only need to notify the regional authorities of their wish to naturalise. They have the absolute right to become Swedish citizens. Persons born in Sweden whose parents are both foreign citizens can also register as citizens. (If one parent is Swedish then they have Swedish citizenship at birth.) Acquisition of citizenship by registration is now the most common means by which foreign citizens naturalise in Sweden.

Sweden is a contracting state to the Convention of Strasbourg of 1963 which aims to reduce the number of cases of multiple citizenship and military obligations. Under this convention, a foreigner applying for citizenship must show that he renounces his former citizenship. Swedish law extends this obligation to citizens applying from non-contracting states. Dual citizenship is, however, not absolutely forbidden, as cases may occur where renunciation is impossible: for example, political refugees are not required to renounce their previous citizenship. Also the costs of renunciation for East Europeans are considered to be too high. A number of Southern European and non-European countries refuse to allow the renunciation of their citizenship.

This principle of requiring the renunciation of previous citizenship only applies in the application process and not for acquisition by registration. As a consequence it is estimated that there are more than 100,000 dual nationals in Sweden. This number is likely to increase in the future as the principles of the 1963 convention become more difficult to operate. In 1981 the Swedish government initiated a debate on dual citizenship within the Council of Europe, but received little support from other immigration countries, apart from France. The debate on dual citizenship is continuing in the council but not very actively.

These liberal arrangements for acquiring citizenship are the result of a policy of encouraging naturalisation which was supported by all political parties. The major area of disagreement in relation to immigration policy in Sweden has been the question of extending voting rights to foreign citizens at the national level. The non-socialist parties argued strongly that only Swedish citizens should be entitled to participate in national elections, otherwise Swedish citizenship would be undermined. This position does not necessarily discourage naturalisation. The right to vote in national elections may be an incentive for some immigrants to naturalise. The policy of encouraging naturalisation and imposing only liberal conditions allows the migrant to choose whether to be a full citizen and participate in national elections without imposing this duty and forcing assimilation.

The Federal Republic of Germany
The Federal Republic of Germany does not consider itself to be an immigration country and generally has a 'protectionist' policy towards the naturalisation of aliens. However, persons of German background coming from former German territories or from other parts of Eastern Europe have a right to claim citizenship. Citizens of the German Democratic Republic receive immediate citizenship. Otherwise, aliens must apply for naturalisation, and to achieve it have to fulfil relatively strict conditions.

Although the law on citizenship acquisition is a federal law, the actual decision in each case is decentralised at the level of the 'Regierungspräsident', the highest civil servant between *Länder* and communes. The law does not regulate every point and officials are expected to comply with guidelines (Einbürgerungrichtlinen, 1977) which lay down the following conditions for naturalisation: (1) own accommodation and the ability to maintain one's family; (2) a positive orientation towards Germany including mastery of the German language both spoken and written; (3) knowledge of the political system of the FRG and loyalty to the basic liberal democratic order; and (4) irreproachable conduct in Germany for at least ten years, defined more widely than just the absence of offences against the criminal law.

These regulations are expressed in rather general terms, which allows considerable scope for official discretion thus causing great uncertainty. Also, as a general rule, dual citizenship has to be avoided and also different citizenships by members of the same family. Bureaucratic procedures are inhibiting. The applicant has to bring about 20 documents and pay a fee of between DM100 and DM5,000 depending on income. The general rule for the fee is three-quarters of one month's salary.

Naturalisation has become a political issue in the last few years, focusing on the report issued in 1983 by the Commission for Migrants Policy (often known as the Zimmerman Commission), made up of representatives of the federal government, the governments of the *Länder* and the chief organisations of communes. The main recommendations of the Zimmerman report were easier naturalisation for long-established migrants and for the second and later generations; acceptance of dual citizenship if the country of origin refuses to accept the change, and the possibility of making migrants decide whether or not to opt for naturalisation within a certain time period. The various representatives on the commission could not agree on specific recommendations and so proposed alternative solutions without supporting any of them. Because of this and also because more liberal naturalisation proposals are very unpopular in Germany, no action has been taken. The debate, however, is likely to continue as the problem of assimilating the second generation becomes more acute.

United Kingdom
The United Kingdom has traditionally been a prime example of a country where the principle of *jus soli* has applied. Until the British Nationality Act of 1981, all persons born in any British territory in any part of the world could claim British citizenship, whether or not their parents were British citizens or legally settled. After the Second World War, countries belonging to the British Commonwealth began enacting their own citizenship legislation, but their citizens continued to be British subjects until the British Nationality Act 1981. Traditionally, therefore, British citizenship has been widely extended and many people with only slight connections with the United Kingdom had the right to British citizenship.

The immigration of West Indians and Asians from British colonies and Commonwealth countries, in the post-war period, caused the introduction of immigration controls in the 1960s and 1970s which undermined the traditional imperial notion of citizenship. The right of entry to, and settlement in, a country is a fundamental right of citizenship. Once immigration controls were erected against colonial and Commonwealth citizens it became inevitable that a new and narrower definition of British citizenship would have to be introduced. This was done by the British Nationality Act 1981.

A person born in the United Kingdom is a British citizen if at the time of his birth his father or mother is a British citizen or is settled in the United Kingdom. A person born outside the United Kingdom is a

British citizen if at the time of the birth his father or mother is a British citizen otherwise than by descent, or if one of his parents is serving in the armed forces, other government service or a European Community institution. A person born in the United Kingdom who is not entitled to British citizenship at birth is entitled to be registered as a British citizen after the age of 10 years, providing he has not been absent from the UK for more than 90 days in any of his first 10 years.

There are two ways for those who are not British citizens to acquire citizenship: registration for those with the right to claim citizenship and naturalisation for other foreign citizens. People entitled to register for citizenship are British overseas citizens who have not acquired the citizenship of their country of origin at independence, and citizens of British dependent territories provided they have lived in the UK for five years (or come from Gibraltar or the Falkland Islands). Registration was also open for a transitional period to Commonwealth citizens who were settled in the UK on 1 January 1973 or who have the right of abode and were living in Britain on 1 January 1983. Women married to British husbands before 1 January 1983 also had the right to registration. These transitional arrangements ended on 31 December 1987. Children under 18 years can ask for registration but without a right to citizenship, whereas adults entitled to register cannot be refused. A registration fee of £55 ($87) has to be paid.

Naturalisation is for all adults who do not qualify to register. It is subject to a condition of residence of between 3 and 5 years, a sufficient knowledge of the English (or Welsh or Scottish Gaelic) language, that he or she is of good character and intends to reside principally in the United Kingdom. Applicants must not be in breach of the immigration laws. Naturalisation is at the discretion of the Home Secretary, who does not have to give any reason for refusal, and there is no appeal against the decision. The fee for naturalisation is £160 ($250) but only £70 ($110) for spouses of British citizens. Foreign nationals must take an oath of allegiance to the Crown when they naturalise.

Dual citizenship is allowed in Britain without qualification. This may encourage the take-up of citizenship by immigrants settled in Britain as they need not renounce their previous citizenship. Dual citizenship is almost obligatory for Irish people as they are considered British in the United Kingdom and Irish in the Republic of Ireland.

The British Nationality Act 1981 marked the abandonment of the common citizenship of all British subjects. Citizens of independent Commonwealth countries no longer had British citizenship as well, though they retain their voting rights and other privileges when in Britain. British subjects in the remaining colonies became citizens of the British Dependent Territories and some others became British Overseas citizens. British citizenship was restricted to those with a close connection by birth, descent or settlement in the United Kingdom. As the trend of government policy has been to give priority and greatest security to those with British citzenship, the Nationality Act 1981 put considerable pressure on Commonwealth immigrants settled in the United Kingdom to register as British citizens. There was thus a very high level of applications for citizenship from Commonwealth citizens in spite of a high increase in fees after 1979. Pressure from parliament caused a reduction in fees from £200 to £160 in 1984.

France

According to the Nationality Code (Code de la nationalité, 1945, revised 1973), a number of persons whose parents have foreign citizenship automatically have, or can acquire, French citizenship. Due to the application of the 'double *jus soli*' principle, a child born in France is French if one of his parents was born in France (or in a French colony before independence); if both parents are foreign-born, then the child acquires citizenship automatically at majority if he or she has lived in France for five years and has not been convicted of a serious criminal offence. The young person may refuse French citizenship, in either case, by making a declaration as long as he has another citizenship and his parents agree. The government can refuse citizenship acquisition at majority for reasons of disqualification or lack of assimilation, but in a practice this has never occurred.

Registration for citizenship is allowed to persons married to a French citizen after six months, if asked for at marriage and to citizens of former African colonies born before independence.

Citizenship can also be obtained by naturalisation or reintegration for former citizens. The conditions are an age of at least 18 years, five years' residence, good behaviour and the absence of deportation orders or convictions for serious criminal offences. Assimilation to the French community is also required, including knowledge of the French language. The five years' residence period can be reduced to two years for persons born in France or married to a citizen, and for university graduates. It can be reduced to nothing for those who have given exceptional service, are former citizens or are the father of three or more children. The administrative fee for naturalization is small and depends on income. People earning less than the minimum legal wage, who make up a high proportion of applicants, are exempt. The Nationality Code does not require the renunciation of the former citizenship. This is requested only from applicants from contracting states to the Convention of Strasbourg 1963.

Although naturalisation remains a discretionary decision of the state it is rarely refused. Costa-Lascoux estimates that refusals do not exceed 10–12 percent of applications and many of these are accepted at the second attempt. However, CIMADE, an organisation supporting migrant workers, estimates refusals at 30 percent of applications.

In March 1986 the new Conservative government proposed to revise the Nationality Code, despite the reluctance of its centrist coalition partners. The new Bill was intended to end the acquisition of citizenship at birth by children born in France who had one parent born in a French colony, and also the automatic acquisition of citizenship at majority by young people resident in France for the previous five years. It would also have ended the right of foreign spouses to register as French citizens six months after their marriage. All these groups would have had to apply for citizenship by declaration, allowing the government discretion to refuse on the grounds of non-integration or criminal convictions. The children of foreigners applying for naturalisation would have to apply separately and would no longer be included in their parents' application. Finally, an oath to the laws of the Republic would become obligatory for all applicants.

The Bill was submitted to the Conseil d'Etat, where it was heavily criticised. Nevertheless, the government made only minor amendments, such as dropping the Oath to the Laws of the Republic, and proposed to submit the Bill to parliament. President Mitterrand and the Church hierarchy opposed the Bill. The most unexpected opposition came from students and young people already agitating against the government's proposed educational reforms. Second-generation immigrants were very active in this opposition and supported the criticisms of anti-racist groups like 'SOS Racism'.

In January 1987 the government made concessions to its critics and withdrew the Bill for further consultations. A 'Commission of Wise Men' was established, and their report was rather different from the government's proposals and was well received except by the National Front and 'SOS Racism' (the latter opposed one recommendation: the ending of automatic citizenship at majority for children born in France). Since President Mitterrand's re-election in May 1988 it appears that a drastic revision of French traditionally liberal policy has been avoided.

The Netherlands

The Law on Netherlands Nationality came into force on 1 January 1985. It allows young foreigners between 18 and 25 resident in the Netherlands since their birth to acquire Dutch citizenship by option. A simple statement that the applicant wishes to become Dutch is all that is required. For a transitional period, which ended in 1987, this option was available to foreign children of Dutch mothers and it was widely used. Applicants from both groups do not have to renounce their previous citizenship and can remain dual nationals. Under the 1985

Nationality Act a person whose father or mother is Dutch has Dutch citizenship. The children of aliens, who were born in the Netherlands, are Dutch citizens provided they were born in the Netherlands too.

Other aliens wishing to become Dutch citizens must naturalise. The conditions are five years' residence, an age of 18 years, the absence of a criminal record and integration in Dutch society, which means the ability to converse in simple Dutch. Foreigners married to, or living permanently with, a Dutch citizen, can apply for naturalisation after a period of three years. There was a special procedure for Surinamese citizens migrating to the Netherlands after the independence of Surinam and wishing to become Dutch citizens. This ended in 1986.

Applicants for naturalisation are required to renounce their former citizenship unless this is unreasonable. Moroccans, Greeks and East Europeans have difficulty giving up their previous citizenship and are allowed to remain dual nationals. The fee for naturalisation is 300 florins ($145). If naturalisation is refused, the applicant has a right to appeal.

The new Nationality Act 1985 replaced an earlier one dating back to 1892. The main innovations were equality for men and women in acquiring or transmitting citizenship, establishing an appeal procedure against refusal of naturalisation and substituting an administrative procedure in place of a legislative procedure. There was some criticism of the new legislation by lawyers who thought it was too restrictive, and also a campaign against it by the anti-immigrant Centre Party concerned that foreign criminals would be able to acquire Dutch citizenship too easily.

The new Act is part of the Dutch 'ethnic minorities policy' which combines strict admissions control with a more liberal naturalisation policy. The government stated that only minimal integration should be a requirement for naturalisation, that the cultural identity of aliens should be respected and that it was opposed to 'forced integration'.

Belgium

There has also been a new Belgian Nationality Act, which came into force in January 1985. This Act was passed to facilitate the acquisition of citizenship and especially to allow a 'double *jus soli*' principle, so that children born in Belgium with one parent also born in Belgium would have the right to become citizens before the age of 12 if their parents wished. If one of the parents is Belgian, the child has Belgian citizenship if born in the country.

Citizenship acquisition by option is possible for young people between 18 and 22 years in a large number of cases if they have lived in Belgium between the ages of 14 and 18 or for a period of nine years and have been resident for one year before applying for citizenship. Other foreigners may acquire citizenship by naturalisation in two stages. First, they apply for 'common naturalisation', which entitles them to all the rights of citizens except voting rights in provincial and national elections. The conditions are five years' residence and an age of 18 years. After five years of common naturalisation, the applicant may ask for 'full naturalisation', allowing all citizenship rights. The conditions for full naturalisation are an age of 25 years and a fee of BF2000 ($150).

In both cases of option and naturalisation the Attorney-General investigates the will to integrate and the moral character of the applicant. If the result of the enquiry is negative, citizenship will be refused. Citizenship acquisition normally implies renunciation of the previous citizenship.

The debate about the new Nationality Act led to divisions between parties on the left who were insisting on a more positive policy for integration immigrants and those on the right who, though they wished to encourage integration through easier naturalisation, were then worried by the great number of applications and pressed for the Act to be applied restrictively.

Switzerland
Citizenship in Switzerland has a three-fold character: every citizen of the Swiss Confederation is also a citizen of a canton (member state of the Confederation) and of a commune (commune d'origine) where he has a hereditary 'right of city' even if he has never lived there. The commune acts as registry office for all his family. This arrangement complicates the naturalisation process. An applicant needs to be accepted at each of these three autonomous levels, as a result of which ease of naturalisation varies considerably across the country.

At federal level citizenship acquisition and transmission is regulated by the Federal Nationality Act 1952 (revised December 1984). This Law is clearly based on the *jus sanguinis* principle. Citizenship acquisition is automatic only by marriage (by a foreign woman to a Swiss man) or by descent or adoption (when one parent at least is a Swiss citizen). People without these direct family connections to Swiss people can acquire citizenship by naturalisation in a canton and a commune. The necessary federal authorisation is given under the conditions of 12 years' residence and 'aptitude for naturalisation' proved by an investigation into his character and that of his family. The condition of 12 years' residence is reduced if the applicant has lived in Switzerland between the ages of 10 and 20, as these years count double. The fee at federal level varies between SF100 and SF200 ($70-140), varying with income. The applicant must renounce his former citizenship, if this is possible, in order to minimise cases of dual nationality. It is not possible to claim citizenship or to have a facilitated naturalisation procedure if both parents are foreign.

Cantons (and, according to cantonal laws, communes) also impose conditions for their acceptance of naturalisation applications. They investigate whether the applicant is well integrated, and approves Swiss political institutions and the Swiss way of life. They also fix fees and allow communes to charge for the acquisition of communal citizenship. As fees also vary with the applicant's income, differences can be extremely great, from SF100 ($70) for a person with low income in Neuchâtel or Thurgau to SF75,000 ($50,000) for a high income applicant in Geneva. Integration into the Swiss way of life is carefully investigated, as has been satirised in Rolf Lyssy's film *The Swissmakers*. As has been emphasised, the procedure is complex and needs positive decisions at three levels. At cantonal and communal levels, naturalisation decisions are usually taken by legislative assemblies (or even assemblies of citizens), and can be influenced by the political climate. It is thus hard for applicants to predict the likely success of an application as there is such wide scope for discretion.

Naturalisation policy has recently become a matter of political debate. In 1974 the anti-immigrant party, National Action Against Overforeignisation of People and Fatherland, launched an initiative to amend the constitution to limit naturalisation to 4,000 per year. This initiative was opposed by the federal government and parliament and was rejected by the electorate in 1977 by a majority of two to one.

In 1982 the government proposed a constitutional revision in order to guarantee equality between men and women in transmitting citizenship to their children and to standardise the conditions for the naturalisation of young foreigners brought up in Switzerland, and refugees and stateless persons. Parliament separated the question concerning the right of mothers to transmit citizenship to their children from that of facilitated naturalisation for foreigners. These were put separately to the vote in a referendum in 1983, with the anticipated result of the first being approved and the second rejected.

The Bill designed to enact the successful constitutional amendment was published by the government in August 1987. One of its main innovations is that men and women will be treated equally in all aspects of naturalisation. For example, automatic naturalisation for women marrying a Swiss man is to be ended and facilitated naturalisation for foreign men or women marrying a Swiss citizen is proposed. The conditions are that the marriage has lasted three years and the applicant is resident in Switzerland. The resumption of citizenship by former citizens is made possible after one year's residence. The criteria for naturalisation, that were undefined, will be made more precise; for example, integration into the Swiss community and way of life, conformity to the laws and absence of threat to the security of the country. This Bill has not yet been passed by parliament.

Attitudes Towards Citizenship Acquisition

There are very few surveys of migrants' attitudes towards acquiring the citizenship of their country of settlement (Hammar, 1985a). These surveys are limited because they only include a few nationalities and also because they are asking hypothetical questions and giving the respondents only a limited choice between keeping their existing citizenship or naturalising. Nevertheless, these surveys give some indication of the willingness of migrants to become full members of their new society.

A small survey in Sweden in 1984 showed that immigrants married to Swedes and members of the second generation have a greater willingness to naturalise than other immigrants. The ownership of property in the country of origin reduced the willingness to naturalise, as did plans to return. Those with passports that give little security in travelling abroad, like Chileans, are more willing to become Swedish citizens. One-third of those interviewed did not know whether to naturalise or not. A survey among Finns in Sweden by Hammar found that many were willing to naturalise providing they could become dual nationals and keep their Finnish citizenship as well.

At least two representative surveys have been carried out in Germany. In the first, in 1980, the Friedrich-Ebert-Stiftung asked migrants if they intended to apply for citizenship of the Federal Republic. Only 6.6 percent of them answered positively, Greeks, Yugoslavs and Italians being more likely to agree, and Turks, Spaniards and Portuguese being least likely. The second survey, carried out by Marplan in 1984, asked 'Would you be very/somewhat/ not interested in obtaining German citizenship?' Among replies, 13.2 percent said they were very interested and 32.1 percent somewhat interested, but a clear majority were not interested. Only 1 percent gave no reply. Greeks and Yugoslavs, as in the first survey, were the most interested, with Turks and Spaniards being the least interested. There was a significant change depending on length of residence, rising from 5.4 percent very interested among those with less than five years' residence, to 21 percent among those with 15 years or more of residence. This rise is due to a considerable decline with residence of those who reply 'somewhat interested', the proportion of 'not interested' remaining around 50–60 percent.

Swiss research in 1976, with a small, representative sample of 100 Italians in Zurich city, who had all lived at least five years in Switzerland, found that 8 percent had considered naturalisation and

19 percent would consider it; 18 percent gave no reply (Ley and Agustoni, 1976). Those from northern Italy, who had migrated earlier and had better jobs, were the most likely to reply positively. Occupational discrimination and fear of losing one's identity and not being accepted in a new one are very important in the decision to naturalise. If dual citizenship were possible, this would greatly increase the attraction of naturalisation, with 38 percent giving positive replies and an additional 29 percent giving conditionally positive replies. A more recent survey in 1983 among second-generation adults aged 25 years in selected areas of French-speaking Switzerland found that only 9.2 percent were considering naturalisation and 71.7 percent were opposed (Fibbi et al., 1983).

It appears from these, admittedly sparse, surveys that a majority of migrants do not plan to acquire the citizenship of the host country even after 20 years' residence. This is consistent with Hammar's assessment of the 'low propensity for naturalisation' (Hammar, 1985a). Acquiring citizenship seems to be generally seen as the final stage of integration by the migrants themselves, and means giving up plans or dreams to return to the country of origin. But even when such a return is not considered, most migrants prefer to keep their native citizenship for reasons of identity with loyalty to their original country. The same seems to be true for the second generation, at least in the case of Switzerland where naturalisation needs evidence of assimilation in the host country.

These surveys concern only willingness to apply for naturalisation and registration and ignore automatic acquisition – for example, as exists in France or citizenship at birth by *jus soli*. It is, however, not absolute: citizenship can be refused in France in spite of automatic procedure, and in all countries citizenship acquisition by persons born abroad is never excluded. In the Netherlands, this is even the most common case, as the number of persons entitled to automatic acquisition along 'double *jus soli*' lines (third generation) is yet limited. Although the statistics are also influenced by the high degree of difficulty in acquiring citizenship in countries like Germany and Switzerland, nevertheless there is evidence of a strong reluctance by migrants to become citizens of the countries where they now work and live.

Comparative Analysis of Citizenship Acquisition Policy

Basic principles

Jus soli *versus* jus sanguinis   The basic principle of *jus soli* is clearly dominant in Great Britain, although there was a slight erosion of the principle in the Nationality Act 1981. It is also dominant in France, the Netherlands and Belgium either directly by acquisition of citizenship at majority (automatically or by option) for aliens born in the country, or under the form of 'double *jus soli*' where children born in the country, having one parent also born in the country, are citizens. It is, however, not exclusive or absolute. Persons born abroad can also acquire citizenship, and in France citizenship acquisition by *jus soli* can be refused.

Jus sanguinis is dominant in Sweden, Germany and Switzerland. Here the children of foreigners, even if born in the country, have no way of acquiring citizenship except by naturalisation. In Sweden aliens born in the country may register for citizenship, but this option is not available in Switzerland and Germany for migrants' descendants.

Table 8.1   *Types of citizenship acquisition in the project countries*

Country	Automatic	Registration	Naturalisation
		Types of citizenship acquisition	
Sweden	None	Nordic citizens[1] Born in Sweden	All others
Germany	None	Former German territory	All others
Britain	Born in UK[1]	British overseas or Dependent Territory citizens	All others
France	Born in France[1]	Married to citizen Former citizens from African colonies	All others
Netherlands	Parent born in Netherlands	Born in Netherlands[1]	All others
Belgium	None	Young people in many defined situations[1]	All others
Switzerland	None	None	All

[1] Under conditions of residence or age.

Level of state control over citizenship acquisition   The automatic acquisition of citizenship for aliens exists in France, applying at majority to persons born in the country, under conditions of residence, and in Britain, where foreign children born and resident in the country can become citizens after 10 years of age. All the seven project countries, except Switzerland, admit by law a right to citizenship by registration or option either for specific categories of foreign citizens or under conditions of birthplace and residence. Citizenship acquisition on request, at the discretion of public authorities, exists in all seven countries.

Conditions of naturalisation

Clear differences between policies of citizenship acquisition appear in the comparison of the conditions legally imposed for obtaining citizenship through naturalisation.

Residence All the countries in this study impose conditions of residence before naturalisation can be applied for. The residence qualification varies considerably but is often relaxed for people born or educated in the country or for refugees and stateless persons. These conditions are summarised in Table 8.2.

Table 8.2 *Residence qualification for citizenship acquisition*

Country	Normal condition	Special condition
Sweden	5 years	Nordic citizens, 2 years Refugees, 4 years Married to Swede, 4 years
Germany	10 years (principle but not required by law)	—
Britain	3–5 years	—
France	5 years	Married to French citizen, 6 months to 2 years Born in France, 2 years University grad., 2 years 'Exceptional service', None Father of 3 children, None Former citizen, None
Netherlands	5 years	—

Belgium	10 years (5 common + 5 full naturalisation)	Young people 18–22:
		  9 years resident or 14–18 years of age
		Married to a Belgian,
		  6 mths

Switzerland	12 years (additional requirements possible from cantons or communes)	Residence 10–20 years of age counts double

Fees Financial requirements for citizenship acquisition vary considerably among the countries under study. A strict comparison would be too complex to make because in a number of countries the fee depends on the applicant's income. The details presented in Table 8.3 concern only fees for naturalisation under normal circumstances. Registration and facilitated procedures where they exist are generally cheaper. Exchange rates for comparison are those valid in April 1987 and the amounts have been rounded.

Table 8.3   *Fees for naturalisation (US$)*

Country	Fixed fee	income-related fee	
		Lowest	Highest
Sweden	—	—	—
Germany	—	55	2,725
Britain	250	—	—
France	—	—	—
Netherlands	145	—	—
Belgium	—	50	—
Switzerland	—	140	50,000

Rules of good conduct   Naturalisation is always subject to conditions of good conduct and positive commitment or loyalty to the new country, defined in different ways. Good conduct is usually defined as absence of a criminal conviction, while positive commitment usually means knowledge of the language, will to integrate in the new society or some test of loyalty.

Table 8.4   *Rules of good conduct and positive commitment required for naturalisation*

Country	Requirement		
	Good conduct	Integration	Language
Sweden	No recent or serious criminal conviction	None	None
Germany	Impeccable living, no convictions, maintaining family	Positive orientation to Germany and democracy	Mastery
Britain	No serious convictions	Oath of loyalty to Crown	Good
France	No serious convictions	None	According to status
Netherlands	Absence of registered convictions	Minimal solidarity with society	Simple
Belgium	Good morality	Will to integrate	Not specified
Switzerland	Variable	Good integration, approval of Swiss political institutions and way of life. (Cantons can make additional conditions.)	Variable

Complexity of procedure   In some countries, procedures for acquiring citizenship, and especially naturalisation procedures, strongly influence both the propensity to apply for citizenship and the likelihood of success. This relates both to the strictness of control by public authorities and to the complexity of the procedures.

Sweden, France and Britain have relatively simple naturalisation procedures. In Germany, Belgium and the Netherlands naturalisation procedures are longer and more difficult as they require that the applicant provides evidence of his commitment to integration for the authorities to assess. The Swiss procedure is the most complex, due to the involvement of each level of government in the naturalisation process. This leads to three autonomous levels of decision-making.

Simplified naturalisation procedures can be found in most countries for family reasons such as marriage, children of mothers who cannot transmit citizenship, adoption and legitimation of children. Registration is always a more simplified procedure than naturalisation, often needing only a declaration to a local or central public authority.

The French case of automatic citizenship attribution at majority for people born in France is the most simple procedure, as it requires no action by the person involved nor by the authorities. Often these people are both unaware of their entitlement to citizenship and continue to be treated as aliens by the authorities. Their citizenship, if contested, can be established in court. In these cases the simplicity of the procedures may cease to be to the advantage of the recipient.

The problem of dual citizenship   In all the countries under study one of the most acute questions is the problem of dual citizenship. Ten European states have signed the Strasbourg Convention of 6 May 1963 on the reduction of the number of cases of multiple citizenship and of dual military obligations. Among the contracting states are Sweden, the Netherlands, the Federal Republic of Germany, France, and the United Kingdom. Only Belgium and Switzerland, among our project countries, have not adhered to the convention.

The Strasbourg Convention aims to minimise cases of dual citizenship by the rule that the original citizenship must be renounced in cases of citizenship acquisition when the applicant is an adult and freely applying for a new citizenship either by naturalisation, registration or recovery. People with more than one citizenship are required to fulfil military service only in one country.

In spite of this, treaty cases of dual citizenship have greatly increased because of international migration. Hammar estimates that there are more than 3 million dual citizens in Europe (Hammar, 1985a), but the numbers could greatly exceed this as it is estimated that people of dual French and North African nationality number 1 million. The Strasbourg Convention has failed to achieve its aims because of the great increase in international migration and because it only applies to naturalisation procedures and not to citizenship acquisition by descent, marriage or automatic attribution. Only two emigration countries, namely Italy and Ireland, have signed the convention. Another reason for its failure is that enforcement has been half-hearted.

Whereas five of the states under study adhere to the convention, two of them – namely, Britain and France – have not integrated renunciation into their laws and only require it from citizens of another contracting state. But even in the other three states, where renunciation of the former citizenship would cause problems for the applicant, he can retain it.

It is understandable why the official policy of many states should be to avoid dual citizenship. It may lead to practical problems of judicial conflict, as in the much publicised cases of 'legal kidnapping' of children from mixed families, conflict over obligations of military service or taxation. There are also symbolic reasons based on the conception of citizenship as allegiance or exclusive membership of a national community. Dual citizenship is thus a contradiction of the total loyalty that states demand from their citizens.

Dual citizenship may have disadvantages for those who have it. This is most evident in the case of dual military obligations for young men, though this is often resolved either by adhering to the recommendations of the Strasbourg Convention or by bilateral agreement between states. More important is uncertain legal status and jurisdiction in personal and family legal questions such as name, marriage, divorce, descent and succession. The laws of Islamic and European states differ considerably in these matters and conflict over 'forced' marriages and custody of children of divorced parents have been much publicised. Finally, dual citizenship may limit the legal protection a state can give to its citizens abroad. This may be most important for naturalised citizens whose former countries refuse to allow renunciation of their citizenship.

The legal advantages of dual citizenship are that the individual is free to live and work in both countries where he enjoys full social and political rights. Dual citizenship may also allow a choice of legal jurisdiction, although this is often limited by the principle of applying the law of the country of residence, which is often defined as predominant.

There are conflicting opinions about the balance of advantages and disadvantages of dual citizenship, and the debate is perhaps just beginning. It is interesting to note the divergent conclusions of two social scientists who have recently examined this issue. Hammar argues for a reconsideration of the Strasbourg Convention and easier access to dual nationality, with priority being given to the country of residence (Hammar, 1985a). Costa-Lascoux (1986) is much more reluctant about dual citizenship because of the division between its symbolic, religious and cultural aspects which continue to link migrants to their country of origin and the functional, economic and legal aspects which predominate in the country of residence. She criticises the idealistic idea of 'choosing one's citizenship', thus leaving to the individual the responsibility of making a choice without being able to assess all the consequences. She would prefer an evolution in the notion of citizenship away from allegiance to a state to membership in a state.

Liberal versus Protectionist Policies

One can contrast the policies of the project countries into liberal and protectionist. A liberal policy is pursued in Sweden, Britain and France. These countries impose only modest conditions on the acquisition of citizenship by resident foreigners; namely, automatic or optional citizenship for children born in the country, five years' residence or less, no or modest cost, limited conditions of good conduct and a simple procedure.

The Netherlands and Belgium have revised their policies in the liberal direction. They are more demanding about evidence of the applicant's will to integrate, requiring an investigation by authorities leading to somewhat more complex procedures.

At the protectionist pole one can find Switzerland and Germany, both of which impose numerous and onerous conditions for naturalisation. There is no facilitated procedure for migrants' descendants, a long residence qualification (10–12 years), high fees and complex and discretionary procedures to prove that the applicant is well integrated or even assimilated into the society. In these two countries naturalisation is seen as the final stage of assimilation. One can only become a citizen having renounced all attachments to the country of origin. In both countries there have been recent debates about liberalising naturalisation procedures but they failed to result in policy changes as no consensus could be achieved.

Comparing the Effects of National Policies

General comparisons
Hammar has compared the rate of citizenship acquisition in the foreign population of six of the seven project countries. This comparison is general in the sense that it does not distinguish between types of acquisition (naturalisation, registration and so on) or between former nationality of the naturalised. This analysis gives a first evaluation of the effects of different policies of citizenship acquisition (Table 8.5). Computing the same percentage for a more recent year leads to broadly similar results (Table 8.6).

There are a number of caveats to be made when analysing these tables. First, the definition of citizenship acquisition and the foreign population vary within and between the countries, as do methods of estimating the numbers. There are also specific national variations and

Table 8.5   *Acquisition of citizenship by country and in relation to the size of the foreign population, 1980*

Country	Foreign population	Acquisition of citizenship	%
Sweden	543,600	19,200	3.5
Netherlands	414,000	20,800	5.0
France	3,500,000	120,000	3.4
Switzerland	909,000	18,100	2.0
Belgium	903,736	8,700	1.0
Germany (Fed. Republic)	4,629,800	14,960	0.3

Source: T. Hammar, 'Dual Citizenship and Political Integration', *International Migration Review*, 19 (3): 438–49

Table 8.6   *Acquisition of citizenship by country and in relation to the size of the foreign population, 1984*

Country	Foreign population	Acquisition of citizenship	%
Sweden	390,565	21,844	5.59
United Kingdom (1986)	1,736,000	45,872	2.64
Netherlands	558,700	8,570	1.53
France (1982)	3,680,100	51,600	1.40
Belgium	890,900 (1983)	8,290 (1982)	0.93
Switzerland	932,400	8,593	0.92
Germany (Fed. Republic)	4,363,700	38,046	0.87

Source and notes: see Tables 8.7–8.13 below

peculiarities; for example, Hammar's figures for Germany exclude acquisition of citizenship by people from former German territories. As such data is included in the 1984 figures and would be included by some of the other countries, one could revise the 1980 figure for Germany to 0.9 percent, which is similar to the official rate given by the Deutscher Bundestag.

Second, there is also a great deal of uncertainty about the French data. The SOPEMI Report for 1985 gives 52,103 as the figures for citizenship acquisition in France for 1980. This excludes automatic acquisition, for which no figures are available. The discrepancy with Hammar's figure of 120,000 is startling. For 1984, the estimates of 15,000 to 17,000 automatic acquisitions have been added to the 35,573 acquisitions by naturalisation or declaration based on SOPEMI. But these estimates only include automatic acquisition at majority age, as automatic attribution at birth by the 'double *jus soli*' principle is considered as just births by French citizens. These latter are estimated by Costa-Lascoux (1987) at 40,000, and the grand total of all these types of citizenship acquisitions comes to nearly 100,000, which is closer to Hammar's figure. Using these figures one could estimate citizenship acquisition at 2.72 percent for 1982/3.

Third, in the cases of Belgium and the Netherlands, the figures do not reflect recent changes in naturalisation policies, which will only be apparent after 1985. Dutch figures include a high proportion of Surinamese and former Dutch citizens readmitted to citizenship. Both of these groups are declining in importance. In the Swiss figures the number of naturalisations for 1980 include citizenship acquisition or adoption and a number, about 4,000, of children of Swiss mothers whose naturalisation was allowed by a revision of the law in 1978. The figures for 1984 do not include these categories.

In spite of the impossibility of obtaining strictly comparable data, some interesting conclusions can be drawn from these tables. First, the gap between Sweden, with over 5 percent of naturalisations, and Germany, at less than 1 percent, is very marked. It means that theoretically, *ceteris paribus*, the foreign population of Sweden could all become citizens in less than 20 years, while in Germany this would take more than 100 years. In between, Britain, the Netherlands and France come around the middle of the list, while Switzerland and Belgium come near the bottom.

These findings confirm the indications given by the comparison of national policies. Sweden has the most open, liberal policy promoting naturalisation. The French liberal policy has also resulted in a great number of citizenship acquisitions, of which about two-thirds are made by attribution at birth or majority and one-third by naturalisation or reintegration (Costa-Lascoux, 1987). British figures tell a similar story, even if the most important characteristics of citizenship policy do not appear here: that is the fact that a large majority of migrants in the UK are British citizens because of (former) colonial or Commonwealth ties. That the Netherlands liberal policy was already clear before the 1985 legal revision, appears equally obvious.

Also one should not be surprised to find Switzerland and Germany at the other extreme. Their restrictive policies are clear in the numerous and difficult conditions imposed on applicants for naturalisation. The position of Belgium is likely to change significantly as the new Nationality Law of 1985 takes effect.

Differences among national groups of migrants The citizenship policies of the receiving countries play a decisive role in the variations of the naturalisation rate among countries. However, in each country there are significant variations among members of different national groups. These variations will be examined for seven representative national groups of migrants in six of the project countries. Detailed data for Belgium were not available to the author.

Due to the difficulties and uncertainties in computing these percentages, we can only draw partial and tentative conclusions from the comparison. However, it is clear that the differences between

Table 8.7   *Absolute and relative acquisition of citizenship by*
selected national groups in Sweden, 1984

Origin	Resident population	Acquisition of citizenship	%
Greece	10,410	1,090	10.5
Italy[1]	4,009	90	2.2
Morocco	1,157	244	21.1
Portugal	1,544	n.d.	—
Spain	2,997	223	7.4
Turkey	21,159	1,281	6.0
Yugoslavia	38,253	687	1.8
All alien	390,565	21,844	5.6

[1] 1985 data (1984 data included in 'other countries').
n.d. No data available.

Source: SOPEMI Report for Sweden, 1985

Table 8.8   *Absolute and relative acquisition of citizenship by*
selected national groups in the Federal Republic of Germany, 1983

Origin	Resident population	Acquisition of citizenship	%
Greece	292,300	344	0.1
Italy	565,000	1,119	0.2
Morocco	44,200	46	0.1
Portugal	99,500	69	0.1
Spain	166,000	258	0.2
Turkey	1,552,300	846	0.1
Yugoslavia	612,800	2,395	0.6
All alien	4,534,900	39,485	0.9

Source: SOPEMI, 1985

Percentages for migrants are lower than the mean rate. This is due to the fact that a majority of cases of citizenship acqusition are those of people of German origin from former German territories, who have a right to apply for citizenship: they amount to 25,252, as compared with 14,334 naturalisations representing only 0.3% of the foreign population.

Table 8.9   *Absolute and relative acquisition of citizenship by*
selected national groups in Great Britain, 1986

Origin	Resident population	Acquisition of citizenship	%
Greece	11,000	178	1.6
Italy	77,000	422	0.5
Morocco	n.d.	209	—
Portugal	n.d.	155	—
Spain	29,000	239	0.8
Turkey	12,000	352	2.9
Yugoslavia	n.d.	209	—
All alien	1,736,000	45,872	2.6

Sources: Population: 3-year average 1984–6 computed from Labour Force Survey; citizenship: *Home Office Statistical Bulletin* 29/87; n.d. No data available

These British data are only partial, and concern statistically small migrant populations. A majority of migrants in Britain are Commonwealth citizens, mainly from the Indian sub-continent and the West Indies.

Table 8.10   *Absolute and relative acquisition of citizenship by selected national groups in France, 1984*

Origin	Resident population[1]	Acquisition of citizenship	%
Non-automatic acquisitions			
Greece	n.d.	n.d.	—
Italy	333,700	2,984	0.9
Morocco	431,100	1,879	0.4
Portugal	764,900	4,318	0.6
Spain	321,400	4,148	1.2
Turkey	123,500	388	0.3
Yugoslavia	64,400	962	1.5
All alien	3,680,100	35,573	1.0
Automatic acquisitions			
All alien		around 16,000	1.4
Attribution at birth			
All alien		around 40,000	
Grand total		around 100,000	2.7

[1] Data from population census, March 1982; n.d. No data available.

Sources: SOPEMI, 1985: Costa-Lascoux, 1986; Costa-Lascoux, 1987

Table 8.11   *Absolute and relative acquisition of citizenship by selected national groups in the Netherlands, 1984*

Origin	Resident population	Acquisition of citizenship	%
Greece	4,000	40	1.0
Italy	20,300	330	1.6
Morocco	111,300	110	0.1
Portugal	7,900	80	1.0
Spain	20,700	130	0.6
Turkey	155,600	280	0.2
Yugoslavia	12,200	80	0.7
All alien	558,700	8,570	1.5

Source: SOPEMI, 1985

In the case of the Netherlands, it is interesting that figures of citizenship acquisition have greatly increased after the enforcement of the new Nationality Act, amounting to 15,740 in 1985 (2.8% of the 1984 alien population) and 11,798 in 1986 (2.1% of the same population).

Table 8.12   *Absolute acquisition of citizenship by selected national groups in the Netherlands, 1984–6*

Origin	Acquisition of citizenship		
	1984	1985	1986
Greece	40	160	n.d.
Italy	330	470	181
Morocco	110	1,190	1,350
Portugal	80	260	158
Spain	130	320	129
Turkey	280	1,400	1,242
Yugoslavia	80	390	209
All alien	8,570	15,740	11,798

Sources: SOPEMI, 1985 and 1986; C.B.S. *Maandstatistiek van de Bevolking*, 1986; n.d. No data available

The increase is especially great for Moroccans and Turks, who were the least likely to naturalise under the former Nationality Act. No increase has occurred for Italians and Spaniards: this might be because they belong to the European Community which guarantees them freedom of movement to the Netherlands and to their country of origin as well as full social rights.

Table 8.13   *Absolute and relative citizenship acquisition by selected national groups in Switzerland, 1984*

Origin	Resident population	Acquisition of citizenship	%
Greece	8,900	81	0.9
Italy	398,600	2,049	0.5
Morocco	1,400	26	1.9
Portugal	24,400	37[1]	0.2
Spain	106,000	344	0.3
Turkey	49,800	136	0.3
Yugoslavia	63,600	374	0.6
All alien	932,400	8,593	0.9

Sources: SOPEMI, 1985, except [1]1985 figure from *La vie economique*, April 1986

Table 8.14   *Percentages of citizenship acquisition by selected national groups in the countries under study*

Origin	Sweden	Germany	Britain	France[1]	Netherl.	Switzerl.
Greece	10.5	0.1	1.6	—	1.0	0.9
Italy	2.2	0.2	0.5	0.9	1.6	0.5
Morocco	21.1	0.1	—	0.4	0.1	1.9
Portugal	—	0.1	—	0.6	1.0	0.2
Spain	7.4	0.2	0.8	1.2	0.6	0.3
Turkey	6.0	0.1	2.9	0.3	0.2	0.3
Yugoslavia	1.8	0.6	—	1.5	0.7	0.6
All alien	5.6	0.9	2.6	1.0 2.7[2]	1.5	0.9

[1] Naturalisations and registrations only.

[2] All citizenship acquisitions.

national groups of migrants are smaller than the differences between immigration countries. This supports the view that citizenship acquisition policy is a more important factor in determining citizenship acquisition than the propensity to naturalise of particular national groups. Sweden and Germany are the polar cases. None of the national groups considered here has lower percentages than 1.8 in Sweden or greater than 0.6 in Germany.

Differences in naturalisation rates obtained by specific national groups are interesting in illuminating the effects of citizenship acquisition policy. The greatest difference concerns Moroccans, whose rate is only 0.1 percent in Germany but over 20 percent in Sweden, a ratio of 1:200. The ratio for other groups in Sweden and Germany is 1:100 for Greeks, 1:60 for Turks, 1:35 for Spaniards, 1:10 for Italians and 1:3 for Yugoslavs.

There are many reasons which contribute to these variations. The size, status and acceptance of immigrant populations may be important. The closeness of the country of origin and the strength or weakness of its economy may influence feelings about likelihood of return. Migrants within the European Community may see fewer and fewer advantages in changing their citizenship, and this may influence naturalisation rates of Spaniards, Greeks, Portuguese and Italians. An important factor is the policy of the country of origin. Morocco and Greece do not allow renunciation of their citizenship. This is bound to reduce the naturalisation rates for these groups, perhaps even in countries which allow dual citizenship. However, Sweden, which officially is opposed to dual nationality, still has higher rates of citizenship acquisition than countries which allow it, like Britain and France.

It is interesting to note that the trends in the Netherlands since the new Nationality Act show the importance of citizenship acquisition policy. Naturalisations by Greeks increased four-fold between 1984 and 1985, by Turks five-fold and by Moroccans more than ten-fold and remained stable or increased in 1986. These groups seem to be sensitive to changes in citizenship acquisition policy. Naturalisations by Italians, Portuguese, Spaniards and Yugoslavs were more limited and even decreased in 1986.

Conclusion

This comparative analysis of citizenship acquisition in the seven countries under study shows a number of uniformities and divergences which can be summarised in a bipolar typology, the poles of which are termed 'liberal' and 'protectionist'. This use of terms from the nineteenth-century debate on political economy is significant but should not be allowed to mislead. One of the main tasks of states in the late twentieth-century seems to be to control the circulation of labour, perhaps because this factor of production is easier to control than capital. However, one should not limit oneself to economic explanations of policy differences as political and cultural explanations may be more important. Institutional arrangements, like federalism in Switzerland, can be influential, but the political and cultural attitudes of decision-makers and citizens can be even more decisive.

Comparisons between rates of citizenship acquisition and the influences of changes in nationality laws, such as the Dutch reforms of 1984, show that propensity to naturalise is closely related to the citizenship policy of the receiving states. It is not surprising that those states which regard migrant workers as 'guest-workers' have the most protectionist policies, while naturalisation is much higher in countries which have policies of permanent immigration. This is confirmed by Hammar's study 'Dual Citizenship and Political Integration' (Hammar, 1985a).

Recent debates and policy changes concerning citizenship acquisition generally go in a liberal direction, even though in Germany and Switzerland attempts to revise the law have been unsuccessful. British policy has moved in the opposite direction, from an extremely liberal definition of imperial citizenship to the more protectionist policy of the British Nationality Act 1981. Proposals in France to become more protectionist have so far been resisted and the debate shows the strength of liberal ideas.

Another trend in the area of citizenship has been the recent emergence of forms of 'collective citizenship', as in the countries of the Nordic Council or the European Community. Within these communities freedom of movement, work and abode are the first benefits of this collective citizenship, with equal economic and social rights coming next. Voting rights at the local level seem to be the third element, and gradually it seems possible that a Nordic and a European Community citizenship have begun to emerge. There seems to be no contradiction between extending most citizenship rights to all immigrants, as in Sweden, and a collective citizenship for people from the regional (in Sweden's case, Nordic) area.

In European countries, citizenship is traditionally the criterion for full rights in every field of social life. Citizenship acquisition is the final stage of acquiring these rights for non-citizens who begin with the right of abode and employment and gradually acquire full economic and social rights as permanent residents and their voting rights as naturalised citizens. This book has emphasised a continuum and a movement from minimal rights (illegal immigrants) to full rights (citizens). But it can be questioned whether citizenship will also be the only end of this evolutionary process. Hammar (1986) has suggested that 'denizenship' might be a way of giving migrants the full range of rights without the necessity of acquiring a new citizenship. This would provide migrants with a choice of complete integration as a citizen or as an alien with equal status to citizens through denizenship.

The remarkable fact is that immigrants are extremely reluctant to change their citizenship even when encouraged to do so by liberal naturalisation policies. The receiving states can encourage or discourage citizenship acquisition but they cannot force migrants to naturalise: migrants are independent political actors. The fundamental stake for migrants is whether they can become significant, collective, political actors. If they can, they may be able to negotiate the creation of the status of 'denizenship' with the aim of preserving ties with the country of their origin and loyalty as citizens, but admit their membership of their country of residence as denizens. Whether they decided to be a citizen or a denizen of either state would be open to their individual choice.

References

Costa-Lascoux, J. (1986) 'Immigration, nationalité, citoyenneté', Paper presented to the ECPR Workshop on 'Migration as a national and international challenge in European immigration countries', Göteborg, 1–6 April.

Costa-Lascoux, J. (1987) 'L'Acquisition de la nationalité française, une condition d'intégration?', in LAACHER Smain (coordinateur), *Questions de nationalité*. Paris, CIEM/L'Harmattan; pp.81–126.

Fibbi, R., O. Virnot and G. de Rham (1983) *'Différenciations sociales et reproduction des appartenances: les jeunes adultes'*, Recherche sur la formation et l'insertion professionnelle des jeunes étrangers et suisses. Rapport sur la troisième population. Lausanne, mimeo.

Freeman, G. (1986) 'Migration and the political economy of the Welfare State', *Annals of the American Academy of Political and Social Science*, 485 (May): 51–63.

Friedrich-Ebert-Stiftung (1981) *Situation der ausländischen Arbeitnehmer und ihrer Familienangehörigen in der Bundesrepublik Deutschland*. Bonn.

Hammar, T. (1985a) 'Dual Citizenship and Political Integration', *International Migration Review*, 19 (3): 438–50.

Hammar, T. (ed.) (1985b) *European Immigration Policy: A Comparative Study*. Cambridge: Cambridge University Press.

Hammar, T. (1986) *Citizenship: Membership of a Nation and of a State*. Paper to the XIth World Congress of Sociology, New Delhi, (Aug.).

Ley, K. and S. Agustoni (1976) 'Die politische Integration von ausländischen Arbeitnehmern: eine Pilotstudie zur Einbürgerungsproblematik in der Schweiz', *Schweizerische Zeitschrift für Soziologie*, 2(3): 119–47.

Marplan Forschungsgesellschaft (1984) *Gastarbeiter in Deutschland*. Bonn.

Sayad, A. (1984) 'Etat, nation et immigration: l'ordre national à l'épreuve de l'immigration', *Peuples méditerranéens*, 27–8, (April–Sept.) 187–205.

SOPEMI, 'Système d'observation permanente des migrations'. Paris: OECD, yearly.

SOPEMI Report: Immigration to Sweden in 1984 and 1985 (1985) Tomas Hammar and Sven Alur Reinans. Stockholm University.

Wihtol de Wenden, C. (1987) *Citoyenneté, nationalité et immigration*. Paris: Arcanthère.

9

Citizenship or Denizenship for Migrant Workers?

Zig Layton-Henry

The basic theme of this book is that the scale, extent and diversity of post-war immigration to Western Europe has confronted these advanced industrial democracies with a number of challenges which are so far unresolved. First, immigration has transformed European nation states into multi-national and multi-cultural societies at the same time as wider regional groupings such as the Nordic Union and the European Community have been created. Thus the traditional concept of the nation state has been challenged at two levels simultaneously. Second, immigration has rendered obsolete accepted definitions of membership in, and citizenship of, a modern state. Third, the permanent settlement of millions of foreign immigrants who are excluded from political participation challenges the liberal democratic values and institutional procedures so greatly prized in these multi-party democracies.

Before the Second World War, most people residing within European states were citizens. Membership of a state implied citizenship either because one was part of the national community by descent under *ius sanguinis* or because birth within the territory of the state conferred citizenship under *ius soli*. Citizenship was associated with a range of rights (as well as duties), such as the right to personal security, freedom of speech, the protection of the law, the right to participate in the labour and business markets and, symbolically the most important of all, the right to participate in the selection of the political leaders of the state.

Citizenship also implied a national and cultural identity. Although most European states had national minorities, some of which were even irredentist, most European states considered themselves to be nation states whose members felt a strong sense of shared history, culture and political experience. Citizenship thus implied a sense of mutual solidarity not only between citizens but also between the governors and the governed, because of this common membership of the national community. In democracies, national unity and the legitimacy of the rulers were reinforced by citizen participation in elections. The relationship between the state and the citizens was seen as reciprocal, and this reciprocity has been strengthened by the rise of the modern welfare state. A citizen can now call upon the assistance of the state if he is in difficulty – for example, if ill, disabled or unemployed, as well as when in trouble abroad. In turn, the state can require its citizens to help implement its policies by co-operating in raising taxes and obeying other laws, and particularly by serving in the armed forces in time of national emergency.

In recent times, citizenship has grown in importance as the world has become more and more dominated by sovereign states. After the First World War, European states introduced passports and controlled access to their territory more stringently. After the Second World War, the growing numbers of sovereign states – often created as the result of the collapse of the European empires – became increasingly jealous of their national rights and interests and strongly opposed to interference in their internal affairs. The regional arrangements in Europe go somewhat against this trend, but even in the European Community and the Nordic Union, states are reluctant to give up much of their sovereignty. In the contemporary world of sovereign states, to be without citizenship or stateless is to be in a nightmare situation without the right to permanent residence, work or sustenance and entirely at the mercy of arbitrary authority.

In Western Europe, as post-war reconstruction developed into the long economic boom of the 1950s and 1960s, and as welfare states were developed and consolidated, two consequences followed. First, the massive migration from the European periphery and the Third World provided the labour to fuel and sustain the expanding European economies. Second, there was a dramatic widening of the economic gulf between the rich advanced industrial states of Western Europe and the rest of the First World, and the poverty, debt and insecurity of the Third World. Membership of an advanced industrial welfare state became an ever more attractive prize for those who could achieve it, giving access to employment, income, decent accommodation, education and health care for family members and social security benefits for the unemployed. Migrant workers could achieve access to these material benefits only after a hard struggle, but the prospects were good for those who could achieve the status of permanent residents or denizens of these states. In a world of violence, war and arbitrary authority, these countries also offered a relatively high degree of personal security.

Some Western European countries such as Britain, Sweden, the Netherlands and France quickly realised that the economic advantages of settlement in Europe were so great that few foreign migrant workers were likely to return to their countries of origin. These states were slower to realise that post-war immigrants would not be integrated and assimilated easily and completely, but would transform West European countries from relatively homogeneous nation states to multi-national and multi-cultural societies.

British policy-makers were the first to realise the difficulties of assimilating Third World migrants, and almost as soon as colonial immigration began they started devising proposals to control non-white immigration. British policy-makers assumed that non-white immigrants would be as unwelcome to the general population as they were to many of the elite and that they would consequently suffer serious discrimination on racial grounds (Layton-Henry, 1988). However, partly because of the serious shortage of labour in the 1950s and 1960s and because of foreign policy objectives in relation to colonial and Commonwealth governments, substantial immigration controls were not introduced until the mid-1960s. The twin thrust of British immigrant policy since then has been a combination of tough immigration controls aimed at reducing Third World immigration, and weak race relations legislation to reduce the most blatant forms of racial discrimination, provide standards of good conduct for individuals and companies, and reassure non-white immigrant citizens that they are entitled to be treated on the basis of equality. As the large majority of immigrants to Britain were legally British subjects, the problems of citizenship and membership of the British political system did not arise. Most immigrants to Britain had the full legal rights of British citizens from the moment they arrived. The problems they faced were practical experiences of racism and racial discrimination from members of a society which saw them as outsiders and unwelcome competitors for scarce resources. The experience of racism and discrimination was particularly severe, since most immigrants expected to be treated as full and equal citizens because of their status as British subjects, and because in many cases early migrants had served in the British forces during the war. Despite their full legal rights, many black British citizens feel that *de facto* they have second-class status.

In the other project countries, however, most immigrants were not citizens and were often seen as a temporary solution to short-term labour shortages. But as so often happens, short-term expedients became long-term solutions. By the 1980s the number of foreign residents in Western Europe had risen to over 15 million, and they were assuming all the characteristics of a permanently settled population. The vast majority had lived and worked in Europe for over 15 years, were living with their families, and were sending their children to school. They had transformed many inner-city areas with their shops, businesses, churches and mosques. They were valued members of their firms and local communities and were increasingly involved in the provision of social and welfare services as well as being the recipients of these services. Above all, they were taxpayers. However, despite the deep roots they had put down in Western Europe, they were excluded from full membership of their countries of residence because they lacked citizenship. The democratic precept 'No taxation without representation' did not apply to them. The precept for foreign citizens was 'No representation without naturalisation'. However, a substantial majority of migrant workers were proving to be unwilling to become naturalised citizens of their new countries of residence. In some cases the complexity and expense of the naturalisation procedure was a major deterrent, and in others there was pressure from their home governments not to naturalise; but overwhelmingly there was reluctance to compromise their national identity and betray their origins.

This raises the question as to whether these long-established members of Western European societies should continue to be excluded from political participation just because they lack citizenship. Should recognition be given to a new form of association between the state and permanent residents who do not wish to change their citizenship? Professor Hammar has suggested that this new term should be 'denizenship' (see Chapter 1, page 13). We have argued that the distinction between citizen and non-citizen has been eroded by recent developements caused by post-war immigration. There is no longer a sharp distinction between the rights enjoyed by citizens and those of non-citizens. In Western Europe, all residents benefit from the legal and constitutional rights which protect all members of liberal democratic states. We have argued that there is something like a continuum of rights between members of European states, from those with almost no rights to those with all the rights and privileges of citizenship.

This continuum of rights is unbalanced, because most residents of West European societies come close to enjoying most rights. Those with the least rights are those who can be described as aspiring to membership of a West European country, or alternatively, '*de facto*' members who have not established legal rights to work and reside. Aspiring members are, for example, political refugees whose status has not been recognised, or people attempting to gain entry but who have been detained as illegal entrants. These aspiring members have very few rights, apart from the basic human rights such as the right to humane treatment and to a fair hearing of their case, and the right of appeal. Other illegal immigrants or illegal workers may have lived and worked in Western Europe for many years but, in spite of this, have very insecure status because they have no legal rights to residence or employment. The best they can hope for is to establish legality through marriage to a citizen or an amnesty which allows them to legalise their status. The relative frequency of amnesties in some countries such as France and the Netherlands is a tacit admission that governments have often condoned or encouraged illegal immigration because of its benefits to the economy, and that the hard work and other contributions of illegal migrants deserves to be acknowledged by legalisation after a period of time, in spite of the fact that they have violated the immigration laws. However, most European countries, such as Britain, Germany and Switzerland, are strongly opposed to amnesties as they believe they encourage further illegal immigration.

Legal immigrants who have established the right to permanent residence and employment often have a status that is very close to full citizenship. This is why we have proposed that a new concept should be used to describe them: namely, *denizen*. Denizens are foreign citizens who have acquired permanent resident status. They can take any employment, and can reside and move freely without restriction. Generally the only privileges they lack are those of voting in local and national elections. In many countries there used to be a range of additional restrictions on foreign nationals such as bans on occupying public offices, limitations on the right to form associations, monitoring of their movements by the police, limitations on the ownership of property, and an insistence on political neutrality. However, in recent years many European countries have removed these restrictions. Sweden, Norway, Denmark, Ireland and the Netherlands have, of course, gone further and extended local voting rights to foreign citizens with qualifying periods of residence. The extension of voting rights is a recognition that denizens are members of society and should be allowed a say in local decision-making at least. The absence of democracy caused by the exclusion of denizens from the franchise is most apparent at the local level, because of the residential concentration of foreign immigrants. In some cities in Germany, for example, a significant proportion of local residents may be unable to vote and local politicians may be very unrepresentative of the actual population. Moreover, a high proportion of local services in these areas, such as education, housing and social welfare provision, may be geared to helping foreign immigrants. There is thus a very strong case for allowing denizens to vote in local elections.

The extension of local voting rights in Sweden and the Netherlands may be seen as positive steps by their parliaments to facilitate the integration of foreign residents. It can also be seen as a recognition that they are permanent members of their new society and that the democratic state needs their consent and participation in decision-making and policy implementation. The state hopes to gain greater co-operation and legitimacy and to avoid a build-up of resentment and alienation among part of its population. The extension of the local franchise means that local politicians, at least, have to take account of the needs of denizens and ensure that they are treated in a fair and civilised way. It may draw foreign migrants into the local political process and become a precursor to naturalisation. It may also reduce native hostility to denizens because as voters they must be wooed by local parties, politicians and the media. They are political participants, not merely political objects who can be blamed and abused for the deficiencies of the local administration. It is noteworthy that even in countries which are opposed to extending voting rights and continue to have tough naturalisation procedures, consultative institutions have been established to involve foreign residents in local decision-making. Some countries have both consultative machinery and local voting rights. Consultative procedures are, however, only likely to be a short-term expedient. They do not tend to work well because of problems of unrepresentativeness. They also tend to emphasise the distinction between foreign citizens and the native community who are their neighbours, workmates and fellow parents.

The introduction of a common passport for citizens of the European Community and the removal of internal barriers in 1992 provides another dimension to the status of foreign immigrants in Western Europe. It may herald two classes of foreign migrant: those who belong to European Community countries (or a similar grouping) and those who do not. The creation of the Nordic Union and the European Community may herald the creation of supra-national forms of citizenship. This would make the Convention of Strasbourg, which attempts to reduce and abolish dual nationality, even more obsolete than it is already. The existence of these supra-national arrangements means that Finns in Sweden, Italians in France and Greeks in Germany may acquire almost all the benefits of citizenship because their country of origin and country of residence both belong to the association, and there may be little to gain by changing nationality. Two types of privileged denizen may thus develop: those who belong to the supra-national community, and those who do not.

It is also likely that the European Community will develop common policies on immigration controls, the status of political refugees, the treatment of illegal immigrants and the position of foreign residents. The recent upsurge in illegal immigration to Spain, Italy and Greece, combined with easier movement within the European Community, makes the development of common policies very likely. Those countries which favour free movement and have negotiated the Schengen accord seem to be taking the lead, though other community members such as Britain will be very reluctant to give up their traditional border controls.

The trend in the seven project countries has generally been towards the gradual extension of industrial, social, civil and political rights to post-war immigrants and their families. They have gradually changed their status from immigrants to denizens. These liberalising trends have been strongest in Sweden, the Netherlands, Belgium and to some extent France. In Sweden and the Netherlands positive policies have been adopted to fund immigrant associations, facilitate mother-tongue education, promote equal opportunities and allow denizens to participate in local elections. The aim of these policies is to encourage denizens to feel part of the national community without forcing them to change their citizenship, although naturalisation is also encouraged. Paradoxically, Chapter 5, on immigrant associations, shows that encouraging these associations and cultural activities is an aid to integration rather than an obstacle.

In Switzerland and Germany – interestingly, both federal states – the fewest concessions have been made. This may be because both Switzerland and Germany are less secure about their national identity. For the Swiss, this is because they belong to a small, rich country, are fiercely proud of their national traditions and independence, but are heavily dependent on foreign labour, which forms a high proportion of their labour force and population. They are thus very anxious not to allow foreign residents to change their unique culture, economic success and political stability. For the Germans, it is because the legacy of the Second World War has left major questions of national identity and territory unresolved, such as the relations between East and West Germany, the position of West Berlin, and the nationality of ethnic Germans in former German territories and other parts of Eastern Europe. Until these national questions recede, German politicians will be reluctant to admit that immigration has permanently changed the nature of West German society. Thus ethnic Germans from Eastern Europe can acquire West German citizenship automatically on request, while long-term foreign residents in the Federal Republic find it almost impossible. Naturalisation has not been facilitated or encouraged and immigrant labour is still seen as temporary. However, even in these countries the dependence of the economy on foreign labour is widely recognised, and fears are growing about the unbalanced age structure of the population and the need to integrate the permanently settled population. The growing use of the term 'ausländische Mitburger', or 'foreign fellow citizen' in Germany suggest a recognition that denizenship status must be conceded to foreign migrant workers.

Britain seems in some ways to be the exception, as it has moved from a more liberal to a less liberal position. This is partly due to the fact that most migrant workers who came to Britain had the status of British subjects. The liberal definition of 'British subject' could not be maintained as pressure grew within Britain for immigration controls against British subjects from the colonies and from Commonwealth countries. This eventually led to the narrower definition of British citizenship in 1981. However, most immigrants in Britain have full political rights, and a very high proportion recognise that they are permanent settlers and have registered as British citizens. The children born in Britain to foreign parents who are permanently settled will be entitled to register as British citizens under the modified *ius soli* provisions of the British Nationality Act of 1981.

British experience is also exceptional in that, despite the citizenship rights enjoyed by immigrants to Britain, it was in Britain that serious inner-city riots occurred in the 1980s. The spark for these riots was often confrontation between young blacks (often the British-born children of immigrant parents) and the police. The second-generation descendants of immigrants in Britain, particularly young Afro-Caribbeans, suffer high levels of unemployment, high levels of police surveillance and strong feelings of alienation caused by educational and economic failure. Racism is an unambiguous explanation for these grievances, and many young blacks have a collective feeling of injustice due to experiences of racism and racial discrimination. The police are seen as the local symbols of an unjust and racist society and are the most likely authority figures to encounter their smouldering resentment. The British experience shows that the granting of *de iure* rights does not necessarily result in *de facto* equality. Slowly, ethnic monitoring procedures and equal opportunity policies are being introduced in Britain to combat racial discrimination. But the struggle to defeat discrimination and other manifestations of racism still have a long way to go.

Elsewhere in Europe, similar problems are emerging. The second generation in France and Germany in particular are doing poorly in the educational system and the labour market. Even in Sweden young immigrants feel discriminated against (Drobnic, 1988), despite all the efforts of the government to promote equality. Most European countries have, like Britain, experienced anti-immigrant, racist parties (Husbands, 1988). The growth of the National Front in France and the achievement of 14.4 percent of the vote by Le Pen in the first round of the French presidential elections in 1988 show the potential for a racist party in mobilising anti-immigrant sentiments among the French electorate. The recent 'successes' of the Republican Party in West Berlin and the National Democratic Party in Hesse in 1989 also show the potential for anti-immigrant parties in West Germany.

Since 1973, all the seven countries which are the focus of this study have implemented tough immigration controls. This has generally been combined with promises of positive initiatives to integrate immigrants already settled in the country. New nationality legislation, for example, has been combined with amnesties for illegal immigrants. The growing length of residence of foreign migrant workers, the increasing numbers of second-generation foreigners born and educated in Europe and their low propensity to naturalise mean that even more positive measures must be taken to ensure fair and equal treatment for these members of European societies. These must include reform of naturalisation procedures, the acceptance of dual nationality, and the recognition that those born and educated in Western Europe should have the automatic right to citizenship if they wish. Even if they do not wish to naturalise, they should be allowed full political rights including voting rights as long as they wish to remain in the country of their birth and upbringing. There is much to be said for a move away from the European tradition of *ius sanguinis* towards *ius soli* or, at the very least, as De Rham describes it, 'double *ius soli* '.

However, the strength of anti-immigrant feeling in Western Europe indicates that there are limits to the extent to which foreign residents can be given the rights of citizens without their showing positive commitment to their new country of residence through naturalisation. This is because anti-immigrant feeling has a high potential to be translated into electoral support for far-right, anti-immigrant parties. This has been true at different times in the post-war period in Britain, France, Germany and Switzerland. Even in Sweden, perhaps the European country with the most positive policies towards foreign residents, the attempt to extend national voting rights to denizens was defeated by the opposition of centre and conservative parties and by the conservative section of public opinion (Hammar, 1985). In France, there is significant support for amending the liberal naturalisation laws, though the strength of liberal opinion makes any change seem unlikely at present. In Germany and Switzerland, substantial increases in the rights of foreign residents seem unlikely.

The argument of this book is that foreign residents who live in a country for longer than a temporary stay gradually become members of their country of residence, and this fact should be recognised, even if most may not wish to become naturalised citizens of their new society. We suggest that a new status of denizenship should be granted to them, entitling them to all the rights of citizens within their country of residence including the right to participate in national elections. This would give them rights similar to those of dual nationals, who have full rights in more than one country. We recognise the political difficulties of extending full national voting rights, although we would emphasise that in Britain full national voting rights have been granted to Commonwealth and Irish citizens without detrimental effects on the

British political system, and in principle there seems no objection to extending full national voting rights to denizens. The children of denizens should have the right to register as citizens if they so wish when they achieve the age of majority.

Unless strong and positive steps are taken to suppress racism and to accept the fact that denizens are members of West European states and have the right to be treated as full and equal members of their countries of residence, then there is the danger that an alienated, disenfranchised minority will be created. This is particularly true for the second generation born and bred in Western Europe. If such positive initiatives are not taken, then the inner-city riots in Britain might be a foretaste of greater uprisings in the future throughout Western Europe.

References

Drobnic, S. (1988) 'The Political Participation of Yugoslav Immigrants in Sweden', *European Journal of Political Research*, 16(6).

Hammar, T. (1985) 'Citizenship, Aliens' Political Rights and Politicians' Concern for Migrants: The Case of Sweden', in R. Rogers (ed.), *Guests Come to Stay*. Boulder, Colo.: Westview Press.

Husbands, C. (1988) 'The Dynamics of Racial Exclusion and Expulsion: Racist Politics in Western Europe', *European Journal of Political Research*, 16(6).

Layton-Henry, Z. (1988) 'The State and New Commonwealth Immigration 1950–56', *New Community*, 14 (1/2): 64–75.

Index

access to rights, 12–17, 19, 42–4
admission, 13, 27–8
advisory councils, 121
Africans, 2, 4, 9, 35, 95
Afro-Caribbeans, in Britain, 9–10,
  149, 193
Algerians, 2, 4, 35, 56, 78, 130
'aliens', as non-citizens, 159
aliens acts, 36, 74, 78, 81
America, North, 2
'Amicales,' Moroccan, 86, 124
amnesties, 31, 190, 194; see also
  regularisation
Amsterdam, 39, 138, 144
Anwar, M., 152
appeal, right of, 189
Arabs, 95
Asians, in Britain, 5, 9, 10, 66,
  149, 163
assembly, freedom of, 85–6
assimilation, 1–2
association, freedom of, 79, 85–6
associational participation, 50
associations, immigrant, 94–112;
  mediating and bridging roles,
  102–4; orientation to country of
  origin or country of residence,
  102–4
asylum-seekers, see political
  asylum
Aufenthaltsrecht (permanent
  residence permit), 81
Ausländer (foreigners), 7, 74
Ausländerbeauftragte, 116–17
ausländische Mitbürger (foreign
  fellow-citizens), 8, 192
ausländischer Arbeitskräfte
  (foreign labour), 7
'autogestion', 53

Baden-Württemberg, 122, 123, 133
Bangladeshis, 2, 10, 97, 108
Bavaria, 117, 133
Belgian Nationality Act (1985),
  167–8
Belgium: civil rights, 82–3, 84, 85,
  90; consultative institutions,
  116, 121, 124; illegal
  immigration, 29, 31, 32–3, 41,
  45; immigrant associations, 94,
  105; immigration policies, 11,
  15; industrial rights, 47, 49, 52,
  53, 58, 62, 64, 66, 67, 68, 69, 70,
  71; legislation, 15, 167–8;
  naturalisation, 167–8, 172, 174–
  5, 177, 179; trends and attitudes,
  8–9, 192; voting rights, 128–30,
  !33, 141
Betriebsräte, 67–8, 69
bills of rights, 19
Birmingham, 95
black workers, in Britain, 9–10,
  58–9, 65, 188, 193
Bonnet law (1980), 34
Brants, K., 140
Brazilians, 128
Britain: civil rights, 82, 84;

consultative institutions, 115,
  117, 118, 119, 120, 125; illegal
  immigration, 29, 30, 32, 36–8,
  42, 43, 44–5; immigrant
  associations, 94, 95, 96, 97, 98,
  99, 100, 101–2, 103, 104, 107–8;
  immigration policies, 36–8, 187–
  8; industrial rights, 51–2, 58–9,
  61, 63, 64–5, 66, 67–8, 70, 71;
  legislation, 17, 29, 32, 36, 163–5;
  naturalisation, 15, 163–5, 171–2,
  177, 179, 180, 183–4; reciprocal
  voting rights with Ireland, 139;
  trends and attitudes, 9–10, 192–
  3, 194–5; voting rights, 117, 127,
  139, 144, 145, 146, 147, 148–9,
  150, 151, 153
British Nationality Act (1981), 43,
  163, 164–5, 172, 184, 193
Buijs, F., 146, 153
business cycle, and immigration
  policies, 59

Caribbeans, 2, 5, 95
Caritas, 104, 123, 133
Casey, J., 21
Castells, M., 19
Castenmiller, P., 140
Castles, S., 19, 57, 62, 67
Catholic Church, 98–9, 104
centralisation, degree of, 118
Centrumpartij, 138, 148, 152
Ceylon, see Sri Lanka
CFDT (Confédération Française
  Démocratique du Travail), 53,
  56, 64, 66
CGT (Confédération Générale du
  Travail), 53, 56, 63–4, 66
chain migration, 95
Cheetham, J., 104
CIMADE, 166
citizens, and non-citizens, 74–5
citizenship: advantages of, 24; by
  declaration, 166; or denizenship,
  186–95; implications of, 186–7;
  legal definition, 22; renunciation
  of former, 161, 171, 176, 183,
  184; supra-national forms, 184,
  191; use of terminology, 159;
  and voting rights, 127, 140
citizenship acquisition: attitudes
  towards, 170–1; comparative
  policies, 171–7; effects, 177–83;
  differences between national
  groups of migrants, 179–83;
  fees, 173–4; general principles,
  159–60; national variations in,
  160–70; politics of, 158–85; see
  also naturalisation
citizenship rights, 11–12; see also
  civil; industrial; political; social
  rights
civil rights, 11, 74–93; extent, 83–
  4; and human rights, 75–6; in
  the 1970s, 77–80; voicing of
  demands, 86–91
class, and voting patterns, 146

class societies, 19
Claude, R.P., 75
colonies, European, 2, 3, 5, 9, 23,
  49; and voting rights, 127, 139
Commission for Migrants Policy,
  German, see Zimmerman
  Commission
Commission Nationale de Travail
  Immigré, 64
Commission for Racial Equality,
  UK, 97, 102, 107–8, 117, 118
committees on migrant affairs,
  121–2
Commonwealth citizens, 4–5, 27,
  29, 163, 164–5, 193, 194
Commonwealth Immigrants Act
  (1962), 32, 36; (1968), 36
community, size and size of
  immigrant population, 119–20
Community Relations Councils,
  UK, 117, 118, 120, 125
conduct, conditions for
  naturalisation, 174
conscription, see military
  service
Conseil Consultatif de
  l'Immigration, Belgium, 116
Conseil National des Populations
  Immigrés, France, 117
Conseils Consultatifs Communaux
  d'Immigrés (CCCI), 117
Conservative Party, British, 52
constitutional rights, and judicial
  review, 82–3
consultative institutions, 113–26,
  191; aims and scope of, 122;
  attitudes towards, 114–15;
  raison d'être of, 119–20; role
  and significance of, 113–15;
  selection and representation in,
  123–5; types of, 120–2
contact groups, 120
continuum of rights, 18, 184,
  189–90
co-ordination groups, 120
corporatism, 50, 119
Costa-Lascoux, J., 165, 176, 178
Council of Europe, 78, 84, 161
crime, 20
cultural defence, and political
  participation, 102–4
cultural pluralism, 7
Cypriots, Greek, in Britain, 10, 96,
  97, 99, 102
Cyprus, 84, 95

De Peiera family, 44
democracy, 11, 19, 45, 50, 127,
  186; and human rights, 75–6
demonstration, freedom of, 85–6
denizens, use of term, 13, 25, 190
denizenship, 159, 184, 189, 194; or
  citizenship, 186–95
Denmark, 15–16, 17, 84, 136, 144,
  148, 190
deportation, 13, 20, 32, 43, 44–5,
  78

Deutsche Gewerkschaften und Fremdarbeiter, 57
Deutsche Gewerkschafts Bund (DGB), 51, 57-8, 61, 64, 65-6, 133
discrimination: based on citizenship, 77; positive, 115; *see also* racial discrimination
displaced persons, 2, 115
dual nationality (or citizenship), 135, 158, 161-2, 164, 166, 175-7, 191, 194
Dutch Antilleans, 9, 147
Dutch East Indies, *see* Indonesians
Dutch Minorities Report (1983), 106
duties, rights and, 141

economic advantages of immigration, 187-8
economic refugees, 6
education, 43; mother-tongue issue, 99-102
Effendi, Rustam, 150
Eidgenössische Kommission für Ausländerprobleme, 117
Eisenstadt, S.N., 94
elections: equilibrium considerations, 141-2; immigrant candidates, 150-5; immigrant turn-out, 143-5
electoral legislation, 128-33
electoral participation, of immigrants, 143-53
emigration, as a political act, 87
employment: legal rights to, 189; permits, 13
equal opportunities policies, 193
equality, and citizenship, 19, 158
Estonians, 3
ethnic groups, as interest groups, 149-50
ethnic minorities, use of term, 6, 9-10
ethnic pluralism, 83, 91
ethnicity, mobilisation of, 149-50
European Commission, employees of, 4
European Community (EC), 184, 186, 191; and change of citizenship, 182-3; common immigration control policies proposed, 191; draft directives on unauthorised employment, 43-4; free labour market, 28, 40; voting rights, 139, 140, 141
European Convention on Human Rights (1953), 19, 77, 85-6
Evian Agreement (1962), 56
exclusionism, 133-4, 158-9
exploitation, 14, 19-20, 33, 43

factory committees, 67, 69
Falkland Islands, 164
family reunification, 14-15
family settlement, 99-100
federal states, 11, 82
Filipinos, in Britain, 45
Finland, 137
Finns, in Sweden, 3, 9, 10, 29, 96, 100-1, 103, 134, 136, 170, 191
FitzGerald, M., 149, 152
Flanders, 9, 53, 105
Flemish Co-ordinating Committee on Migration, 105
Fontanet decree (1972), 34
foreign workers, 5-6; *de facto* and *de jure* treatment, 20; of Western Europe (1984), 3

France: civil rights, 79-80, 81, 82, 84, 89; consultative institutions, 117; illegal immigration, 14, 15, 27, 31, 33-6, 45; immigrant associations, 94, 96, 98-9, 101; immigration policies, 14, 33-6, 187, 190; industrial rights, 49, 53, 62-3, 63-4, 66, 67, 68-9, 70, 71; legislation, 165-6; naturalisation, 3, 15, 165-6, 171, 172, 174, 175, 177, 178, 179, 181, 184; trends and attitudes, 8, 192, 193, 194; voting rights, 127, 130-1, 133, 142-3, 151
Fraser, J., 96
fraternal organisations, homeland, 98
freedoms, *see* assembly; association; demonstration; opinion
Freeman, G., 12
Fremdarbeiter (foreign workers), 7
Friedrich-Ebert Stiftung survey, 170

Gastarbeiter (guest-workers), 2, 5, 7-8, 183
German Federal Institute of Employment, 40
Germany, Democratic Republic (GDR), 8, 49, 162
Germany, Federal Republic of: civil rights, 77, 79, 81, 82-3, 84, 85, 88, 89, 90; consultative institutions, 94, 115, 116, 118-20, 121-2, 123, 124; illegal immigration, 28, 30, 31, 40, 41; immigrant associations, 94, 97-8, 99, 104; immigration policies, 14-15, 40; industrial rights, 46, 49, 51, 52, 57-8, 61-2, 63, 64, 65-6, 67, 68; legislation, 82-3, 162; naturalisation, 15, 162-3, 170, 171, 172, 175, 177, 178, 179, 180, 182; trends and attitudes, 7-8, 192, 193, 194; voting rights, 131-3, 141, 142, 145, 146, 150, 151, 190
Gibraltar, 164
Giscard d'Estaing, Valéry, 22
Goffman, E., 143
government policies, towards illegal immigrants, 33
Grahl-Madsen, Atle, 74-5
Greater London Council (GLC), 104, 108
Greece, 84, 183, 191
Greek Orthodox Church, 96, 99
Greeks, 40, 61, 167, 191

Haiti, 35
Hamburg, 24, 132, 133
Hammar, Tomas, 74-93, 146, 147, 171, 175, 176, 177-8, 183, 184, 189
Heisler, Martin, 21
Hesse, 118, 121, 123, 132, 133
Hirschman, Albert, 'Exit-voice-loyalty' theory, 87
human rights, 189; and civil rights 75-6; and voting rights, 140
'Human Rights of Aliens in Europe' colloquy (1983), 78, 84
Hungarians, in Britain, 10
Hussain, Safdar, 37

Iceland, 84, 137
identity, national, 11, 22-3, 158, 186, 192

Idrish, Mohammed, 44-5
illegal immigrants, 2, 14-15, 27-46, 189-90; campaigns by, 45; categories of, 30; government policies towards, 33; national policies towards, 33-41; numbers of, 31-3
illegality, definitions of, 28-31
immigrants, official definition, 5
immigration: nature of, 49-50; post-war, 1-10; type of and industrial rights, 48-54
Immigration Act, British (1971), 29, 32, 36
Immigration Appeal Tribunal, 44-5
Immigration Appeals Act (1969), UK, 36
Immigration (Carriers' Liability) Bill (1987), UK, 17
immigration control policies, 23, 84, 188, 193-4; *see also* government policies; national policies
independence, national, 22-3
India, 35
Indians, in Britain, 9, 10, 95, 108
Indonesians, in the Netherlands, 4, 9
industrial councils, 67-8
industrial rights, 12, 47-73
industrialisation, degree of, 11
information, access to, 90-1
information campaigns, for foreign voters, 148
Inländer (permanent residents), 74, 75
Inner Cities Partnership schemes, UK, 107
inner-city riots, Britain (1980s), 120, 193
integration, 1, 2, 91-2; and citizenship, 158, 171; and role of immigrant associations, 109-10; and voting behaviour, 146-7; voting rights and, 140-1
interest groups, ethnic groups as, 149-50
International Covenant on Civil and Political Rights (1966), 77
international law, 78, 139
international organisations, employees of, 4
Ireland, Republic of, 2, 29, 36, 84, 127, 175, 190; reciprocal voting rights with Britain, 16, 139
Ireland Act (1949), 4
Irish, in Britain, 1, 4, 10, 23, 194
Islam, 66, 176; *see also* Muslims
Israel, 94
Italians, 3, 4, 57, 127, 170-1, 191
Italy, 2, 84, 134, 175, 191
ius sanguinis, 159-60, 168, 171-2, 186
ius soli, 131, 159-60, 163, 171-2, 186, 193; double, 165, 167, 171, 172, 194

Jamaicans, in Britain, 9
Jews, 1; in Britain, 10
Josephides, S., 96
judicial review, constitutional rights, 82-3
jus sanguinis, see ius sanguinis
jus soli, see ius soli

Kamal, Djelali, 130
Katznelson, I., 115

Kevenhorster, P., 123
kidnapping, 'legal' cases, 176
Kohl, Helmut, 8
Kosack, G., 19, 57, 62, 67
Kühn, Heinz, 132

labour, foreign, 42–3, 50, 192
labour market: and immigration
   policies, 59; marginality to, 60–
   1; protection of, 27–8, 33
Labour Party, British, 52; Black
   sections, 125, 153
labour recruitment policies, 2, 14,
   17, 96–9
Lagarde, Paul, 20
Landesorganizationen, 51
language issues, 9; *see also*
   mother-tongue education
Lawrence, D., 148
Layton-Henry, Zig, 149, 152
Le Lohé, M.J., 152, 153
Le Pen, J.M., 130, 193
liberalism, 177, 192–5
Libya, 22
Lichtenstein, 84
Lijst Rammelaere, 145
LO/TCO (National Federation of
   Workers/Tjäanstemännens
   Centralorganisation), 51, 59, 64,
   135
local advisory boards, migrants,
   24
Luxemburg, 84
Lyssy, Rolf, 169

McAllister, I., 148
Maghrebians, in France, 4, 8
Malakka, Tan, 150
Manchester, 43, 44
Manpower Services Commission,
   107
Marplan survey, 170
marriage, arranged, 95
Marshall, T.H., 11
medborgarskap (citizenship), 159
media, for immigrants, 90–1
membership of a state, 17–19, 177,
   186, 189, 194
Mendis, Viraj, 43
Midlands, 96
migrant workers: defined, 5;
   different terms used, 7;
   industrial rights, 47–73; status
   and rights, 14; use of term, 5
migrants, 5
Migrants Action Group, Britain,
   45
migration: first phase, 96–9;
   second phase, 99–100
military service, 187; and
   citizenship, 175, 176; and voting
   rights, 141
Miller, M.J., 20–1, 50–1, 57, 87,
   88, 89, 92, 97
minorities, term of description, 8
minorities policies, 91, 106, 143,
   167
minority rights, 91
Mitbestimmung, 69
Mitterand, François, 130, 166
Moluccans, in the Netherlands, 4,
   117, 118
Moroccans, 2, 4, 90, 127; in the
   Netherlands, 3, 39, 45, 86, 167
Morocco, 6, 35, 182–3
mosques, in Britain, 95, 96, 100
mother-tongue education, 91, 99–
   102

Mouvement des Travailleurs
   Arabes (MTA), 89
movement, freedom of, 84
multi-cultural education, 103
multinational companies, 4
municipal councils, committees on
   migrant affairs, 121–2
Muslims, 22; in Britain, 96, 99,
   100, 108

NALGO, 44–5, 65
Naorji, Dadabhai, 150
nation states, 158, 186
National Advisory Council for
   Immigration, Belgium, 64
National Front, France, 130, 131,
   142–3, 166, 193
national interest, 80, 109
national policies, towards illegal
   immigrants, 33–41
nationalism, 22
nationalité (citizenship), 159
nationality, 22–3; *see also* dual
   nationality
nationality legislation; *see under*
   countries
naturalisation, 14, 141, 158–85;
   conditions of, 173; process of,
   14, 15, 23; reform of, 194; and
   representation, 189
Netherlands, the: civil rights, 82,
   84, 91; consultative institutions,
   117, 118, 124, 125; immigrant
   associations, 94, 96, 104, 106–7;
   immigration policies, 38–40,
   106, 167, 187, 190; industrial
   rights, 49, 52–3, 55, 59, 63, 67,
   68, 69, 70; legislation, 15, 117,
   166–7; naturalisation, 15, 166–7,
   171, 172, 174–5, 177, 179, 181–2,
   183; trends and attitudes, 8–9,
   192; voting rights, 8–9, 117, 127,
   137–9, 143, 144, 147, 148, 151,
   152–3
Neuchâtel, 125, 128, 145
neutrality, obligation of political,
   78–80, 140
newspapers, for immigrants, 90
Niederlassungsrecht (right of
   permanent residence), 80
Nordic Council, 134, 136, 184
Nordic countries, 127, 134–7; *see
   also* Denmark; Finland; Iceland;
   Norway; Sweden
Nordic Cultural Agreement, 101
Nordic labour market agreement,
   29, 59, 101
Nordic Language Agreement, 101
Nordic Union, 3, 101, 186, 191
North-Rhine Westphalia, 118–19,
   122, 133
Norway, 15–16, 84, 136–7, 190;
   Commission on Aliens, 74
Nuremburg, 123

Objectif '82 (now '88), 128, 129
opinion, freedom of, 84–5
Oszunay, E., 78, 84

Pakistanis, 2, 4, 35, 95; in Britain,
   4–5, 10, 97, 99, 100, 108
Palme, Olaf, 135
parliaments of migrant workers,
   121
passports, 187; common EC, 191
Pearson, D.G., 149
person, liberty and security of the,
   83–4, 187

Philippines, 6
Pieters, R.A.M., 147
Poles, 1, 3, 10, 145
police, 20, 44, 83–4; and blacks in
   Britain, 193
political asylum, 17, 18, 41–2
political participation, 11, 191;
   alternative, 113–26, 147;
   backlash fear, 152–3; cultural
   defence and, 102–4; levels of,
   86–91; *see also* consultative
   institutions
political parties: admission of
   foreign citizens, 79; anti-
   immigrant, 142–3, 193, 194;
   branches of homeland, 97–8,
   127, 141; ethnic loyalty and
   loyalty to, 153; immigrant, 151;
   immigrant preferences, 145;
   relationships with trade unions,
   51–4
political quiescence thesis, 20–1
Portugal, 2, 84, 95, 128
Portuguese, 32, 40, 127; in France,
   4, 10, 96, 98–9, 101
Powell, Enoch, 21
press: freedom of the, 84;
   minority, 90–1
prisoners of war, 2
protectionism, 162, 177, 183–4
public order, 79–80

Qur'anic schools, 99, 100

race relations legislation, 117, 188
racial discrimination, 10, 18, 119,
   148, 188, 193
racism, 7, 10, 188, 193, 195
receiving countries, problems of,
   6, 97–8
recruitment agencies, 29
refugees, 2, 17; *see also* economic
   refugees; political refugees
registration for citizenship, 164,
   165, 173, 175
regularisation, case for, 44–5
religious organisations, for
   immigrants, 98–9
representation, 22, 24; and
   naturalisation, 189; taxation
   and, 22; in unions by foreign
   workers, 68–70
residence: conditions for
   naturalisation, 173; legal rights
   to, 189; permits, 13; right of
   permanent, 13, 80–2
revolutionary organisations, in
   foreign communities, 20–1, 97–8
Rex, J., 148
rights: absence of, 27–46; trends in
   extension of, 192–5
Rotterdam, 24, 39, 138, 144, 148

Saudi Arabia, 22
Sawyer, P., 96
Saxony, Lower, 118, 122, 123, 133
Schengen accord, 191
Schleswig-Holstein, 24, 132
Schmitter, B., 63
Schmitter Heisler, B., 48
Schoeneberg, U., 110
schools, part-time community, 99–
   100, 102
Schwarzenbach, James, 7, 57

Schweizerischer Gewerkschaftsbund (SGB), 53, 56–7, 62, 64, 69
Scots, 10, 23
seasonal workers, 2
second generation immigrants, 6, 110, 193, 195
security, national, 11, 80, 109, 158
Senegal, 39
separatism, 22–3
settlement, *see* family settlement
shop stewards, 70; committees, 67–8
Sikhs, in Britain, 97, 98, 108
social mobility, upward, and political participation, 146, 152
social rights, 11–12, 76
social security, contributions to, 12
social taxes, on foreign workers, Switzerland, 41
SOPEMI, 178, 180–2
sovereign states, 187
sovereignty, protection of, 140
Spain, 2, 84, 101, 134, 191
Spanish, 3, 4, 40, 61
Sri Lanka, 6, 17, 35
Staatsangehörigkeit (citizenship), 159
state: discretionary power and its limitations, 160; legitimacy and citizenship, 158, 190–1; level of control over citizenship acquisition, 172; relationship with citizens, 186–7; role in relation to immigrant associations, 104–8
Stemrecht '82 (now '88), 128
Stoleru, Lionel, 34
Strasbourg, Convention of, 161, 165, 175–6, 191
strikes, participation by immigrant workers, 66–7, 88–9
Studlar, D., 148–9, 152
Surinamese, in the Netherlands, 4, 9, 40, 95, 167, 179
Sweden: civil rights, 77, 79, 81–2, 83, 84, 90, 91; consultative institutions, 118, 119, 121; illegal immigration, 32, 40,
41–2, 44; immigrant associations, 94, 96, 100–2, 103, 104, 105–6; immigration policies, 10–11, 40, 105–6, 187, 192; industrial rights, 49, 51, 54, 59, 60–1, 63, 64, 65, 70, 71, 72; legislation, 17, 78, 81, 161; naturalisation, 3, 15, 161–2, 170, 172, 177, 179, 180, 182, 183; trends and attitudes, 8–9, 192, 193, 194; voting rights, 8–9, 117, 134–6, 142, 143, 146, 147, 148, 151, 152, 190
Switzerland: civil rights, 80–1, 82, 84, 85, 88; consultative institutions, 117, 123–4, 125; illegal immigration, 28–9, 30, 31–2, 41; immigrant associations, 96, 99; immigration policies, 14, 41; industrial rights, 47, 53–4, 56–7, 62, 63, 69, 70, 71; legislation, 7, 17, 80, 168–9; naturalisation, 15, 168–70, 170–1, 172, 175, 177, 179; trends and attitudes, 7, 192, 194; voting rights, 128, 133

Tamils, in Britain, 17
taxation, 12, 41, 187; and citizenship, 176; and representation, 22, 140
terrorism, 78, 82, 109
Third World, 2, 17, 41, 95, 187
trade unions, 40, 47–8; attitudes to migrant workers, 63–5, 71–2; and labour migration, 54–9; membership, 51–4, 60–3; militancy and involvement of migrant workers within, 65–7, 79; organisation of migrant workers within, 63–5; participation, 60–7; and political parties, pillarisation, 52–3; position in society and industrial rights, 48–54
Trades Union Congress (TUC), 51–2, 59, 65
Tung, Roger Ko-Chih, 87
Tunisia, 35, 39

Turkey, 6, 28, 35, 39, 84, 88, 101
Turks, 2, 3, 4, 32, 40, 90, 106–7, 124; in Germany, 3, 8, 61, 88

Überfremdung (over-foreignisation), 7, 56–7, 169
unemployment, 31, 33, 193
unionisation, degree of, 51–4, 60
unitary states, 11, 82
United Nations Declaration of Human Rights, 19, 76–7, 85–6
Urban Programme, 107

Varki, Meena, 44
Varki, Verghese, 44
Versailles peace treaties (1919), 91
Vietnamese, in France, 4
voluntary organisations, 48
voting behaviour, explanations, 145–50
voting rights, 15–16, 127–57, 194; local, 24, 190–1; pros and cons, 134, 139–43; reciprocity of, 141
Vranken, Jan, 47–73

Wales, 96
Wallonia, 9, 105, 116
war, suspension of civil rights to aliens, 84
Welch, S., 152
welfare benefits, 12–13, 43
welfare services, and immigrant associations, 103–4
welfare states, 12–13, 19, 187
Welsh, 10, 23
West Africans, 2, 4
West Indians, in Britain, 9, 66, 108, 149, 163
work councils, 67–8
workers' delegates, 70
workers' participation, migrant, 67–70
working groups, 120–1

youth organisations, 110
Yugoslavia, 2–3, 6, 101, 183
Yugoslavs, 3, 32, 61, 90

Zamir case, 38
Zimmerman Commission, 163

Notes on the Contributors

Uwe Andersen
Professor of Political Science at the Ruhr University of Bochum since 1979. He is author of numerous articles and books, especially in political economy. He is editor of *Kommunale Selbstverwaltung und Kommunalpolitik in Nordrhein-Westfalen* (1987) and *Kommunalpolitik und Kommunalwahlen in Nordrhein-Westfalen* (2nd edn. 1989).

Tomas Hammar
Professor of Research in International Migration and Ethnic Relations at the University of Stockholm. Head of the Swedish Commission on Immigration Research 1978–83. Author of numerous articles on immigration policy and the political participation of immigrant ethnic minorities in Sweden. He is editor of *European Immigration Policy* (1985) and author of *International Migration, Citizenship and Democracy* (1989) and *Democracy and the Nation State: Aliens, Denizens and Citizens in a World of International Migration* (1990).

Zig Layton-Henry
Senior Lecturer in Politics at the University of Warwick where he teaches Comparative Race Relations, Political Sociology and Research Methods in Political Science. He is author of *The Politics of Race in Britain* (1984) and editor of *Conservative Party Politics* (1980), *Conservative Politics in Western Europe* (1982) and *Race, Government and Politics in Britain* (1986). He recently edited a special issue of the *European Journal of Political Research* (1988) on Immigration and Politics in Western Europe.

Jan Rath
Research and teaching fellow at the Centre for the Study of Multi Ethnic Society and the Department of Cultural Authropology at the University of Utrecht. He was previously a research assistant at the Centre for the Study of Social Conflict at the University of Leiden. His major research interests are the political response to immigration and the political participation of immigrant ethnic minorities. He is the author of various articles, notably in the *European Journal of Political Research, International Migration, International Migration Review* and the *Netherlands Journal of Sociology*.

Gérard de Rham
Researcher and teacher at the Institut d'Etudes Sociales in Geneva. He obtained his doctorate in political science in 1977. He is author of *La politique étrangère de la République de Zambie* (1977) and joint author of *Xénophobie?* (1978), *Qui sont-ils, Suisses ou Espagnols? La deuxième génération* (1980). *L'asile dans notre quotidien. Discours populaire sur les réfugiés* (1986) and *Portrait des salariés romands* (1988).

Jan Vranken
Professor of Sociology and head of the Department of Sociology and Social Policy at the University of Antwerp where he teaches Sociology, Social Problems and Social Ecology. He has published widely in the areas of poverty and the welfare state, including *Zorgen om de Verzorgingsstaat* (1984), *De toegankelijkheid voor migranten van algemene sociale voorzieningen in Vlaanderen* (1985) and *De maatschappij en haar bouwstenen: Een inleiding tot de sociologie* (1988). He is honorary president of the Flemish Co-ordinating Committee for Migrants.

Catherine Wihtol de Wenden
Researcher at the CNRS and member of the Centre d'Etudes et de Recherches Internationales, Fondation Nationale des Sciences Politiques, Paris. She is author of numerous articles on immigration and politics in France. She is also author of *Les immigrés dans la cité* (1978), *Citoyenneté, Nationalité et Immigration* (1987), *Les immigrés et la politique: cent-cinquante ans d'evolution* (1988) and editor of *Citizenship* (1988).